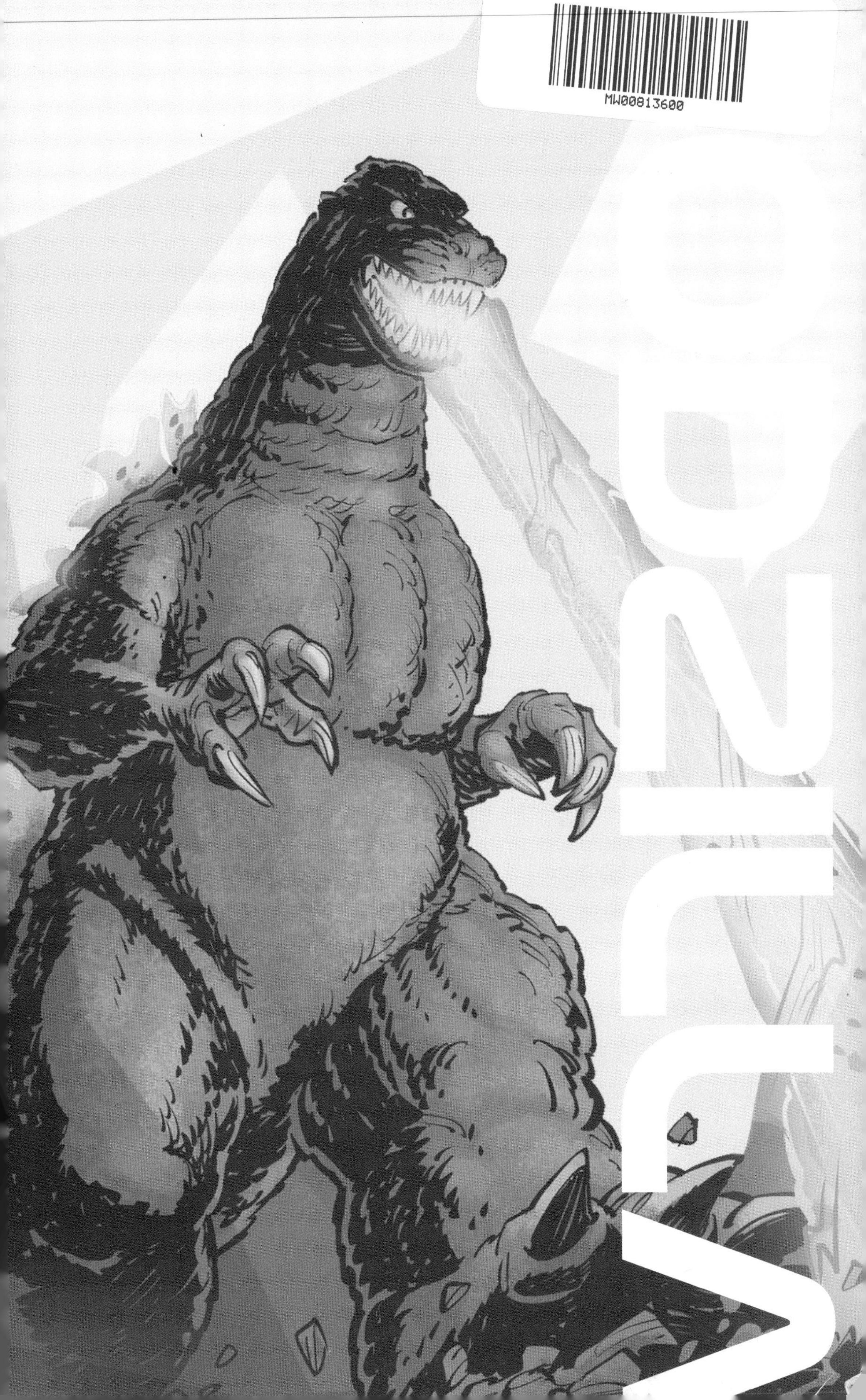

Become our fan on Facebook **facebook.com/idwpublishing**
Follow us on Twitter **@idwpublishing**
Subscribe to us on YouTube **youtube.com/idwpublishing**
See what's new on Tumblr **tumblr.idwpublishing.com**
Check us out on Instagram **instagram.com/idwpublishing**

IDW
www.IDWPUBLISHING.com

Ted Adams, CEO & Publisher
Greg Goldstein, President & COO
Robbie Robbins, EVP/Sr. Graphic Artist
Chris Ryall, Chief Creative Officer/Editor-in-Chief
Laurie Windrow, Senior VP of Sales & Marketing
Matthew Ruzicka, CPA, Chief Financial Officer
Dirk Wood, VP of Marketing
Lorelei Bunjes, VP of Digital Services
Jeff Webber, VP of Licensing, Digital and Subsidiary Rights
Jerry Bennington, VP of New Product Development

Cover Art by
BRIAN CHURILLA

Collection Edits by
JUSTIN EISINGER
and ALONZO SIMON

Collection Design by
CLAUDIA CHONG

Publisher
TED ADAMS

ISBN: 978-1-63140-733-8   19 18 17 16   1 2 3 4

GODZILLA: OBLIVION. OCTOBER 2016. FIRST PRINTING. © 2016 Toho Co., Ltd. All Rights Reserved. GODZILLA ®, Gojira, the related characters and the Character Designs are trademarks of Toho Co., Ltd. © 2016 Idea and Design Works, LLC. The IDW logo is registered in the U.S. Patent and Trademark Office. IDW Publishing, a division of Idea and Design Works, LLC. Editorial offices: 2765 Truxtun Road, San Diego, CA 92106. Any similarities to persons living or dead are purely coincidental. With the exception of artwork used for review purposes, none of the contents of this publication may be reprinted without the permission of Idea and Design Works, LLC. Printed in Korea.
IDW Publishing does not read or accept unsolicited submissions of ideas, stories, or artwork.

Originally published as GODZILLA: OBLIVION issues #1–5.

Special thanks to Yoshiko Fukuda, Rui Machida, and everyone at Toho for their invaluable assistance.

Written by
JOSHUA FIALKOV

Art by
BRIAN CHURILLA

Colors by
JAY FOTOS

Creative Consultant and Letters by
CHRIS MOWRY

Series Edits by
BOBBY CURNOW

Art by BRIAN CHURILLA

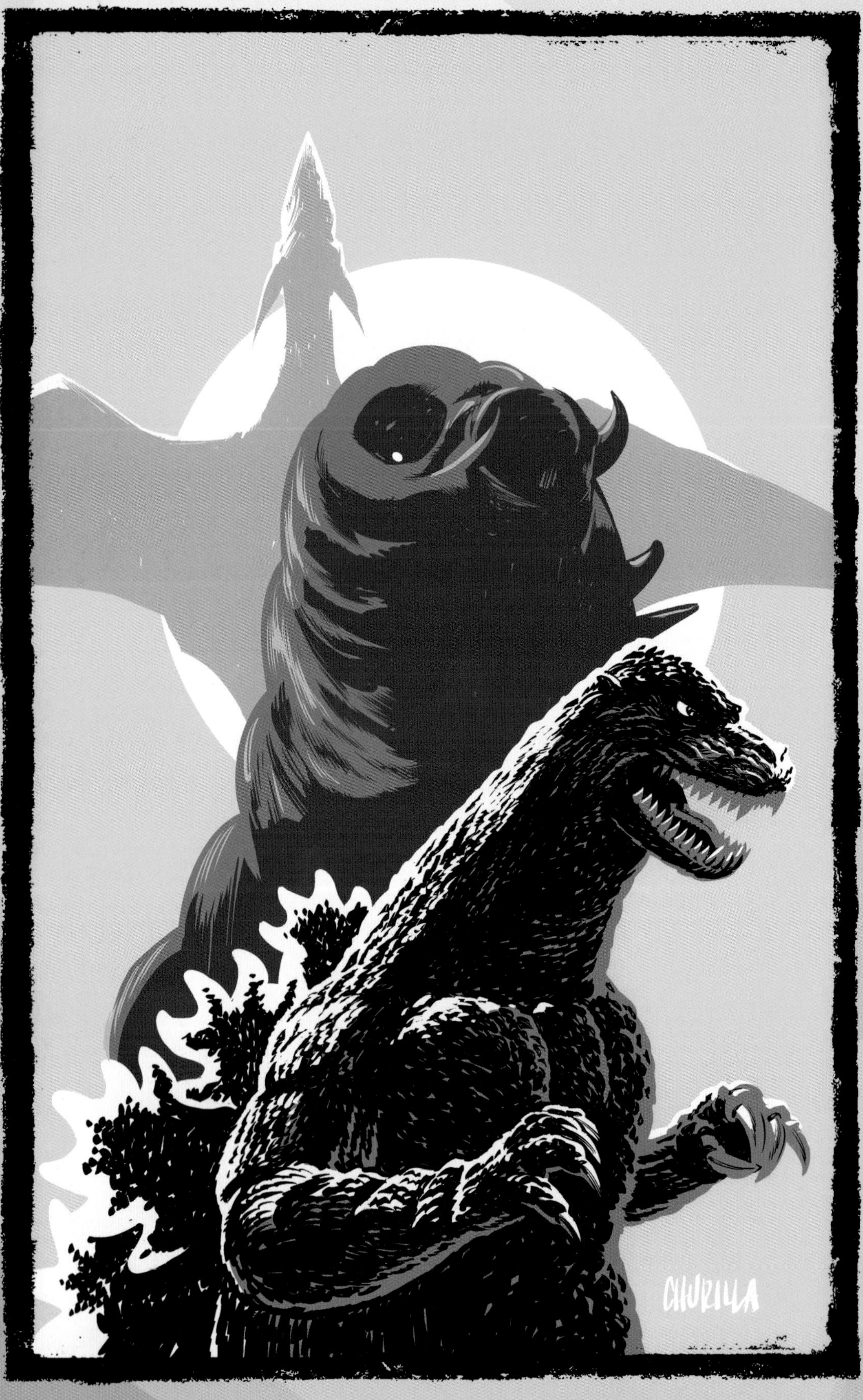
CHURILLA

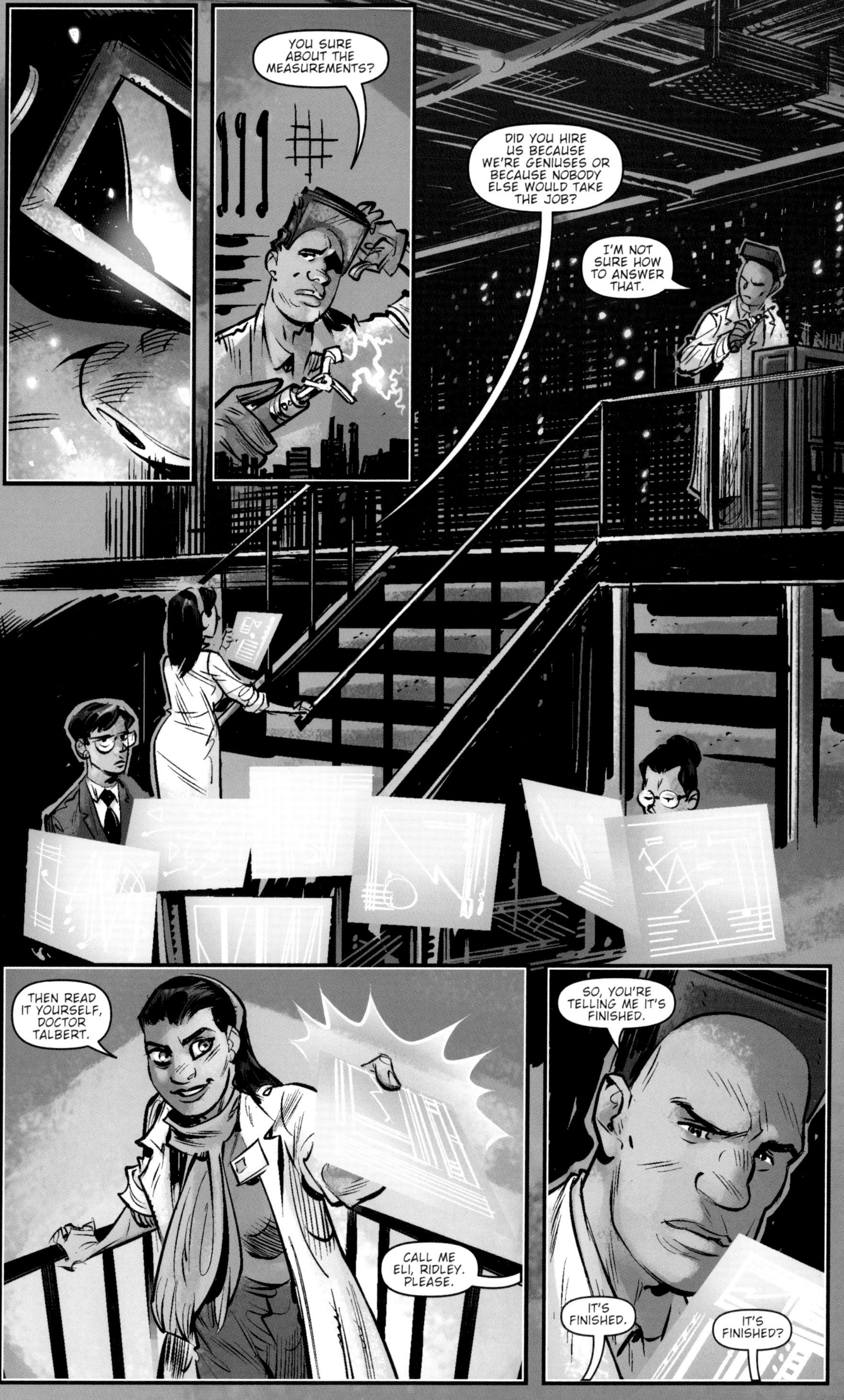

YOU SURE ABOUT THE MEASUREMENTS?
DID YOU HIRE US BECAUSE WE'RE GENIUSES OR BECAUSE NOBODY ELSE WOULD TAKE THE JOB?
I'M NOT SURE HOW TO ANSWER THAT.
THEN READ IT YOURSELF, DOCTOR TALBERT.
CALL ME ELI, RIDLEY. PLEASE.
SO, YOU'RE TELLING ME IT'S FINISHED.
IT'S FINISHED.
IT'S FINISHED?

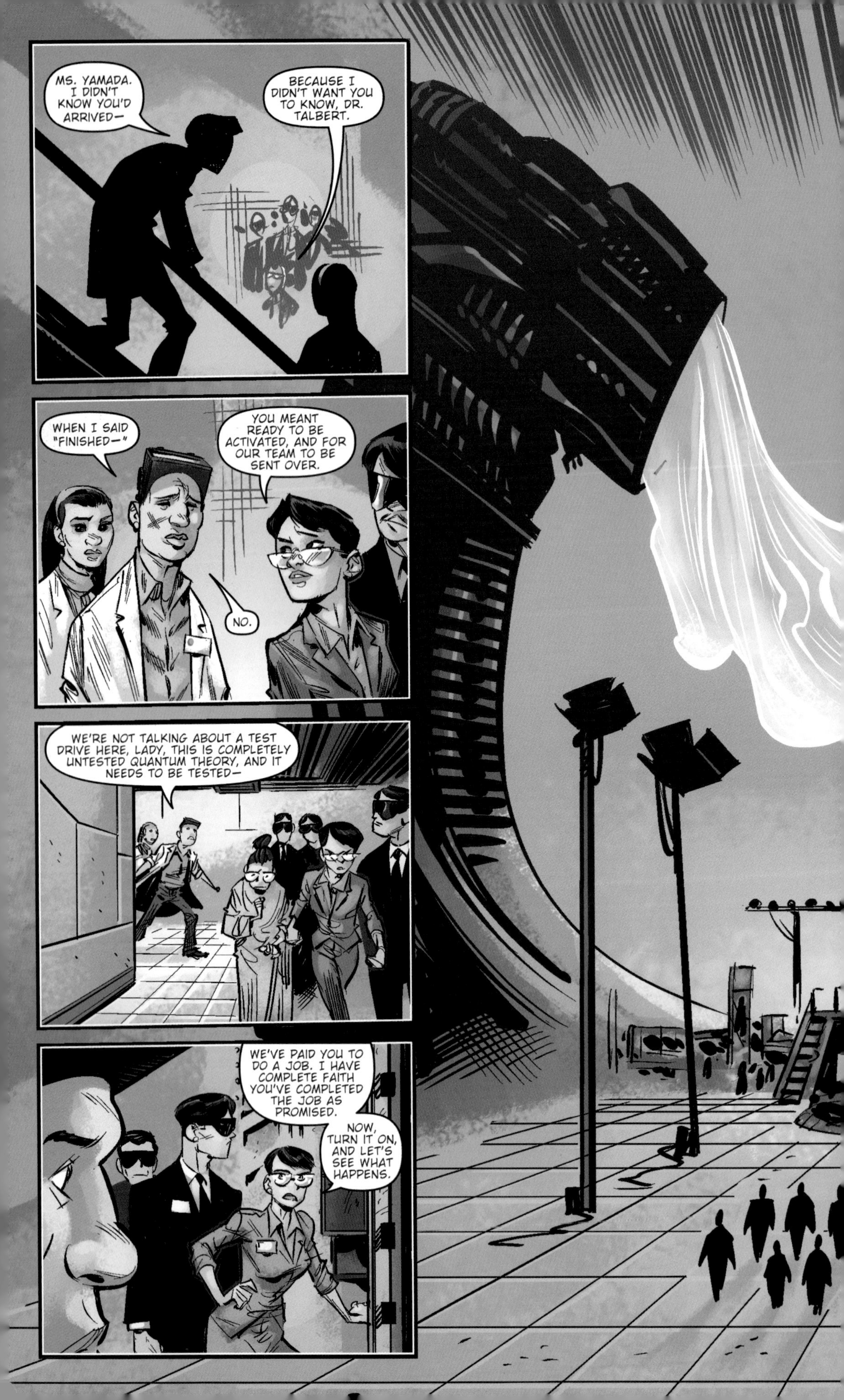
MS. YAMADA. I DIDN'T KNOW YOU'D ARRIVED—
BECAUSE I DIDN'T WANT YOU TO KNOW, DR. TALBERT.
WHEN I SAID "FINISHED—"
YOU MEANT READY TO BE ACTIVATED, AND FOR OUR TEAM TO BE SENT OVER.
NO.
WE'RE NOT TALKING ABOUT A TEST DRIVE HERE, LADY, THIS IS COMPLETELY UNTESTED QUANTUM THEORY, AND IT NEEDS TO BE TESTED—
WE'VE PAID YOU TO DO A JOB. I HAVE COMPLETE FAITH YOU'VE COMPLETED THE JOB AS PROMISED.
NOW, TURN IT ON, AND LET'S SEE WHAT HAPPENS.

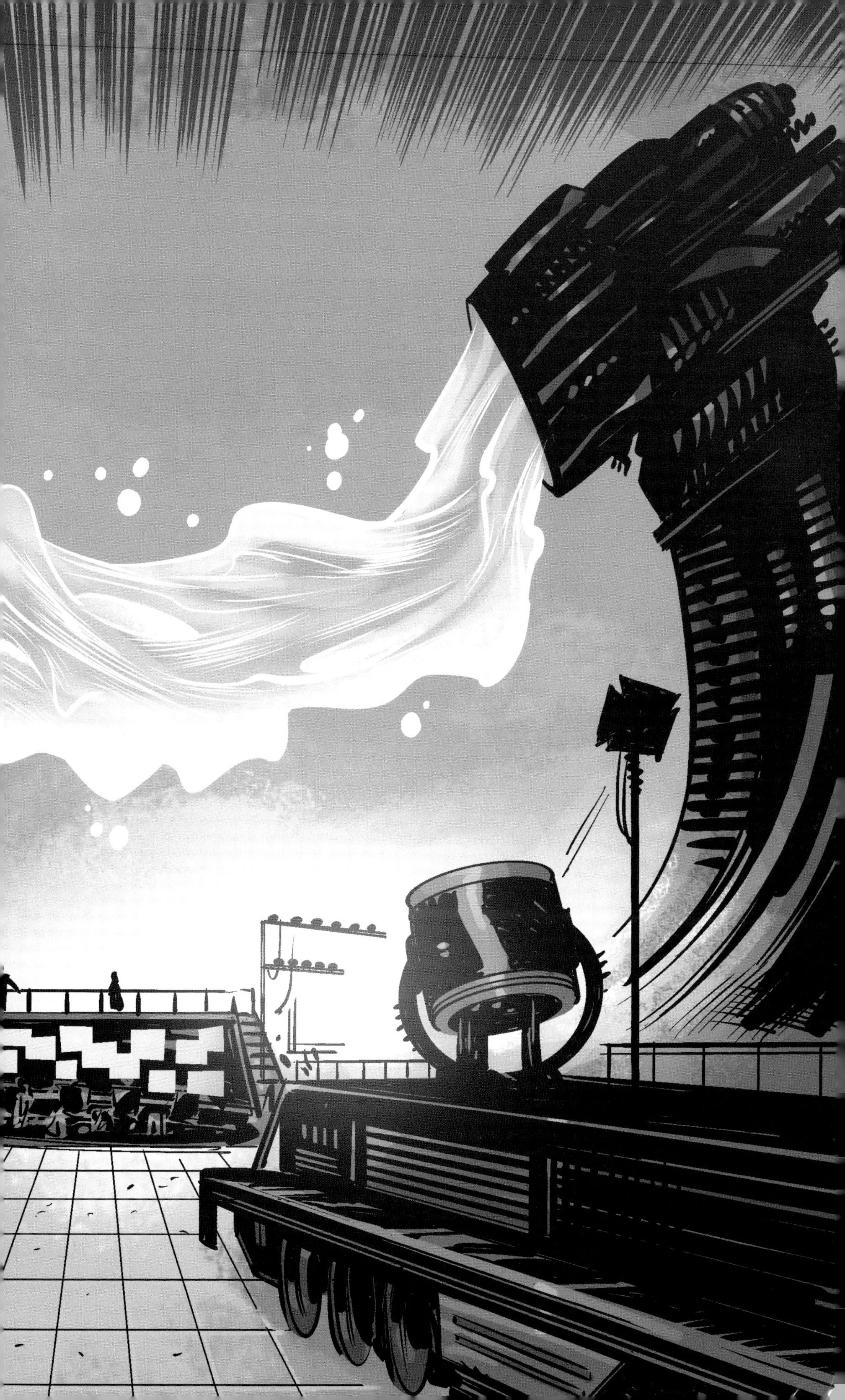

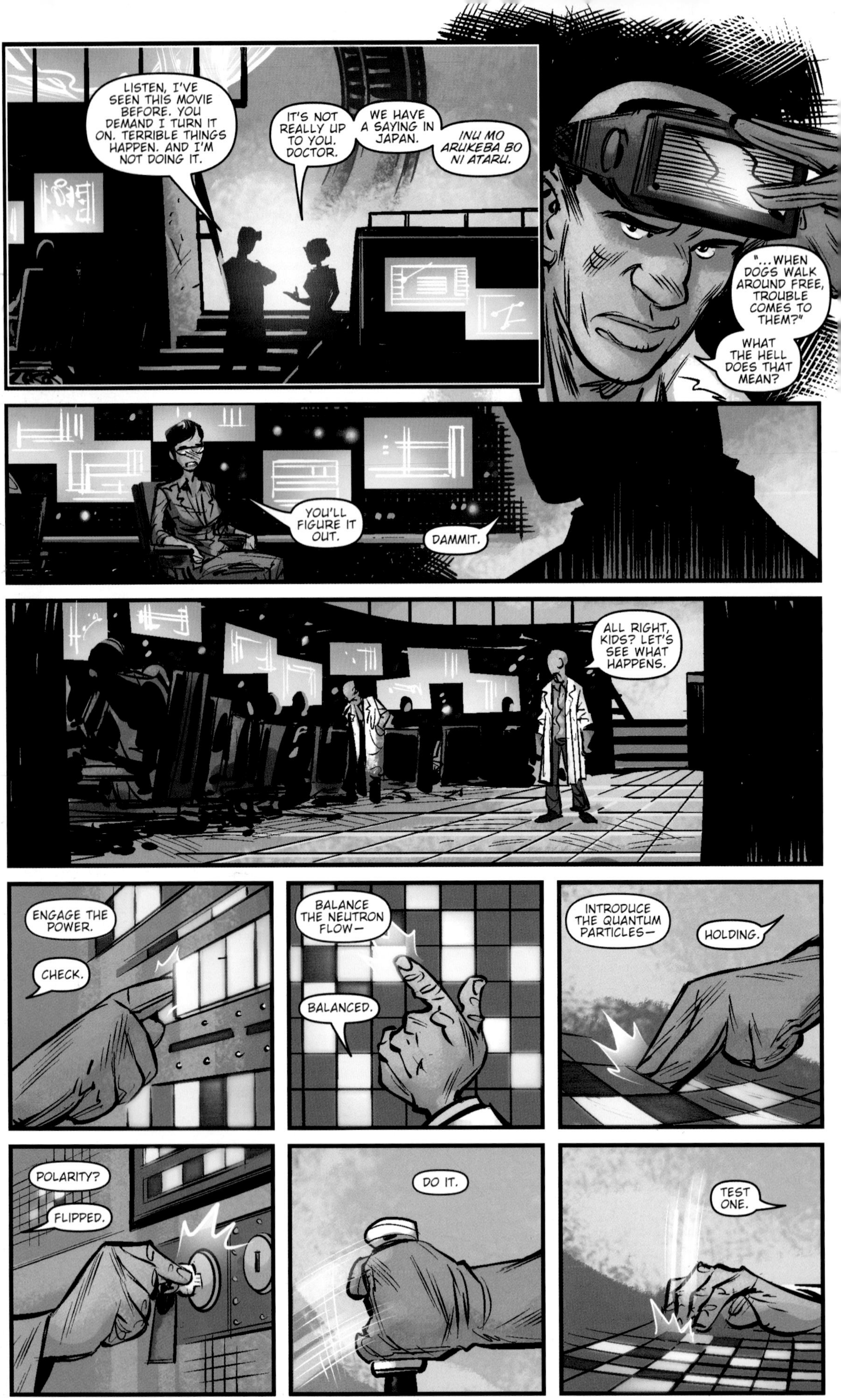
LISTEN, I'VE SEEN THIS MOVIE BEFORE. YOU DEMAND I TURN IT ON. TERRIBLE THINGS HAPPEN. AND I'M NOT DOING IT.
IT'S NOT REALLY UP TO YOU. DOCTOR.
WE HAVE A SAYING IN JAPAN.
INU MO ARUKEBA BO NI ATARU.
"...WHEN DOGS WALK AROUND FREE, TROUBLE COMES TO THEM?"
WHAT THE HELL DOES THAT MEAN?
YOU'LL FIGURE IT OUT.
DAMMIT.
ALL RIGHT, KIDS? LET'S SEE WHAT HAPPENS.
ENGAGE THE POWER.
CHECK.
BALANCE THE NEUTRON FLOW—
BALANCED.
INTRODUCE THE QUANTUM PARTICLES—
HOLDING.
POLARITY?
FLIPPED.
DO IT.
TEST ONE.

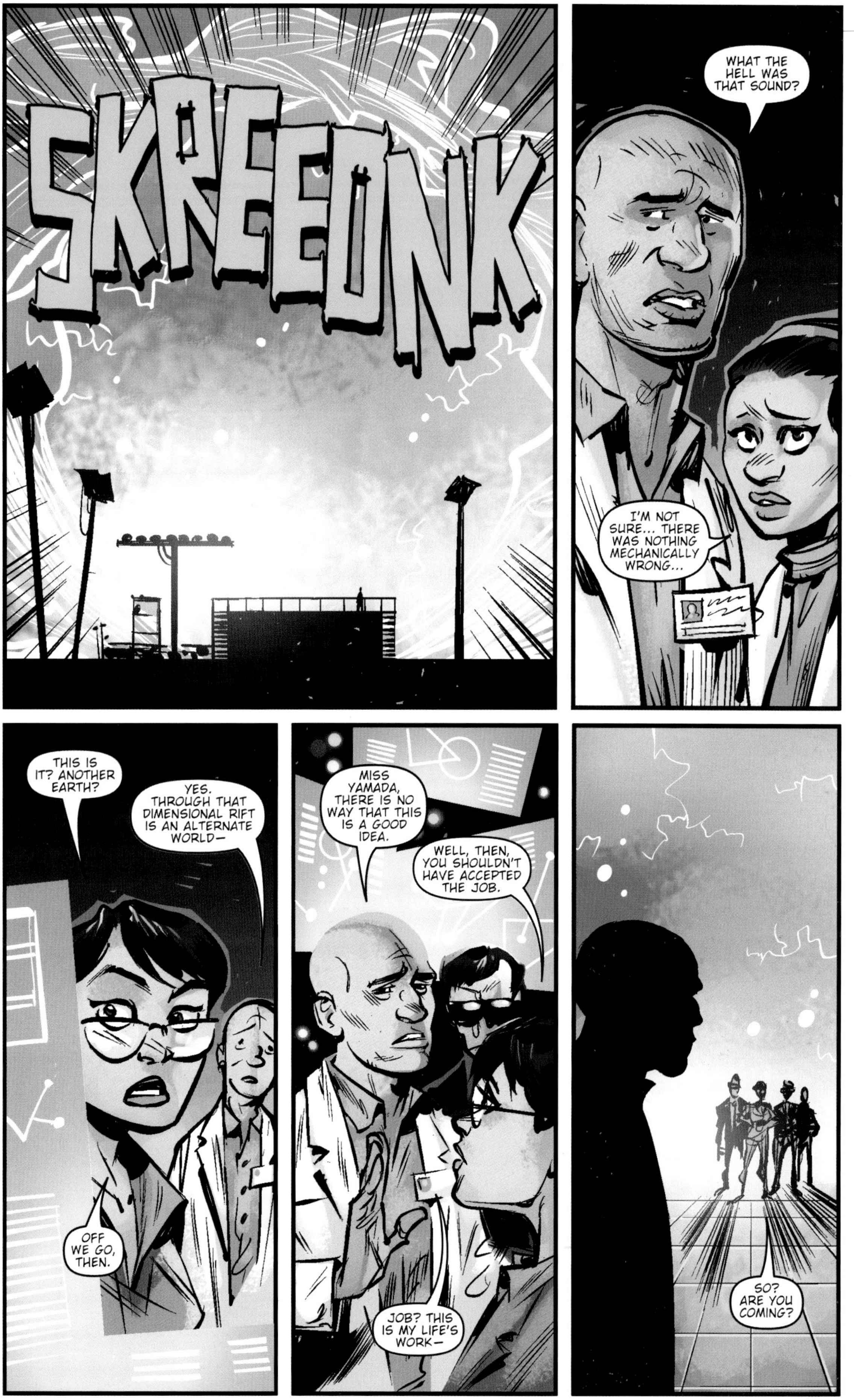
SKREEONK
WHAT THE HELL WAS THAT SOUND?
I'M NOT SURE... THERE WAS NOTHING MECHANICALLY WRONG...
THIS IS IT? ANOTHER EARTH?
YES. THROUGH THAT DIMENSIONAL RIFT IS AN ALTERNATE WORLD—
OFF WE GO, THEN.
MISS YAMADA, THERE IS NO WAY THAT THIS IS A GOOD IDEA.
WELL, THEN, YOU SHOULDN'T HAVE ACCEPTED THE JOB.
JOB? THIS IS MY LIFE'S WORK—
SO? ARE YOU COMING?

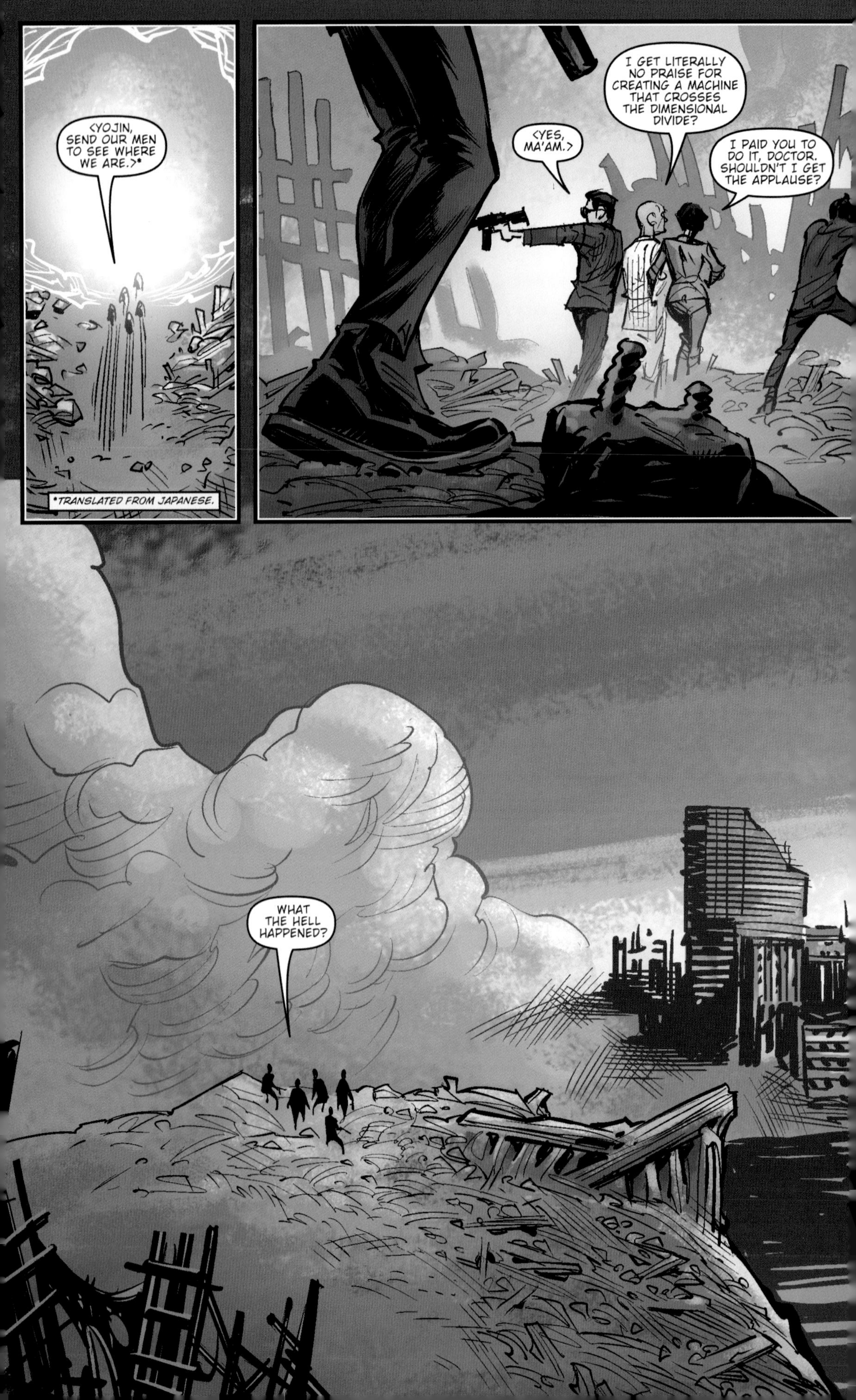
<YOJIN, SEND OUR MEN TO SEE WHERE WE ARE.>*
*TRANSLATED FROM JAPANESE.
<YES, MA'AM.>
I GET LITERALLY NO PRAISE FOR CREATING A MACHINE THAT CROSSES THE DIMENSIONAL DIVIDE?
I PAID YOU TO DO IT, DOCTOR. SHOULDN'T I GET THE APPLAUSE?
WHAT THE HELL HAPPENED?

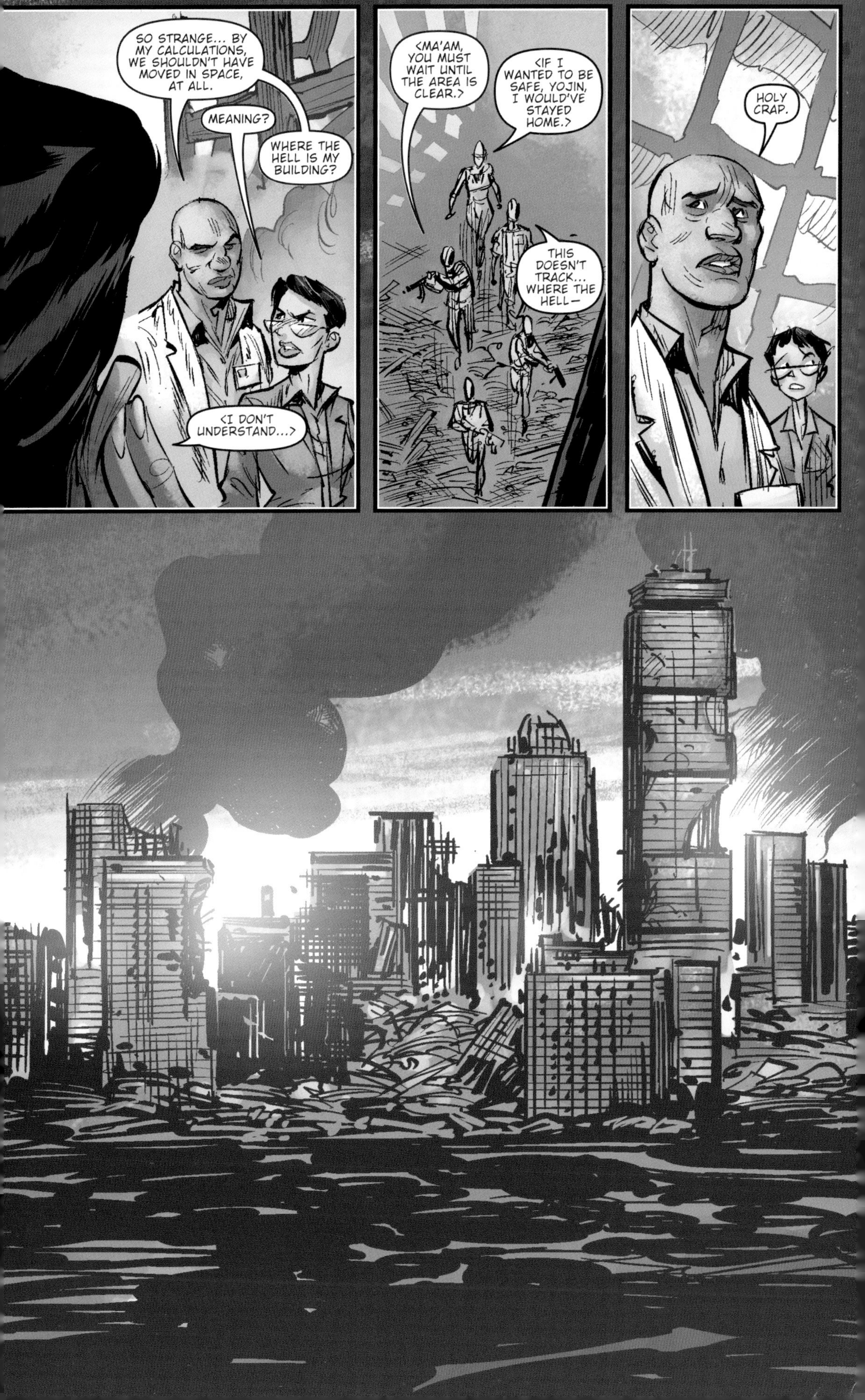
SO STRANGE... BY MY CALCULATIONS, WE SHOULDN'T HAVE MOVED IN SPACE, AT ALL.
MEANING?
WHERE THE HELL IS MY BUILDING?
<I DON'T UNDERSTAND...>
<MA'AM, YOU MUST WAIT UNTIL THE AREA IS CLEAR.>
<IF I WANTED TO BE SAFE, YOJIN, I WOULD'VE STAYED HOME.>
THIS DOESN'T TRACK... WHERE THE HELL—
HOLY CRAP.

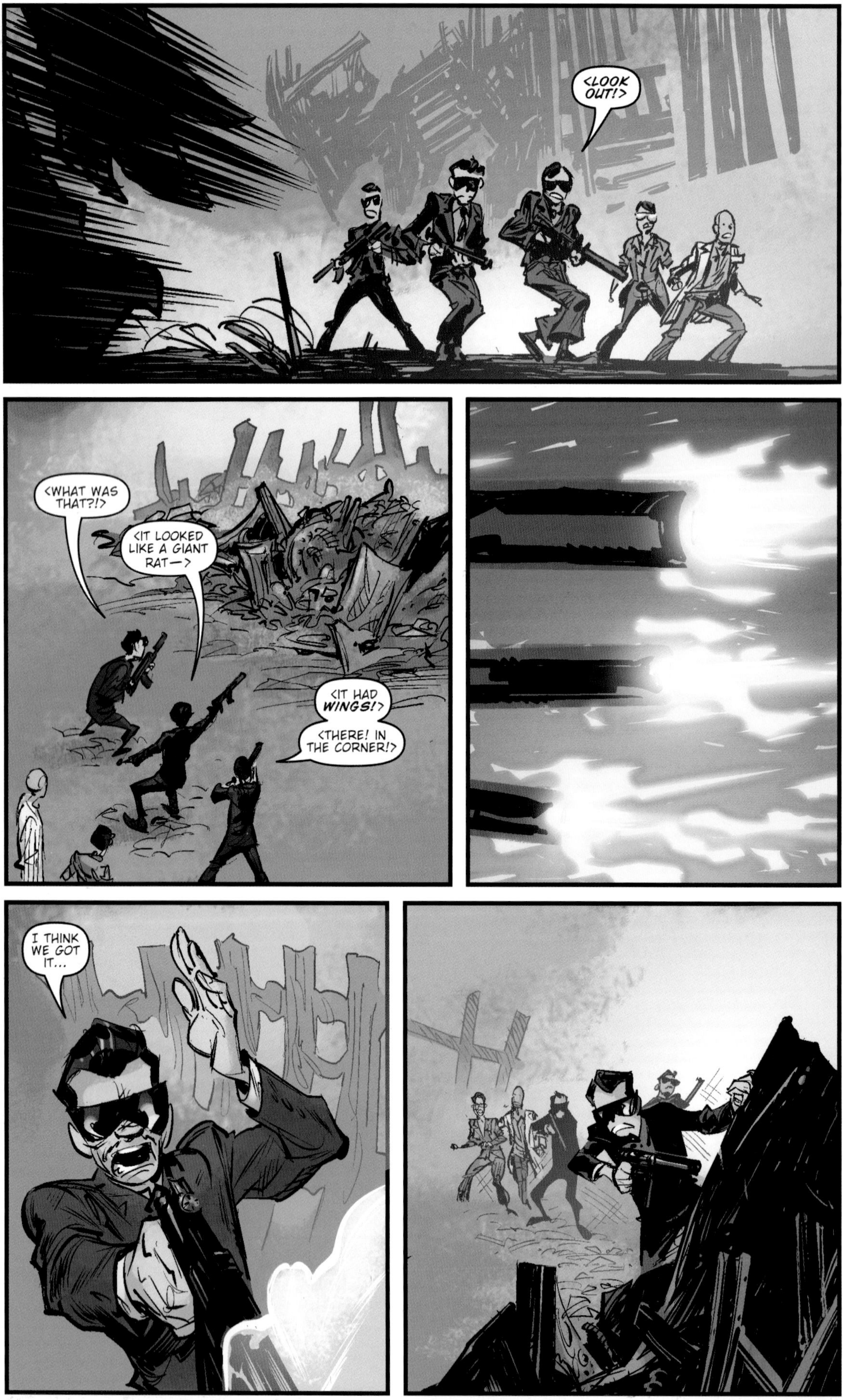
<LOOK OUT!>
<WHAT WAS THAT?!>
<IT LOOKED LIKE A GIANT RAT—>
<IT HAD *WINGS!*>
<THERE! IN THE CORNER!>
I THINK WE GOT IT...

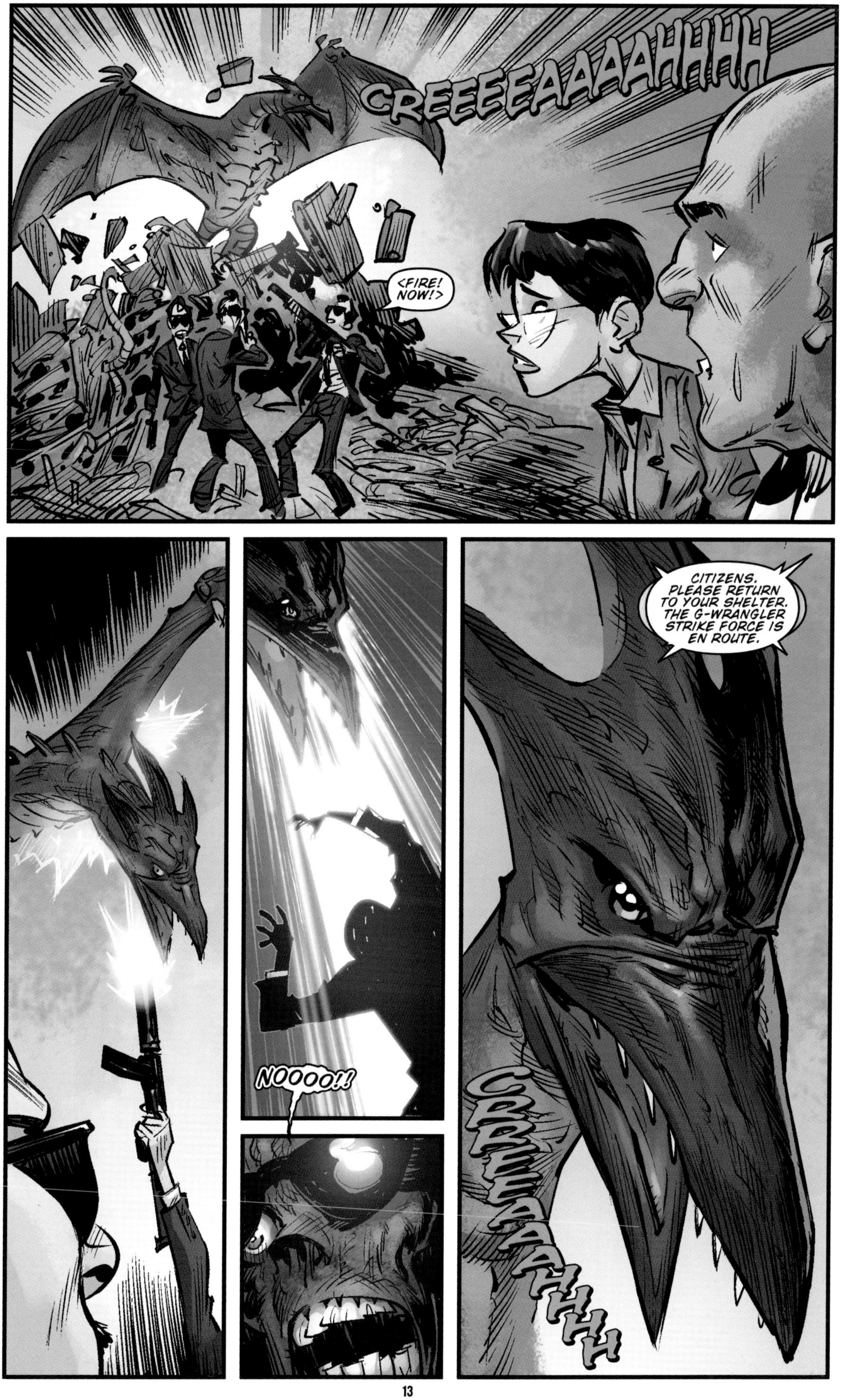

CREEEEAAAAHHHH
<FIRE! NOW!>
CITIZENS. PLEASE RETURN TO YOUR SHELTER. THE G-WRANGLER STRIKE FORCE IS EN ROUTE.
NOOOO!!

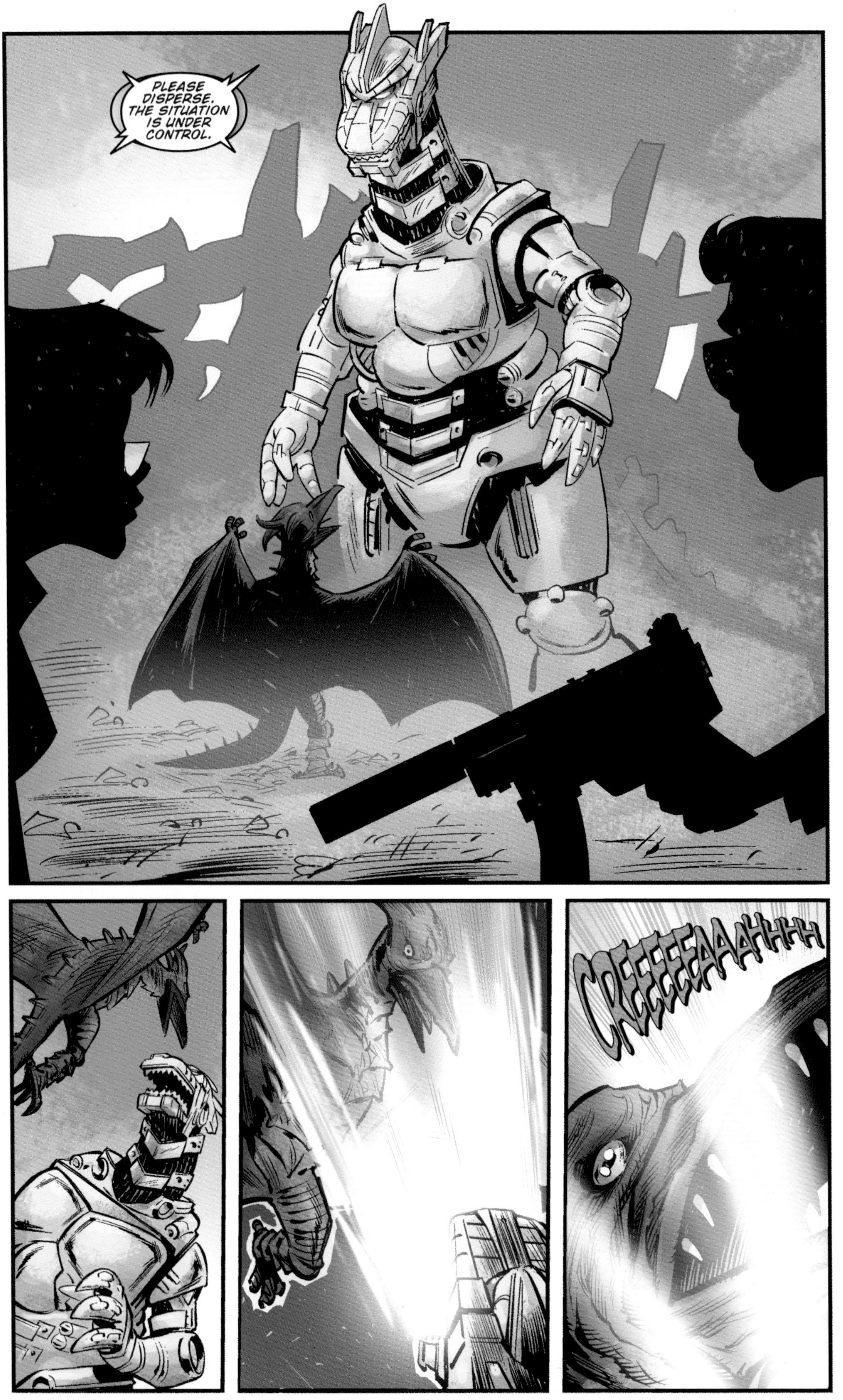
PLEASE DISPERSE. THE SITUATION IS UNDER CONTROL.
CREEEEEAAAHHHH

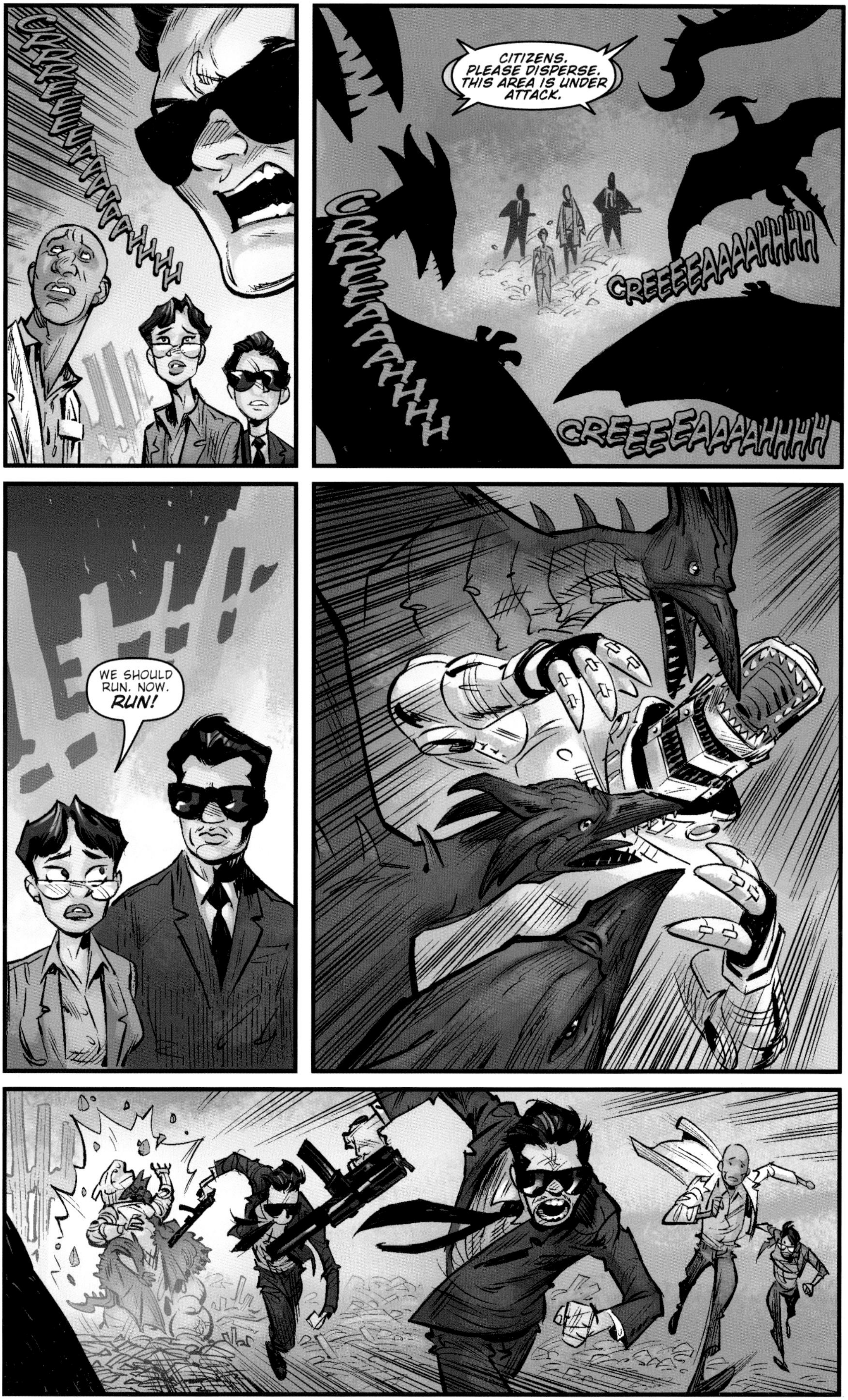

CRREEEEAAAAAAAAHHHHH
CITIZENS. PLEASE DISPERSE. THIS AREA IS UNDER ATTACK.
CRREEEAAAHHHH
CREEEEAAAAHHHHH
CREEEEAAAAAHHHHH
WE SHOULD RUN. NOW. ***RUN!***

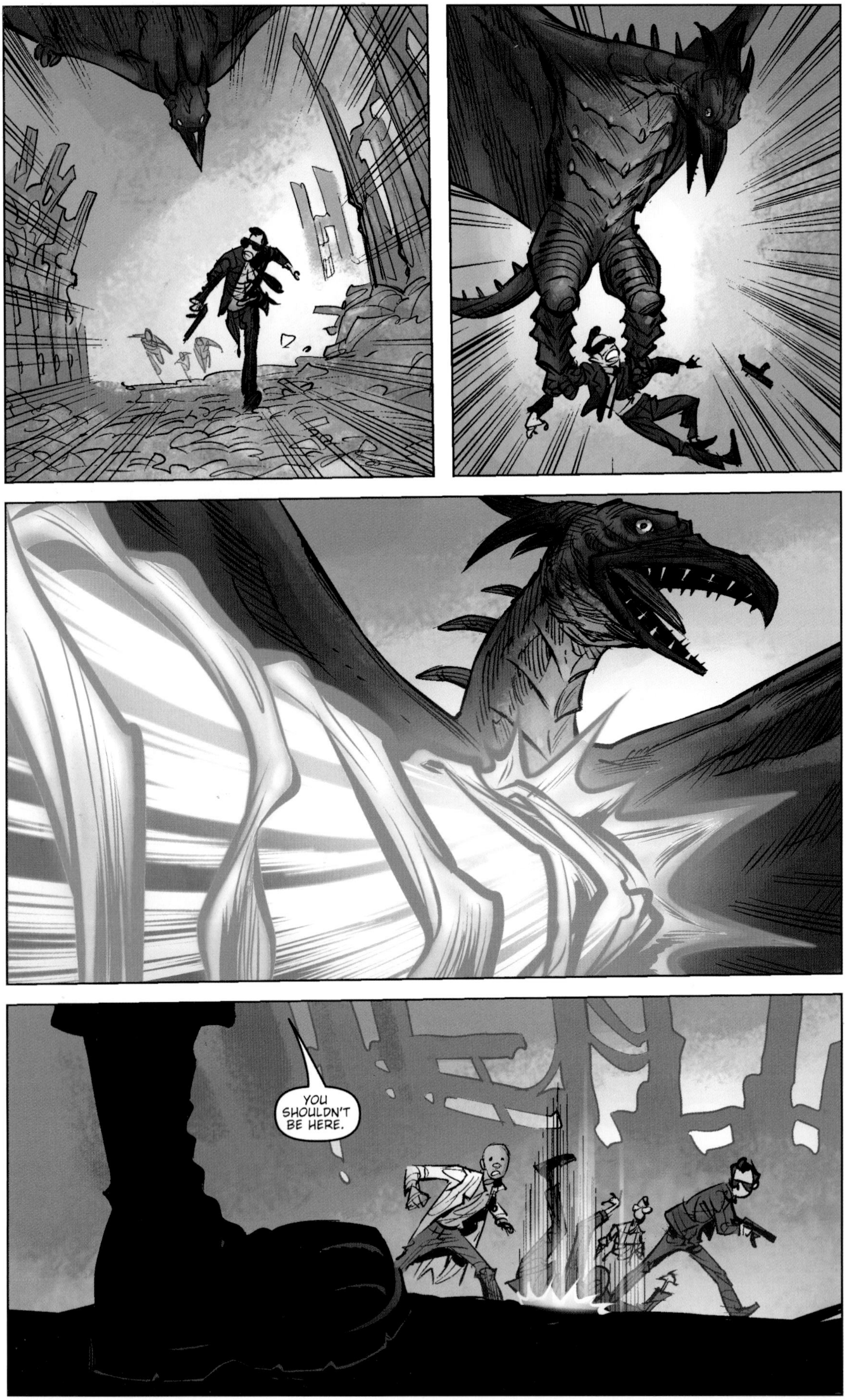
YOU SHOULDN'T BE HERE.

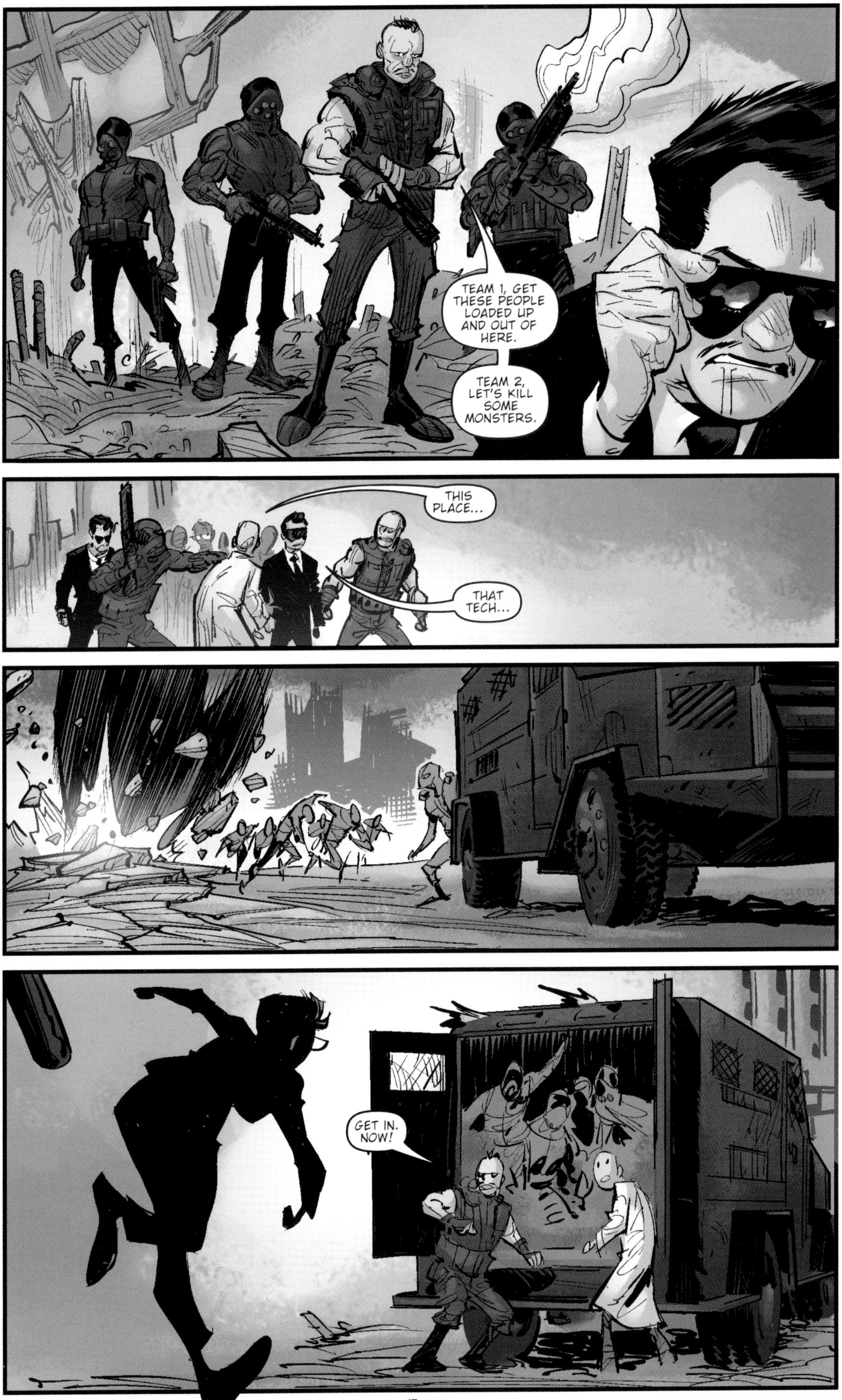
TEAM 1, GET THESE PEOPLE LOADED UP AND OUT OF HERE.
TEAM 2, LET'S KILL SOME MONSTERS.
THIS PLACE...
THAT TECH...
GET IN. NOW!

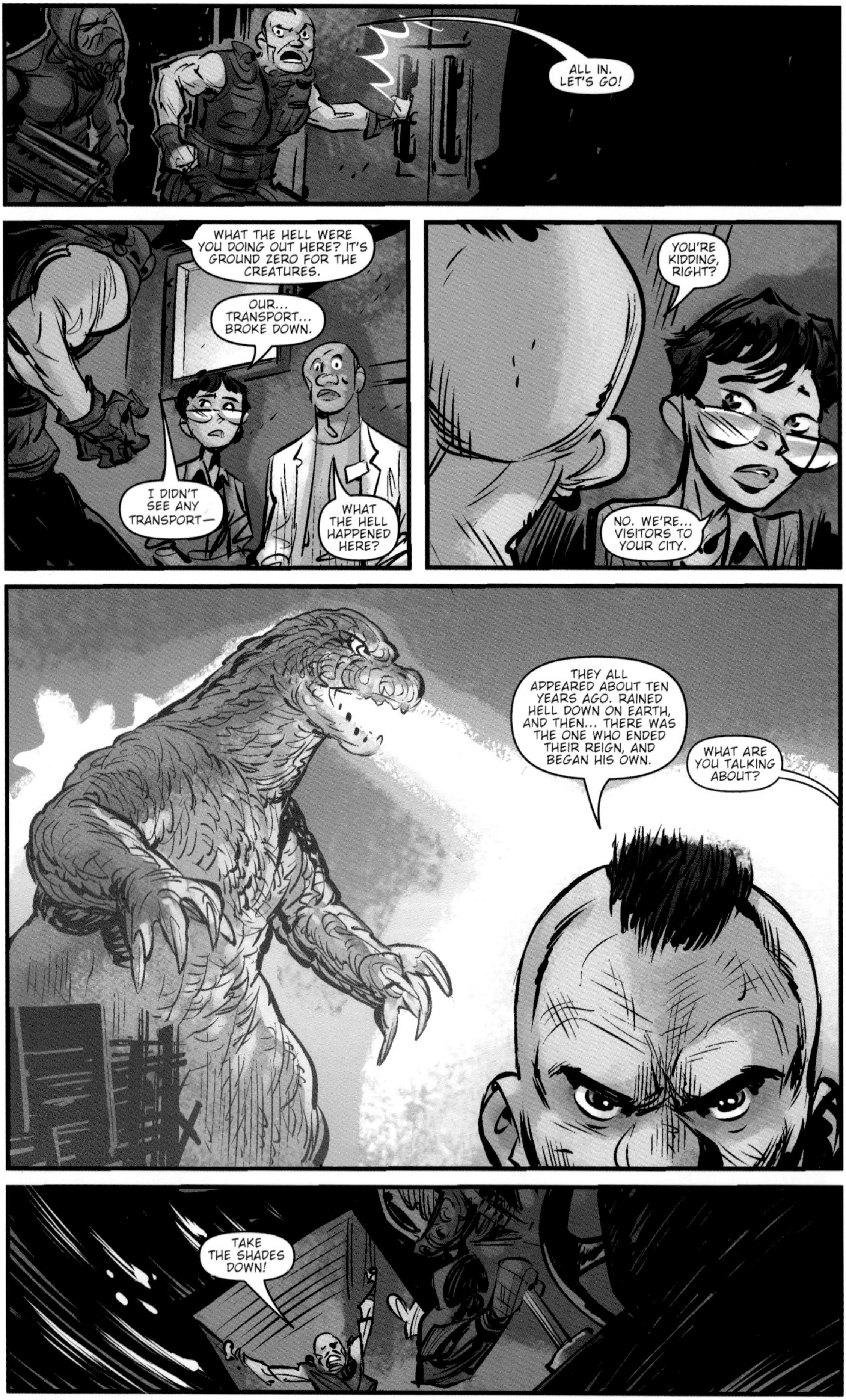
ALL IN. LET'S GO!
WHAT THE HELL WERE YOU DOING OUT HERE? IT'S GROUND ZERO FOR THE CREATURES.
OUR... TRANSPORT... BROKE DOWN.
I DIDN'T SEE ANY TRANSPORT—
WHAT THE HELL HAPPENED HERE?
YOU'RE KIDDING, RIGHT?
NO. WE'RE... VISITORS TO YOUR CITY.
THEY ALL APPEARED ABOUT TEN YEARS AGO. RAINED HELL DOWN ON EARTH, AND THEN... THERE WAS THE ONE WHO ENDED THEIR REIGN, AND BEGAN HIS OWN.
WHAT ARE YOU TALKING ABOUT?
TAKE THE SHADES DOWN!

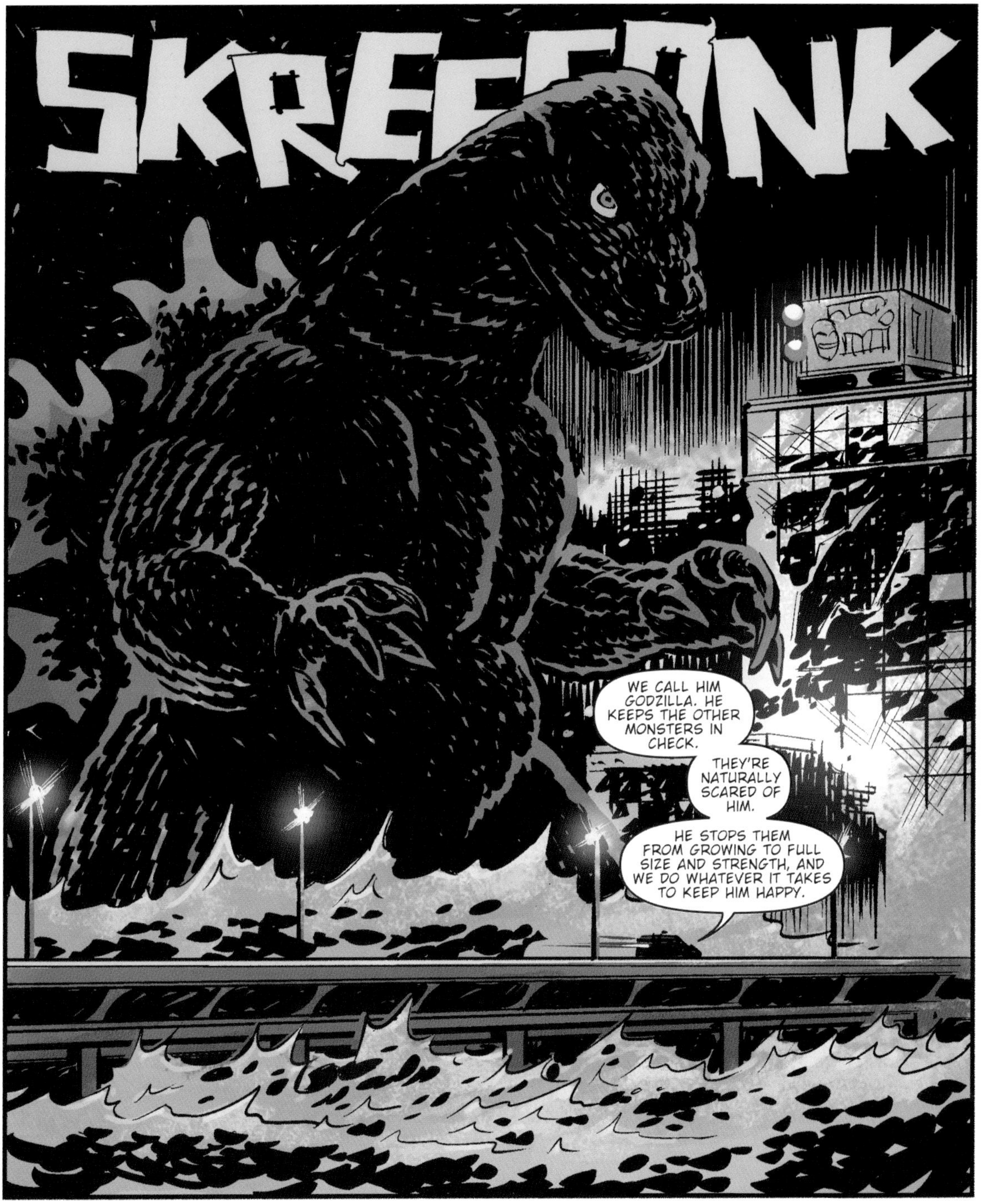
SKREEONK
WE CALL HIM GODZILLA. HE KEEPS THE OTHER MONSTERS IN CHECK.
THEY'RE NATURALLY SCARED OF HIM.
HE STOPS THEM FROM GROWING TO FULL SIZE AND STRENGTH, AND WE DO WHATEVER IT TAKES TO KEEP HIM HAPPY.

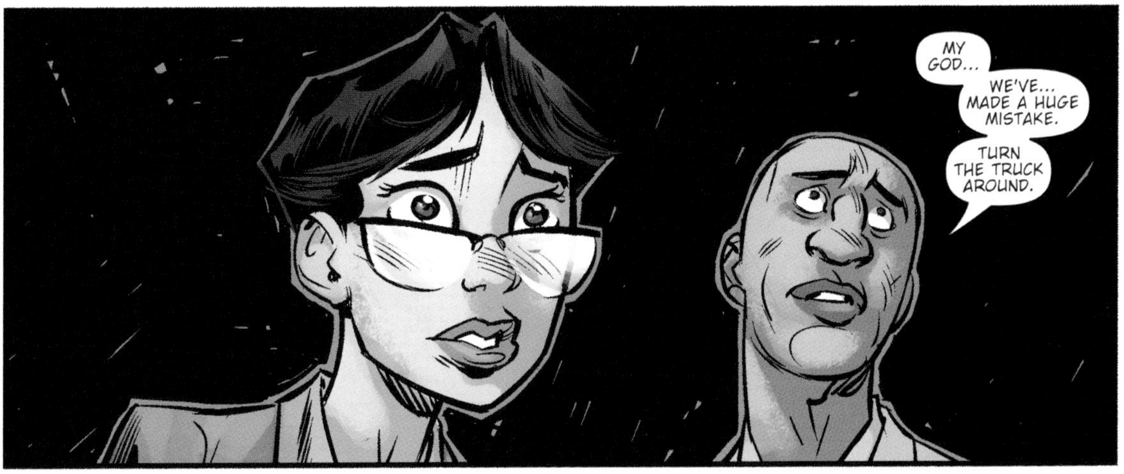
MY GOD...
WE'VE... MADE A HUGE MISTAKE.
TURN THE TRUCK AROUND.

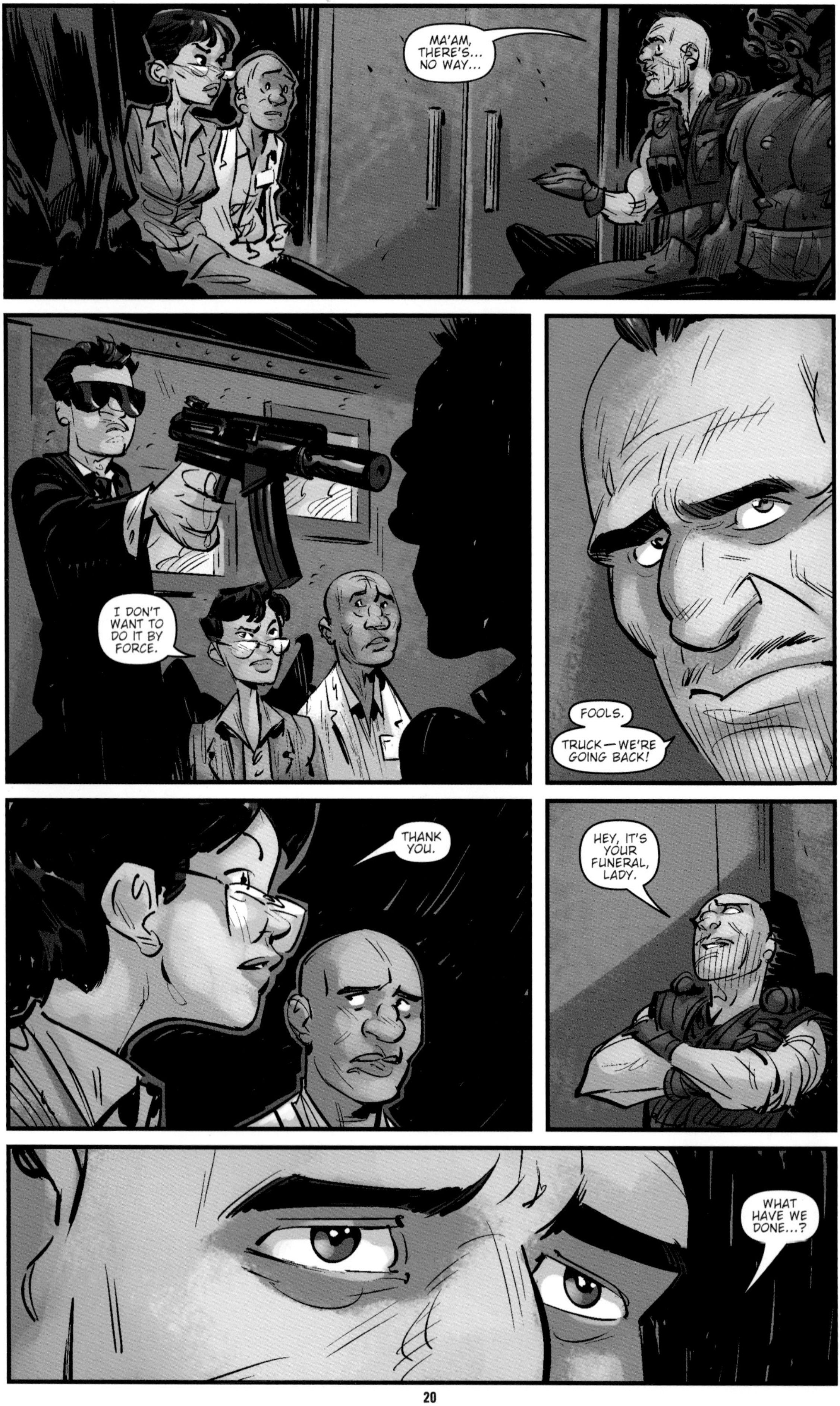
MA'AM, THERE'S... NO WAY...
I DON'T WANT TO DO IT BY FORCE.
FOOLS.
TRUCK—WE'RE GOING BACK!
THANK YOU.
HEY, IT'S YOUR FUNERAL, LADY.
WHAT HAVE WE DONE...?

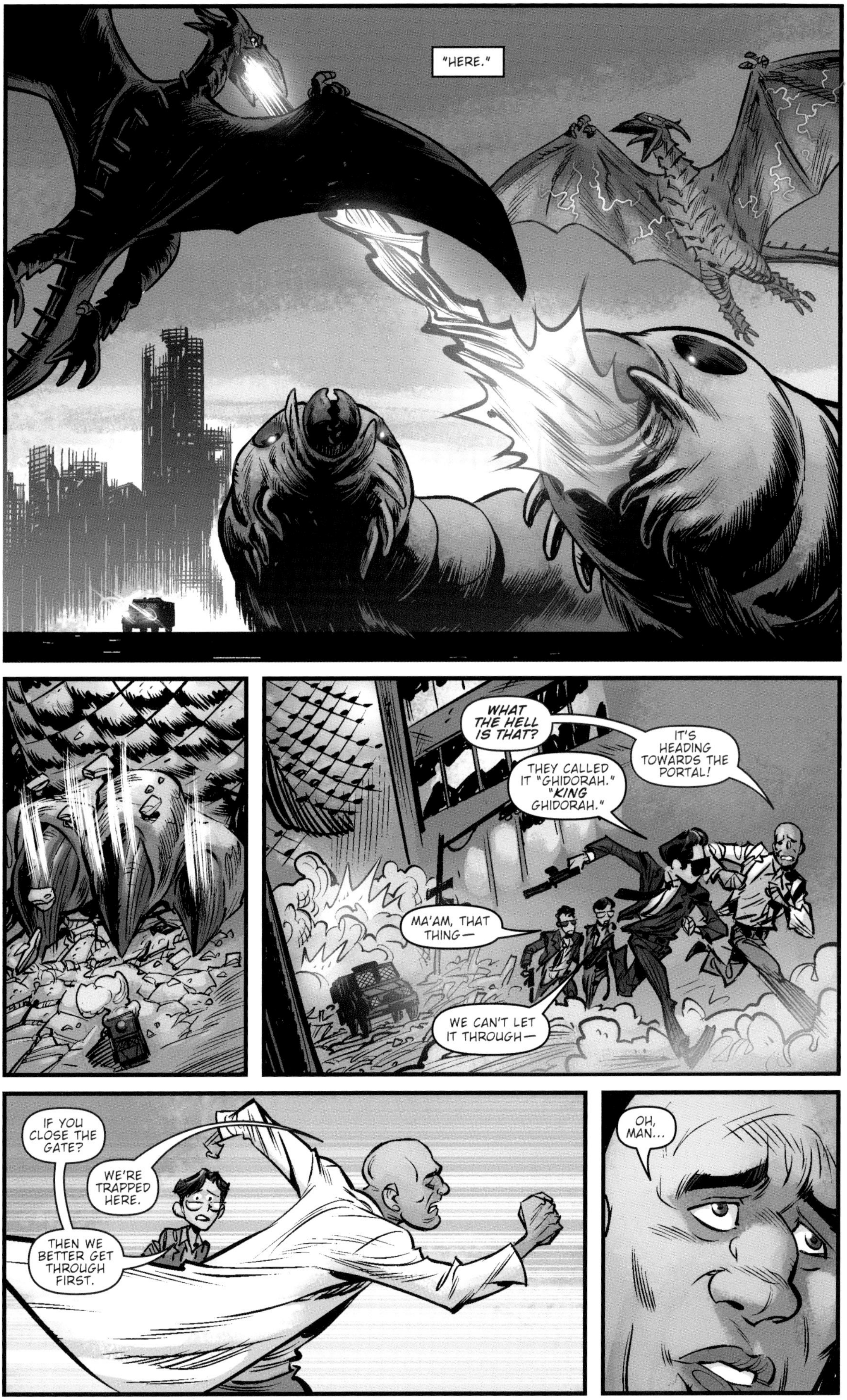
"HERE."
WHAT THE HELL IS THAT?
IT'S HEADING TOWARDS THE PORTAL!
THEY CALLED IT "GHIDORAH." "KING GHIDORAH."
MA'AM, THAT THING—
WE CAN'T LET IT THROUGH—
IF YOU CLOSE THE GATE?
WE'RE TRAPPED HERE.
THEN WE BETTER GET THROUGH FIRST.
OH, MAN...

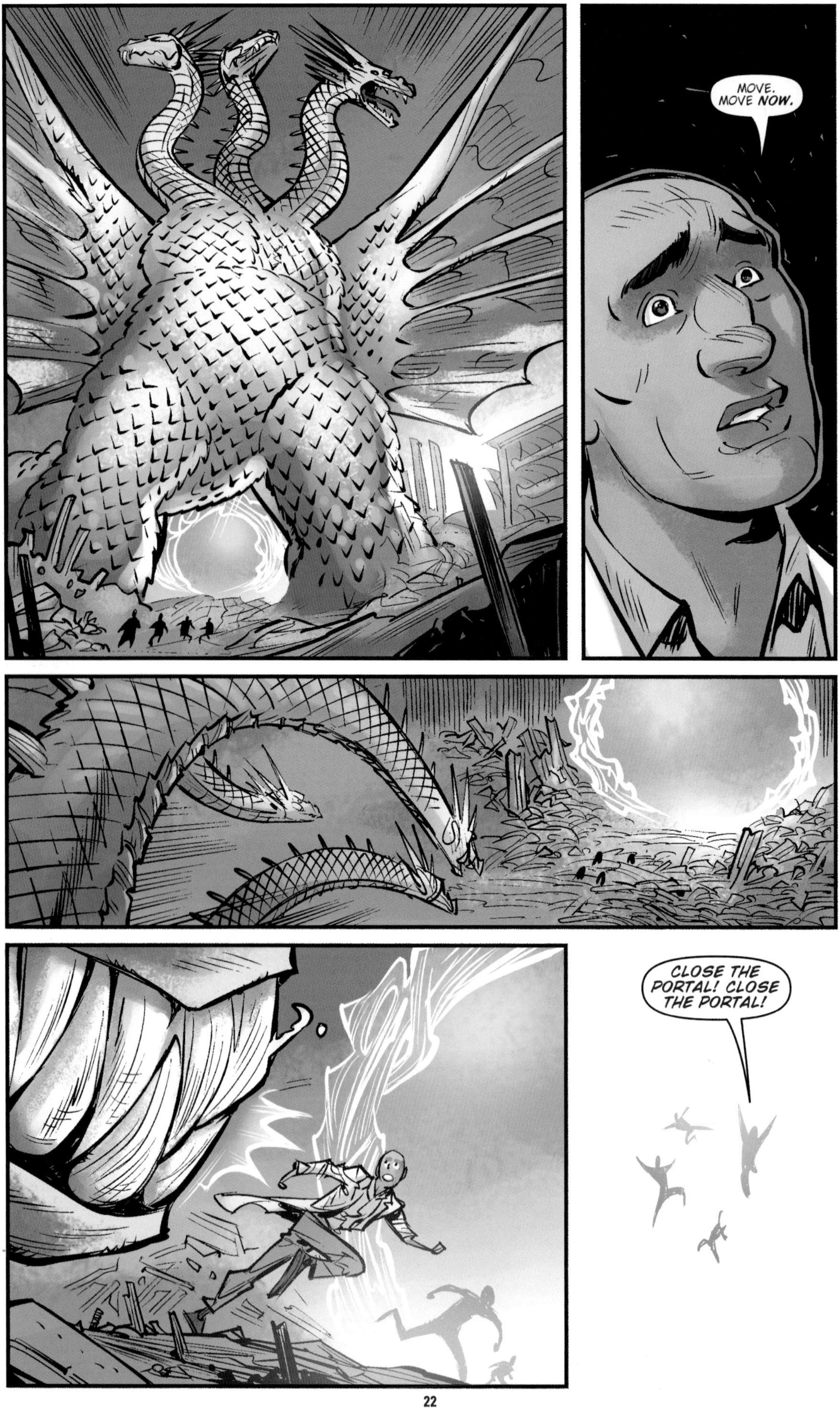
MOVE. MOVE NOW.
CLOSE THE PORTAL! CLOSE THE PORTAL!

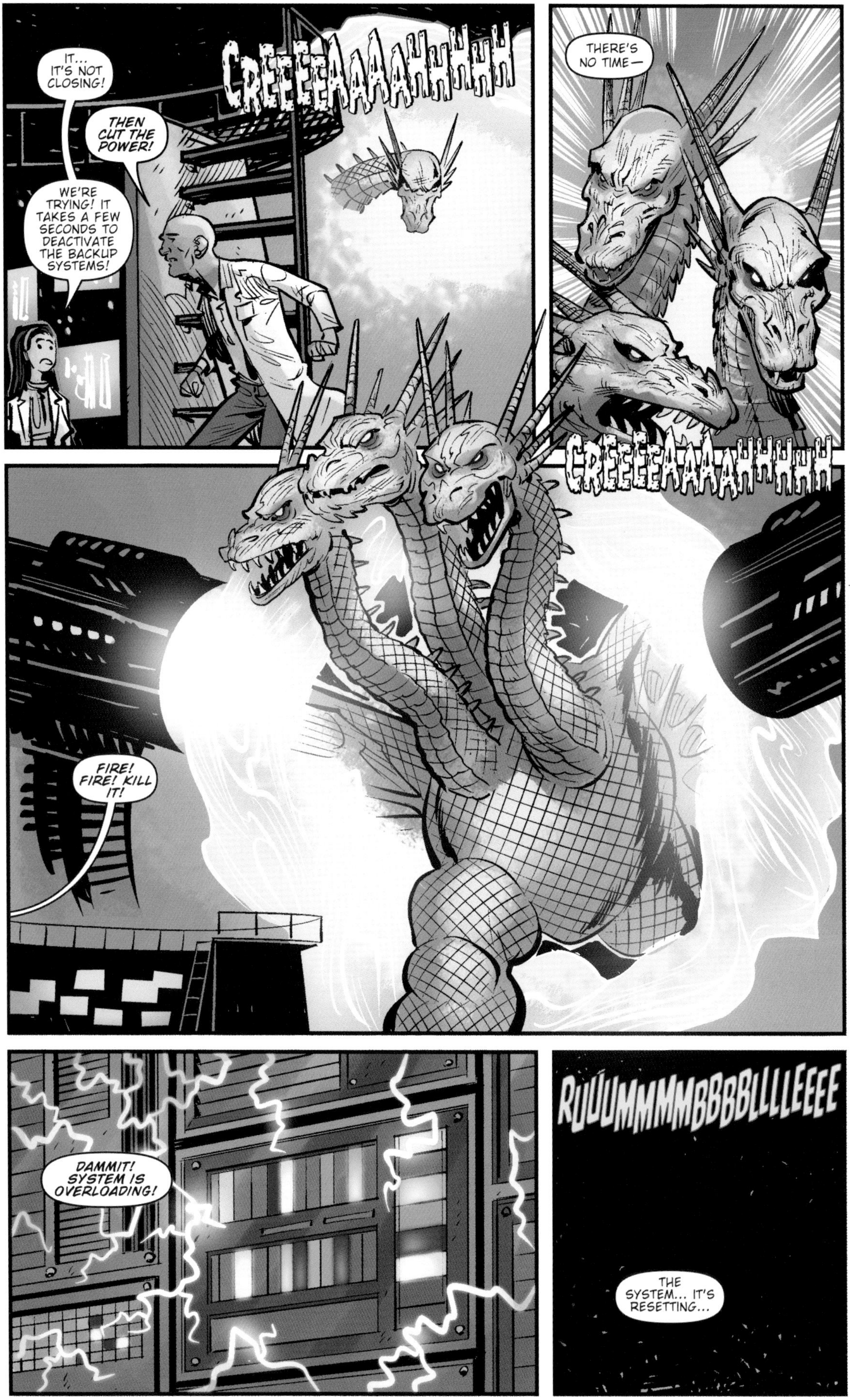
IT... IT'S NOT CLOSING!
THEN CUT THE POWER!
WE'RE TRYING! IT TAKES A FEW SECONDS TO DEACTIVATE THE BACKUP SYSTEMS!
CREEEEAAAAHHHHHH
THERE'S NO TIME—
CREEEEAAAAHHHHHH
FIRE! FIRE! KILL IT!
DAMMIT! SYSTEM IS OVERLOADING!
RUUUMMMMBBBBLLLLEEEE
THE SYSTEM... IT'S RESETTING...

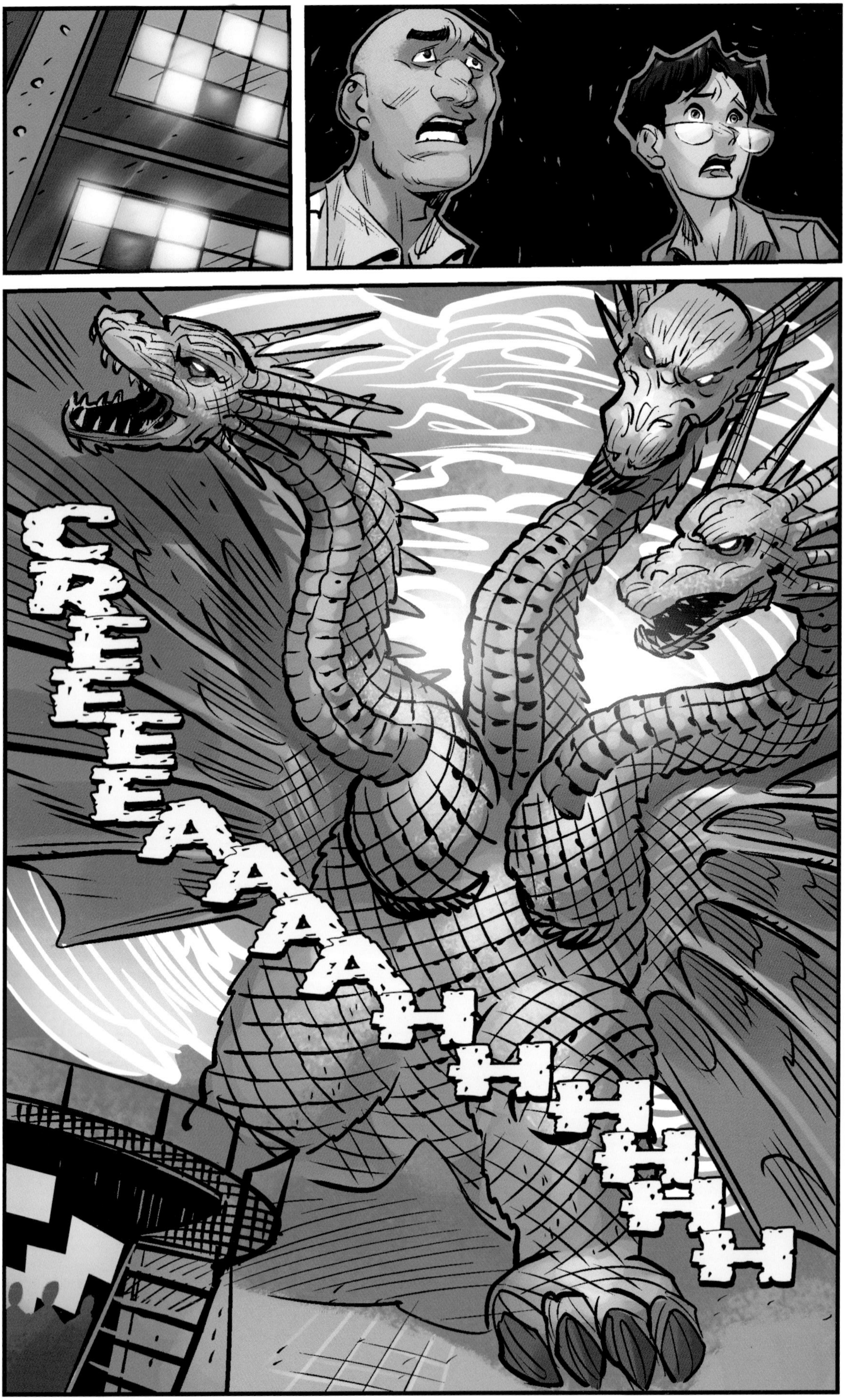
CREEEEAAAAHHHHHH

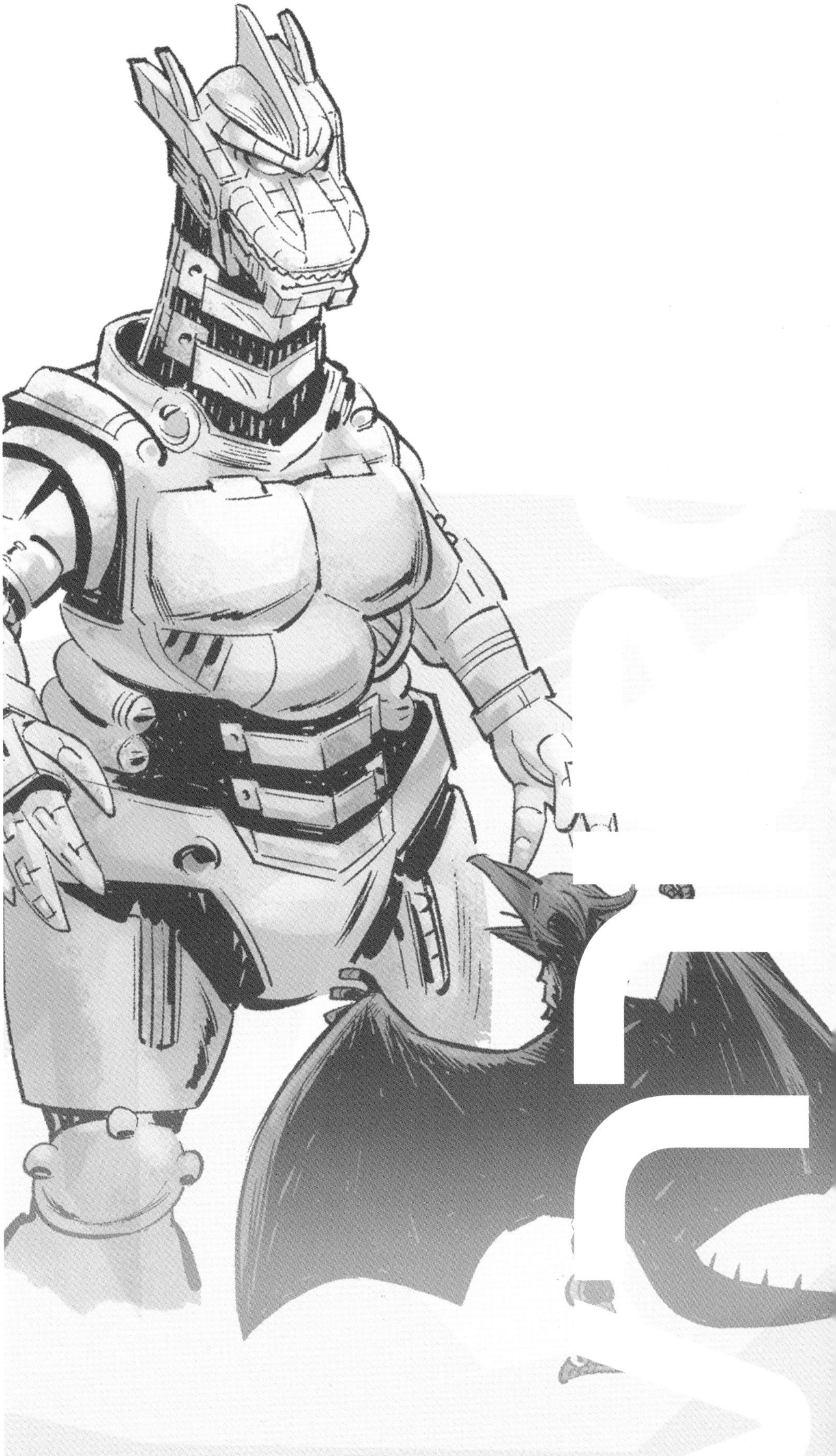

Art by BRIAN CHURILLA

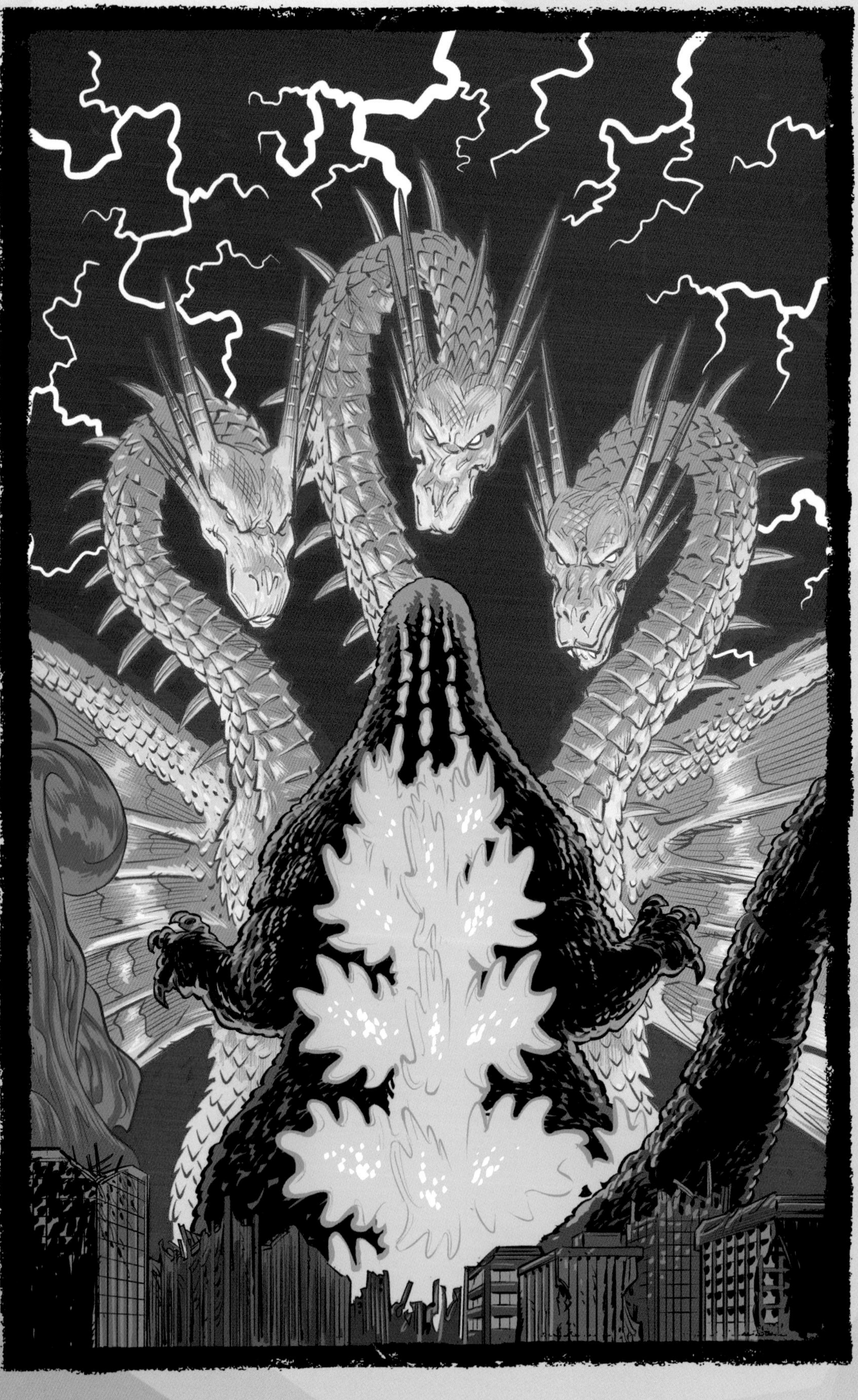

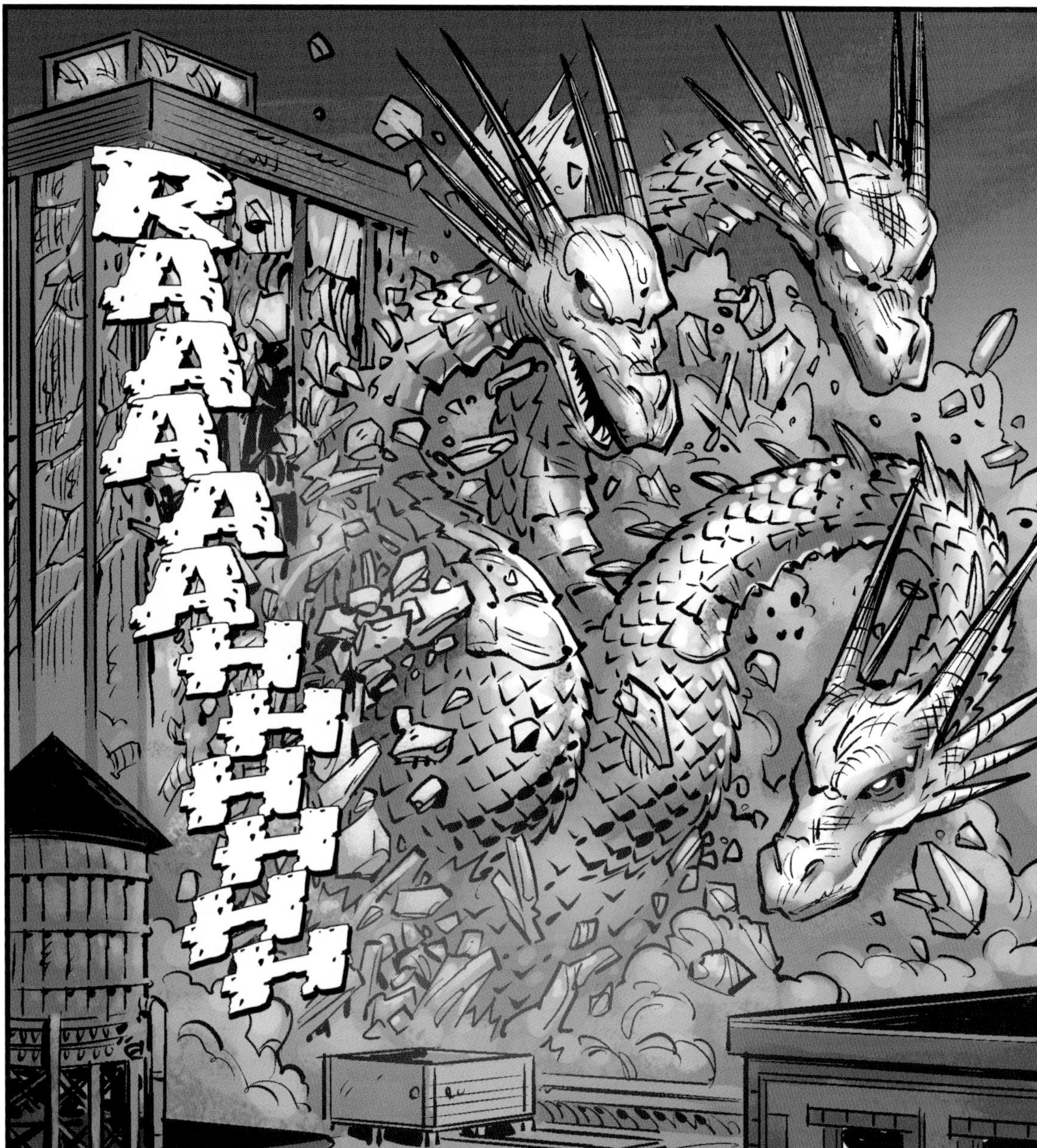
RAAAAAHHHHHH

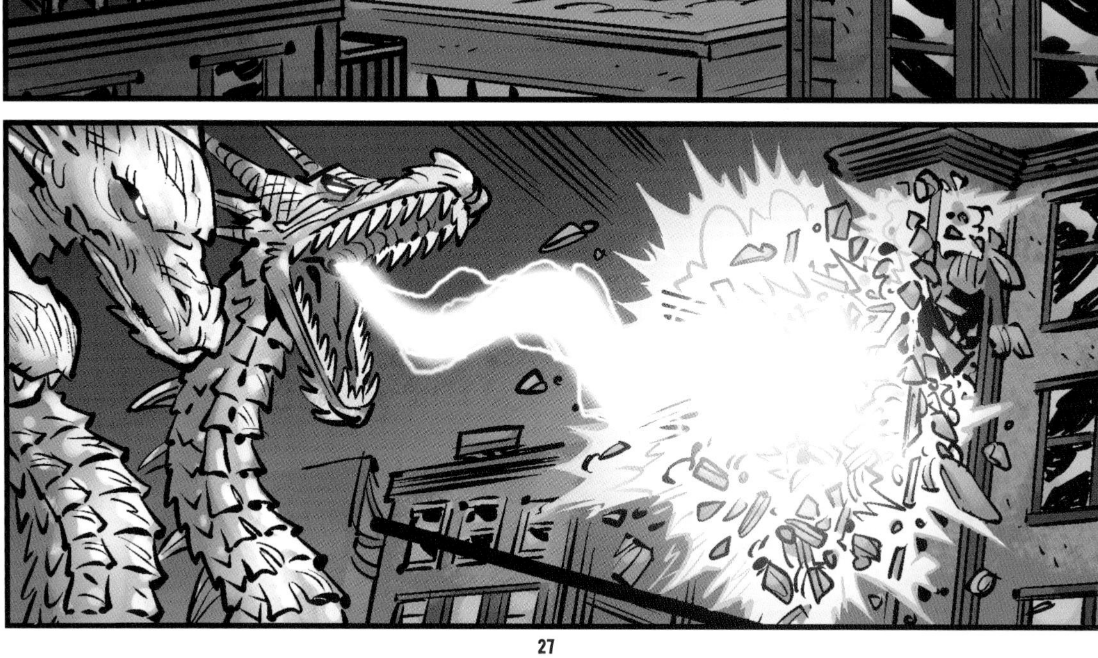

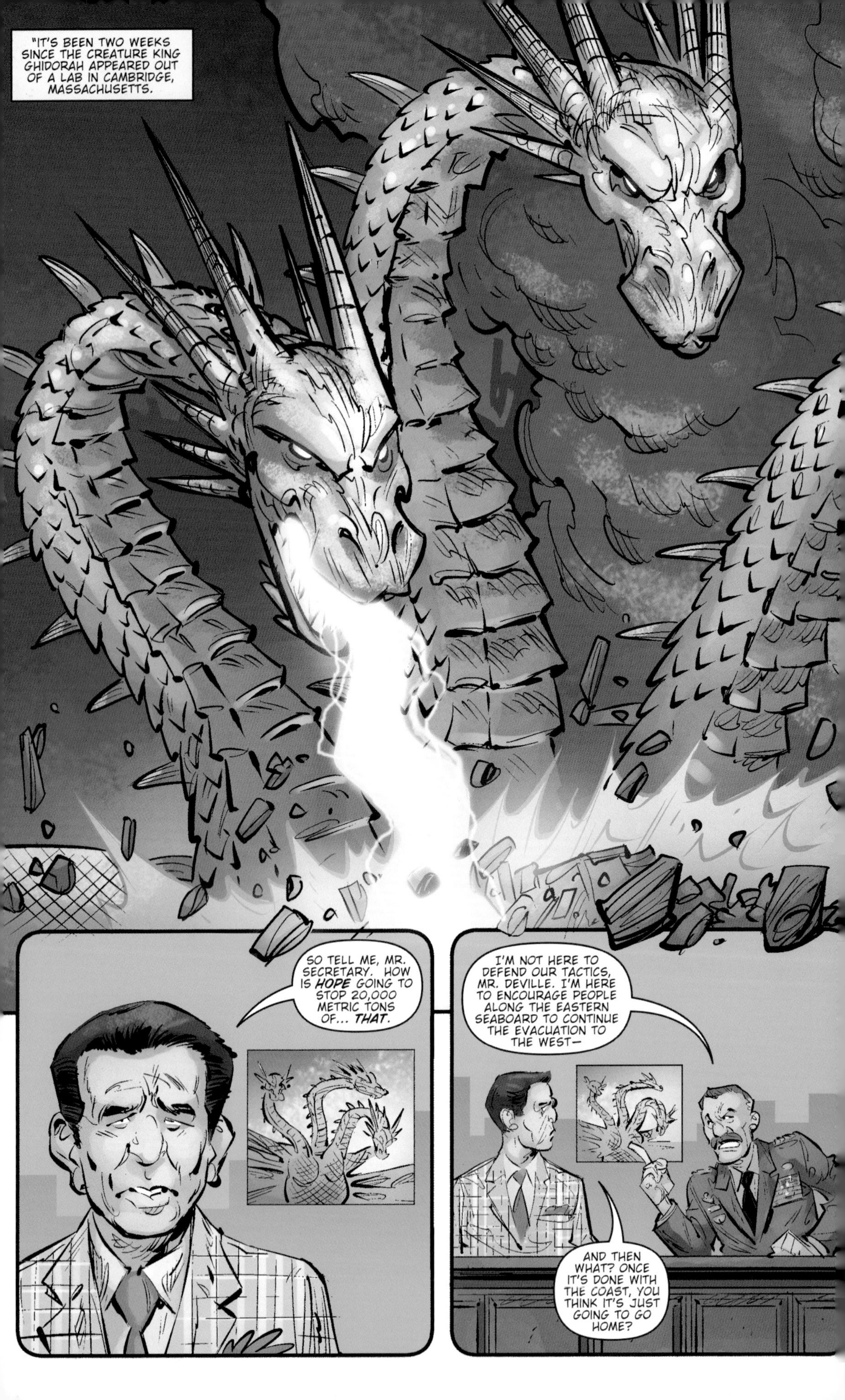
"IT'S BEEN TWO WEEKS SINCE THE CREATURE KING GHIDORAH APPEARED OUT OF A LAB IN CAMBRIDGE, MASSACHUSETTS.
SO TELL ME, MR. SECRETARY. HOW IS *HOPE* GOING TO STOP 20,000 METRIC TONS OF... *THAT*.
I'M NOT HERE TO DEFEND OUR TACTICS, MR. DEVILLE. I'M HERE TO ENCOURAGE PEOPLE ALONG THE EASTERN SEABOARD TO CONTINUE THE EVACUATION TO THE WEST—
AND THEN WHAT? ONCE IT'S DONE WITH THE COAST, YOU THINK IT'S JUST GOING TO GO HOME?

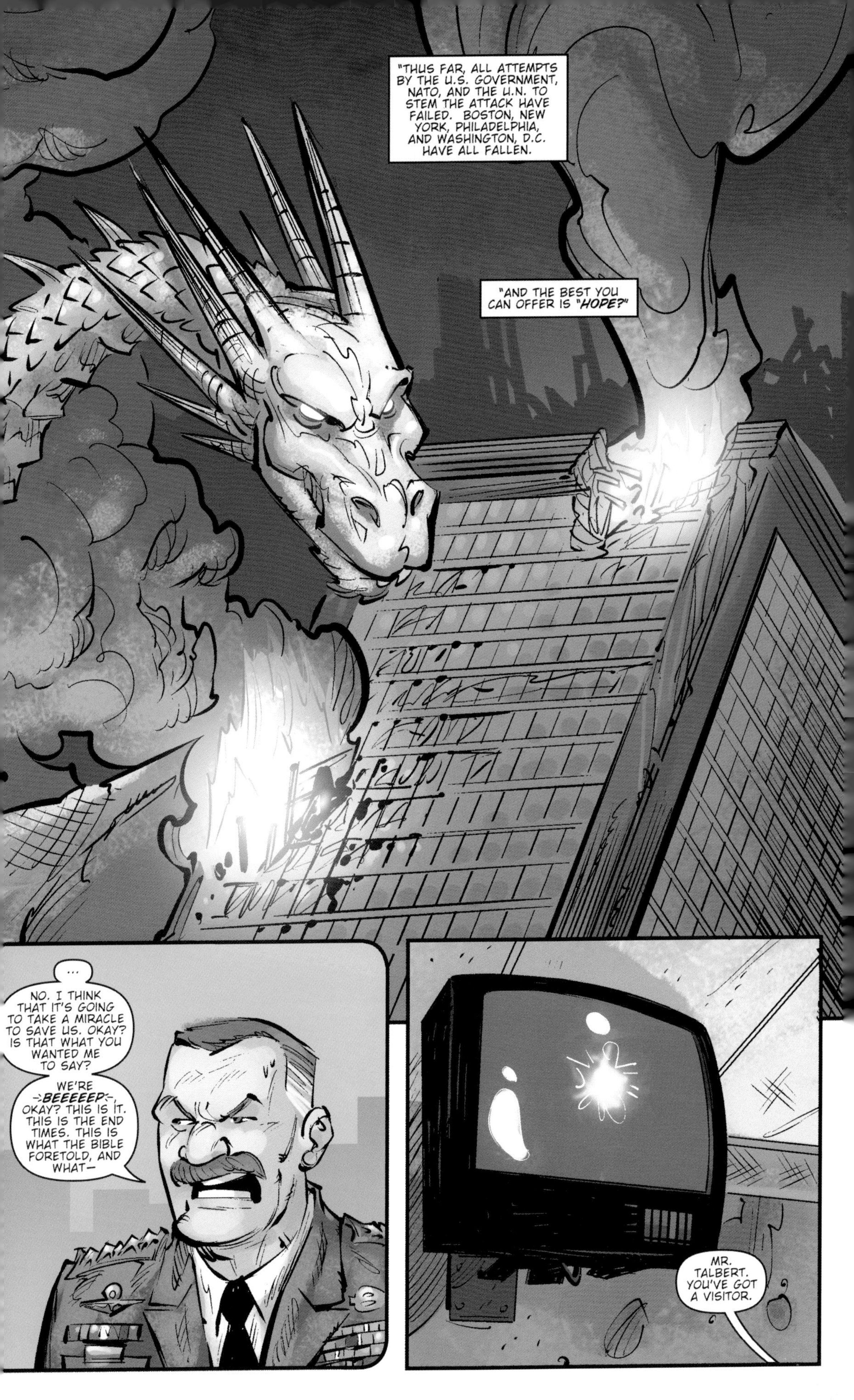
"THUS FAR, ALL ATTEMPTS BY THE U.S. GOVERNMENT, NATO, AND THE U.N. TO STEM THE ATTACK HAVE FAILED. BOSTON, NEW YORK, PHILADELPHIA, AND WASHINGTON, D.C. HAVE ALL FALLEN.
"AND THE BEST YOU CAN OFFER IS "*HOPE?*"
...
NO. I THINK THAT IT'S GOING TO TAKE A MIRACLE TO SAVE US. OKAY? IS THAT WHAT YOU WANTED ME TO SAY?
WE'RE -*BEEEEEP*-, OKAY? THIS IS IT. THIS IS THE END TIMES. THIS IS WHAT THE BIBLE FORETOLD, AND WHAT—
MR. TALBERT. YOU'VE GOT A VISITOR.

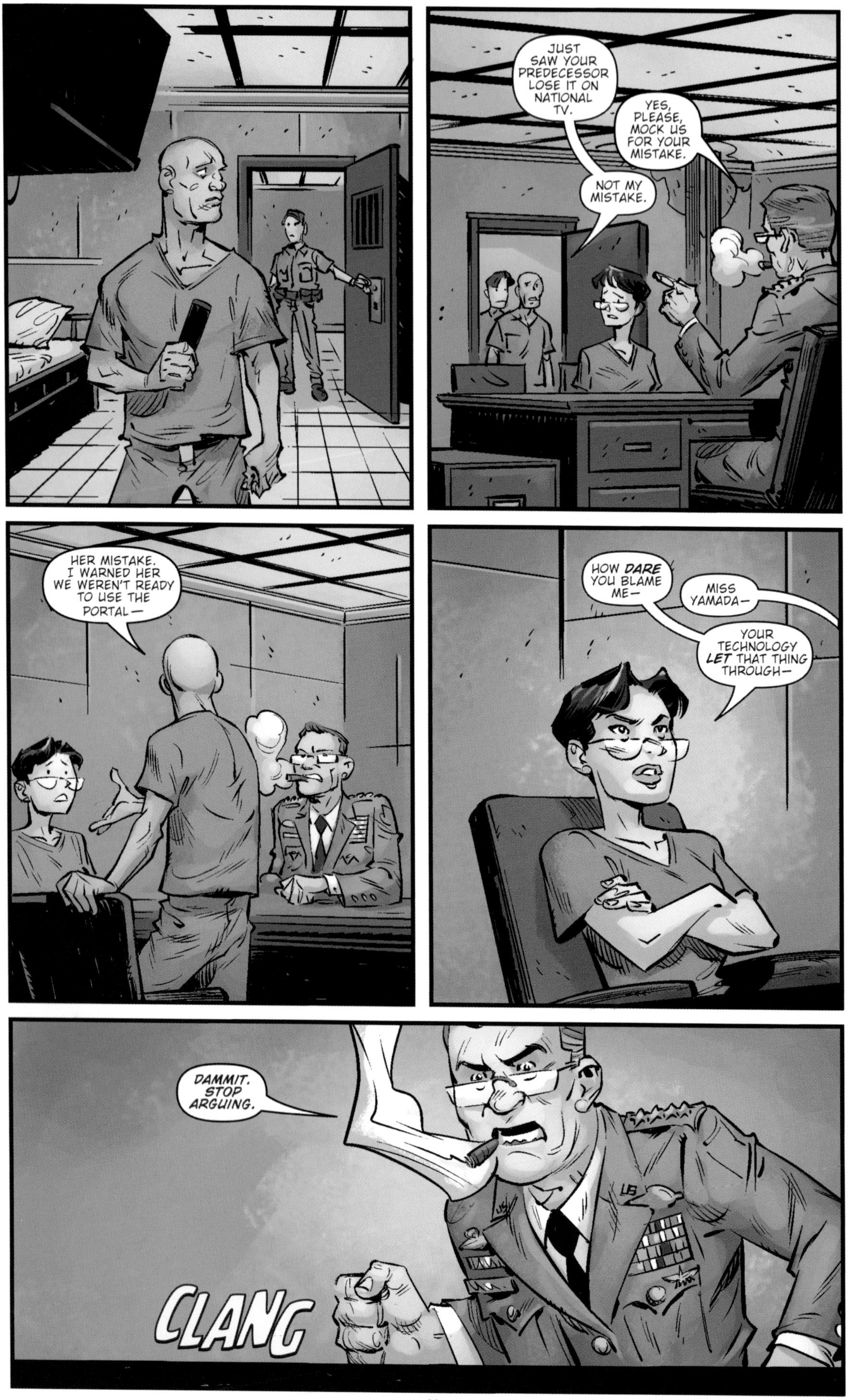
JUST SAW YOUR PREDECESSOR LOSE IT ON NATIONAL TV.
YES, PLEASE, MOCK US FOR YOUR MISTAKE.
NOT MY MISTAKE.
HER MISTAKE. I WARNED HER WE WEREN'T READY TO USE THE PORTAL—
HOW DARE YOU BLAME ME—
MISS YAMADA—
YOUR TECHNOLOGY LET THAT THING THROUGH—
DAMMIT. STOP ARGUING.
CLANG

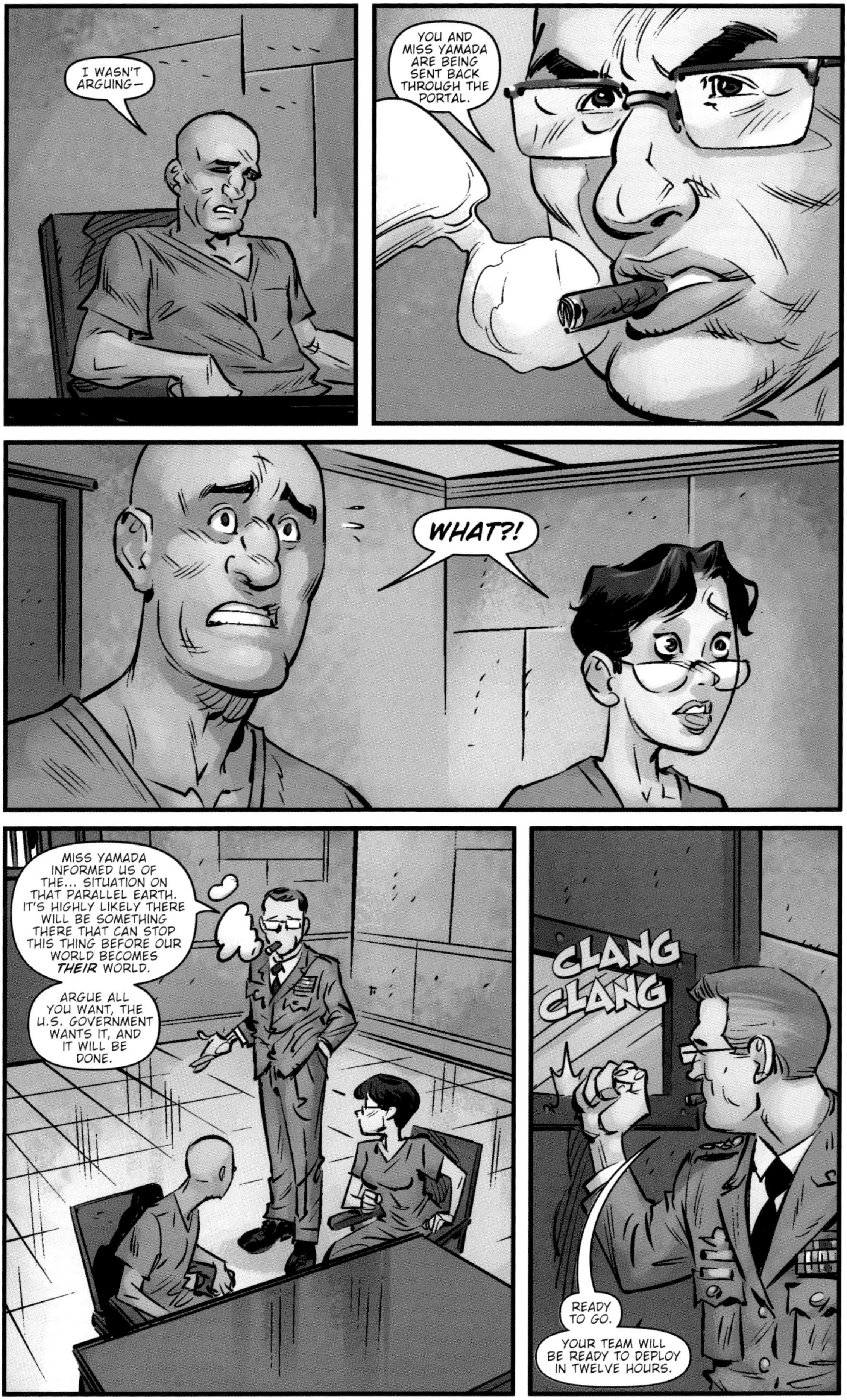
I WASN'T ARGUING—
YOU AND MISS YAMADA ARE BEING SENT BACK THROUGH THE PORTAL.
WHAT?!
MISS YAMADA INFORMED US OF THE... SITUATION ON THAT PARALLEL EARTH. IT'S HIGHLY LIKELY THERE WILL BE SOMETHING THERE THAT CAN STOP THIS THING BEFORE OUR WORLD BECOMES *THEIR* WORLD.
ARGUE ALL YOU WANT, THE U.S. GOVERNMENT WANTS IT, AND IT WILL BE DONE.
CLANG CLANG
READY TO GO.
YOUR TEAM WILL BE READY TO DEPLOY IN TWELVE HOURS.

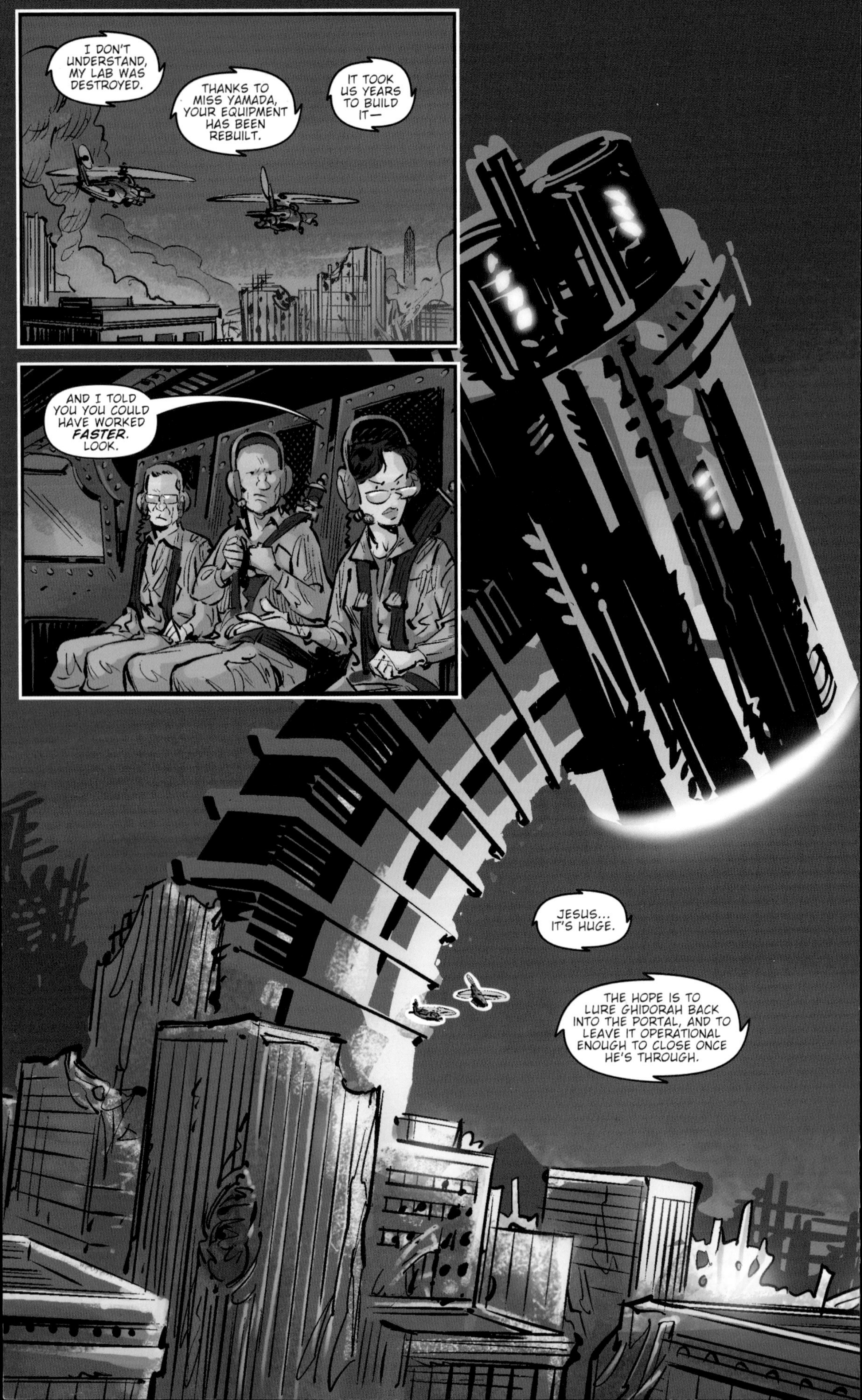
I DON'T UNDERSTAND, MY LAB WAS DESTROYED.
THANKS TO MISS YAMADA, YOUR EQUIPMENT HAS BEEN REBUILT.
IT TOOK US YEARS TO BUILD IT—
AND I TOLD YOU YOU COULD HAVE WORKED **FASTER**. LOOK.
JESUS... IT'S HUGE.
THE HOPE IS TO LURE GHIDORAH BACK INTO THE PORTAL, AND TO LEAVE IT OPERATIONAL ENOUGH TO CLOSE ONCE HE'S THROUGH.

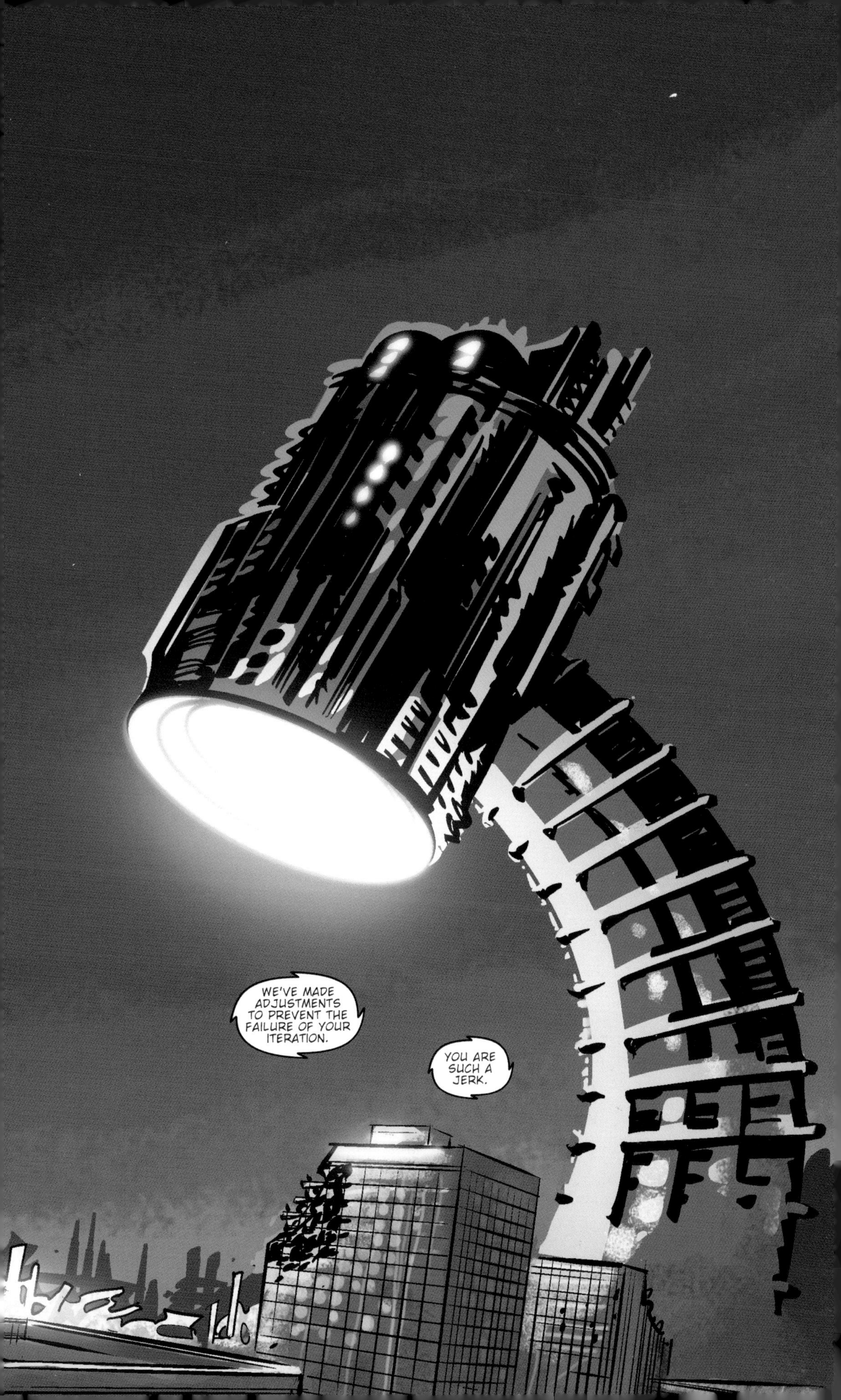
WE'VE MADE ADJUSTMENTS TO PREVENT THE FAILURE OF YOUR ITERATION.
YOU ARE SUCH A JERK.

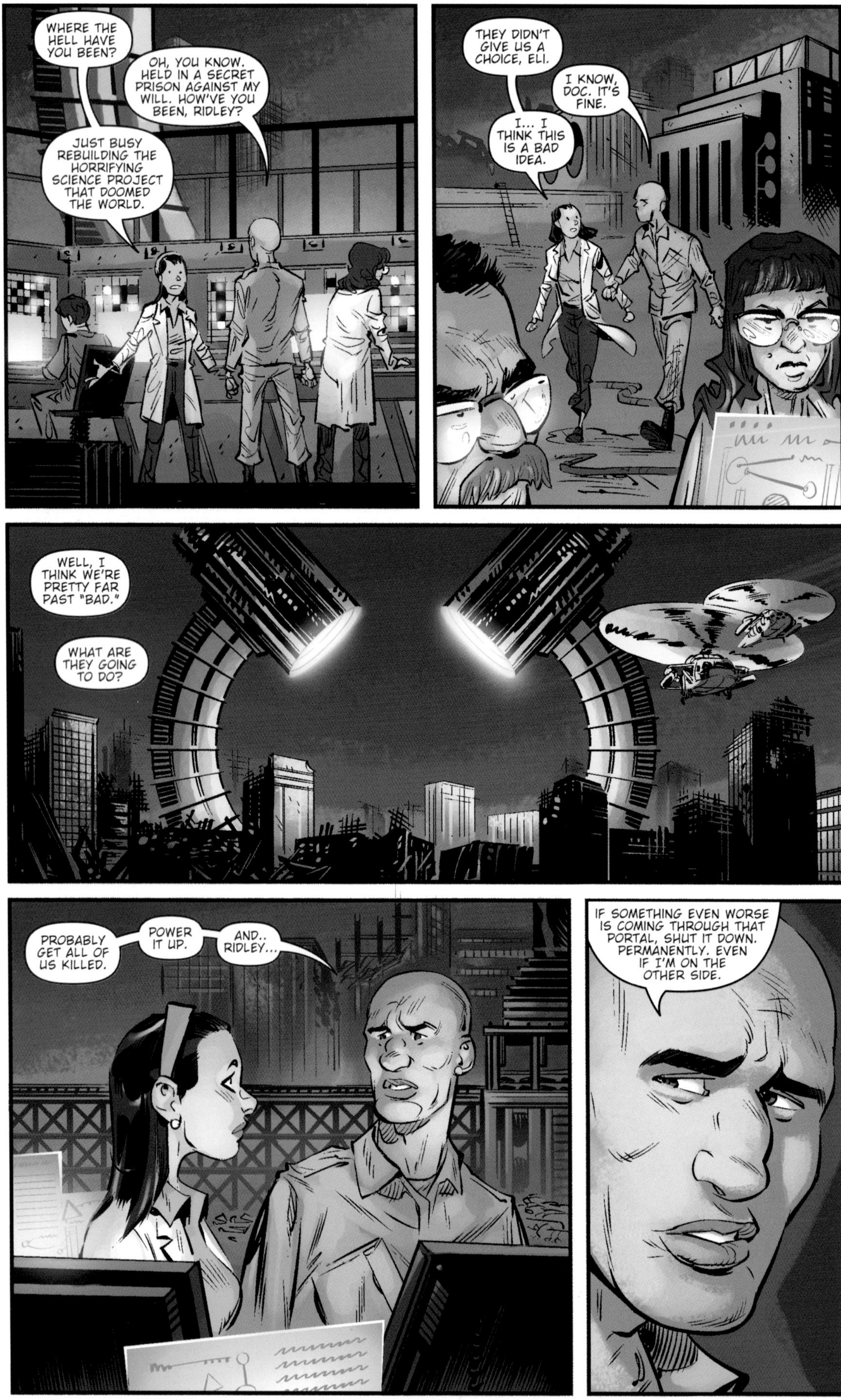
WHERE THE HELL HAVE YOU BEEN?
OH, YOU KNOW. HELD IN A SECRET PRISON AGAINST MY WILL. HOW'VE YOU BEEN, RIDLEY?
JUST BUSY REBUILDING THE HORRIFYING SCIENCE PROJECT THAT DOOMED THE WORLD.
THEY DIDN'T GIVE US A CHOICE, ELI.
I... I THINK THIS IS A BAD IDEA.
I KNOW, DOC. IT'S FINE.
WELL, I THINK WE'RE PRETTY FAR PAST "BAD."
WHAT ARE THEY GOING TO DO?
PROBABLY GET ALL OF US KILLED.
POWER IT UP.
AND.. RIDLEY...
IF SOMETHING EVEN WORSE IS COMING THROUGH THAT PORTAL, SHUT IT DOWN. PERMANENTLY. EVEN IF I'M ON THE OTHER SIDE.

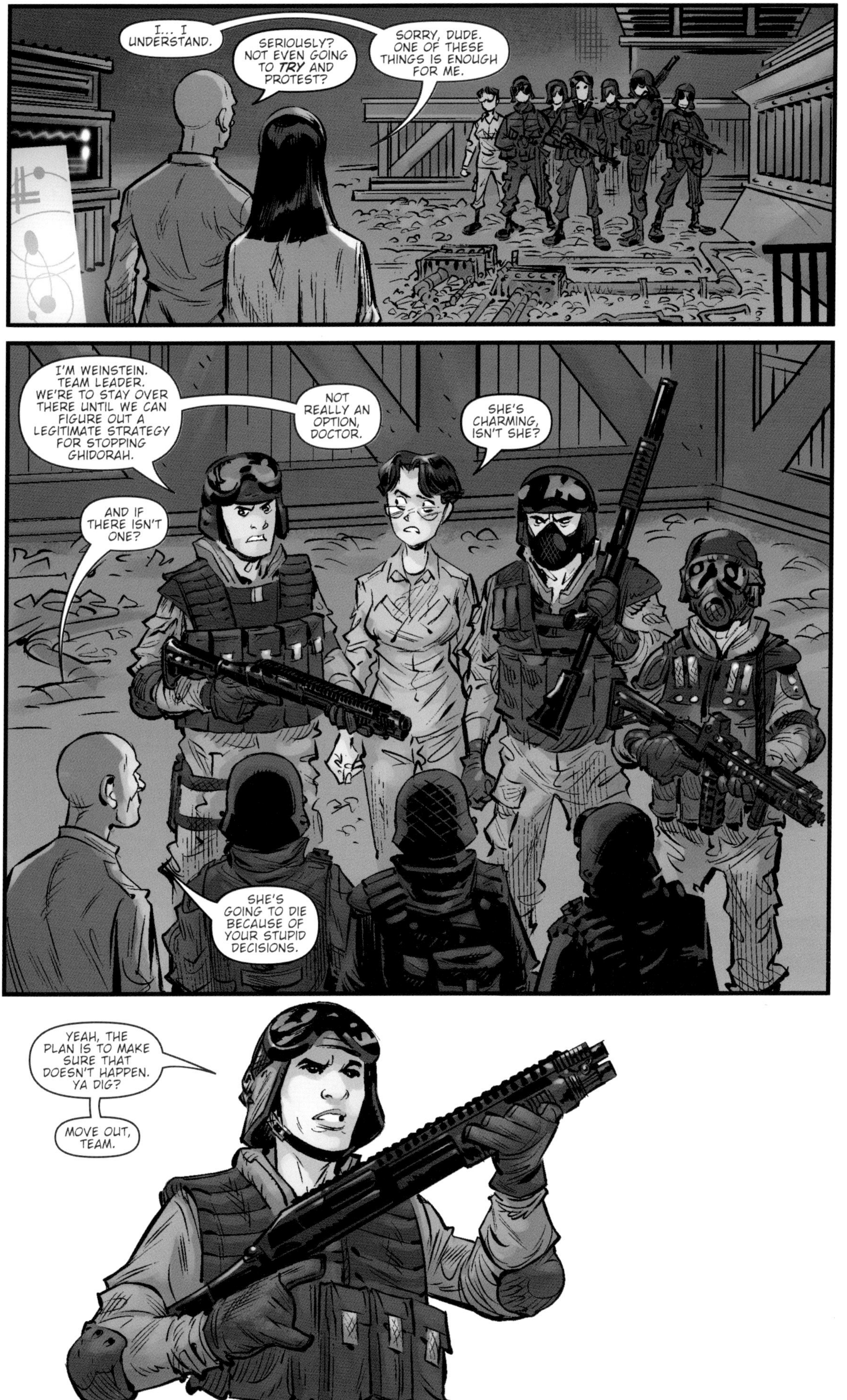
I... I UNDERSTAND.
SERIOUSLY? NOT EVEN GOING TO **TRY** AND PROTEST?
SORRY, DUDE. ONE OF THESE THINGS IS ENOUGH FOR ME.
I'M WEINSTEIN. TEAM LEADER. WE'RE TO STAY OVER THERE UNTIL WE CAN FIGURE OUT A LEGITIMATE STRATEGY FOR STOPPING GHIDORAH.
NOT REALLY AN OPTION, DOCTOR.
SHE'S CHARMING, ISN'T SHE?
AND IF THERE ISN'T ONE?
SHE'S GOING TO DIE BECAUSE OF YOUR STUPID DECISIONS.
YEAH, THE PLAN IS TO MAKE SURE THAT DOESN'T HAPPEN. YA DIG?
MOVE OUT, TEAM.

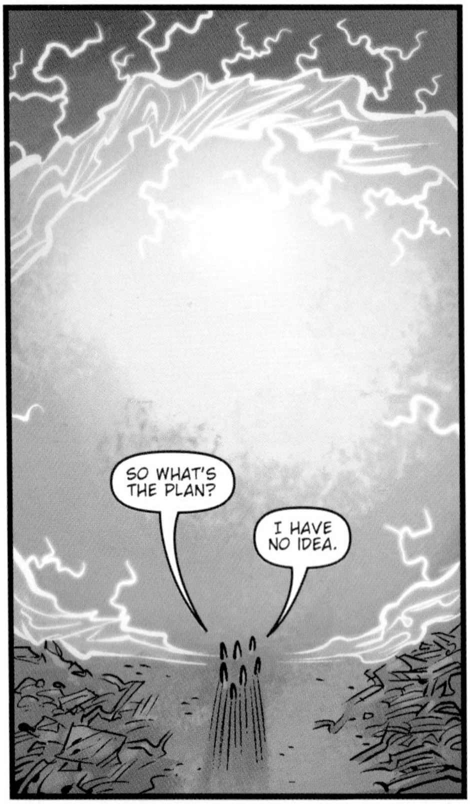
SO WHAT'S THE PLAN?
I HAVE NO IDEA.

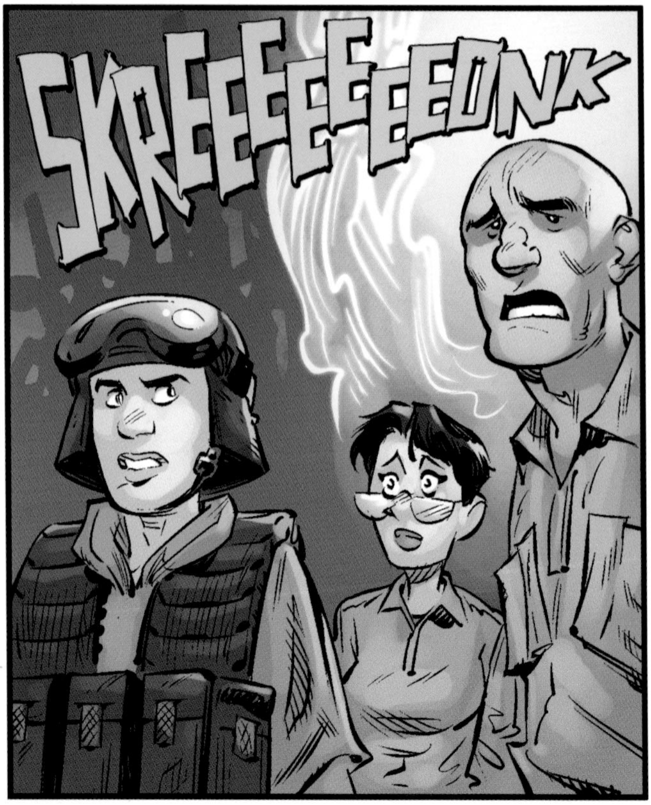
SKREEEEEEEEONK

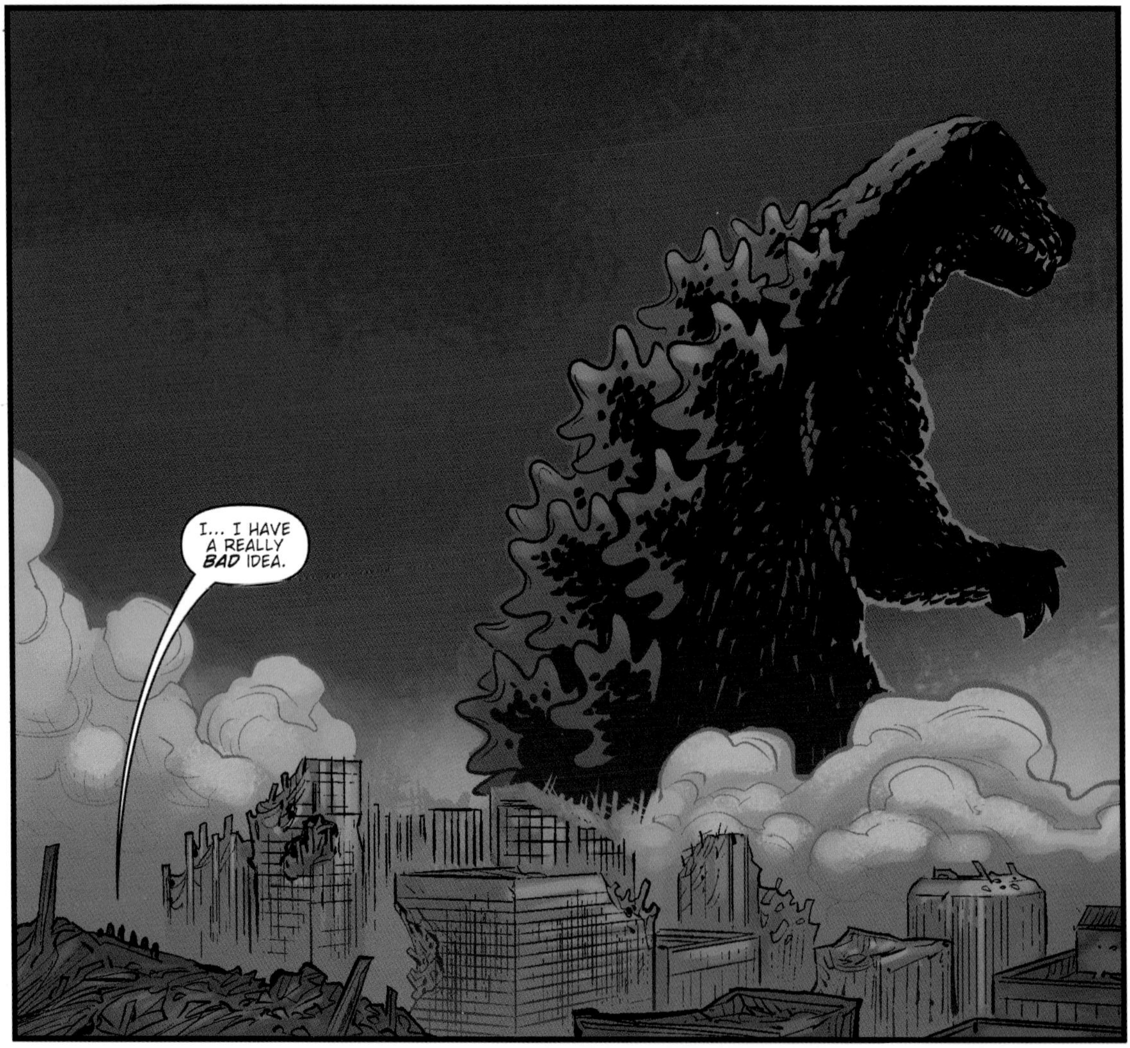
I... I HAVE A REALLY *BAD* IDEA.

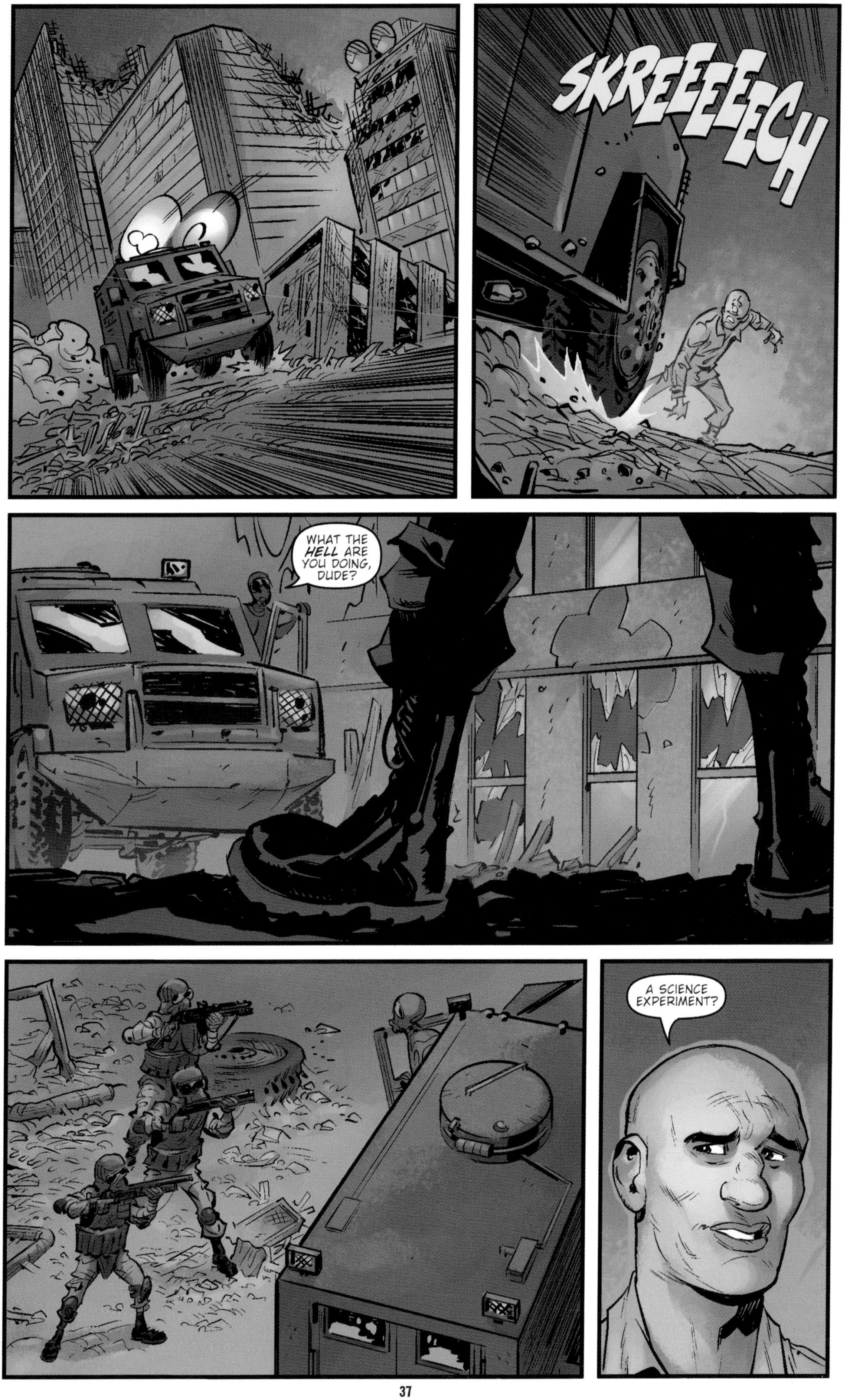
SKREEEEEECH
WHAT THE HELL ARE YOU DOING, DUDE?
A SCIENCE EXPERIMENT?

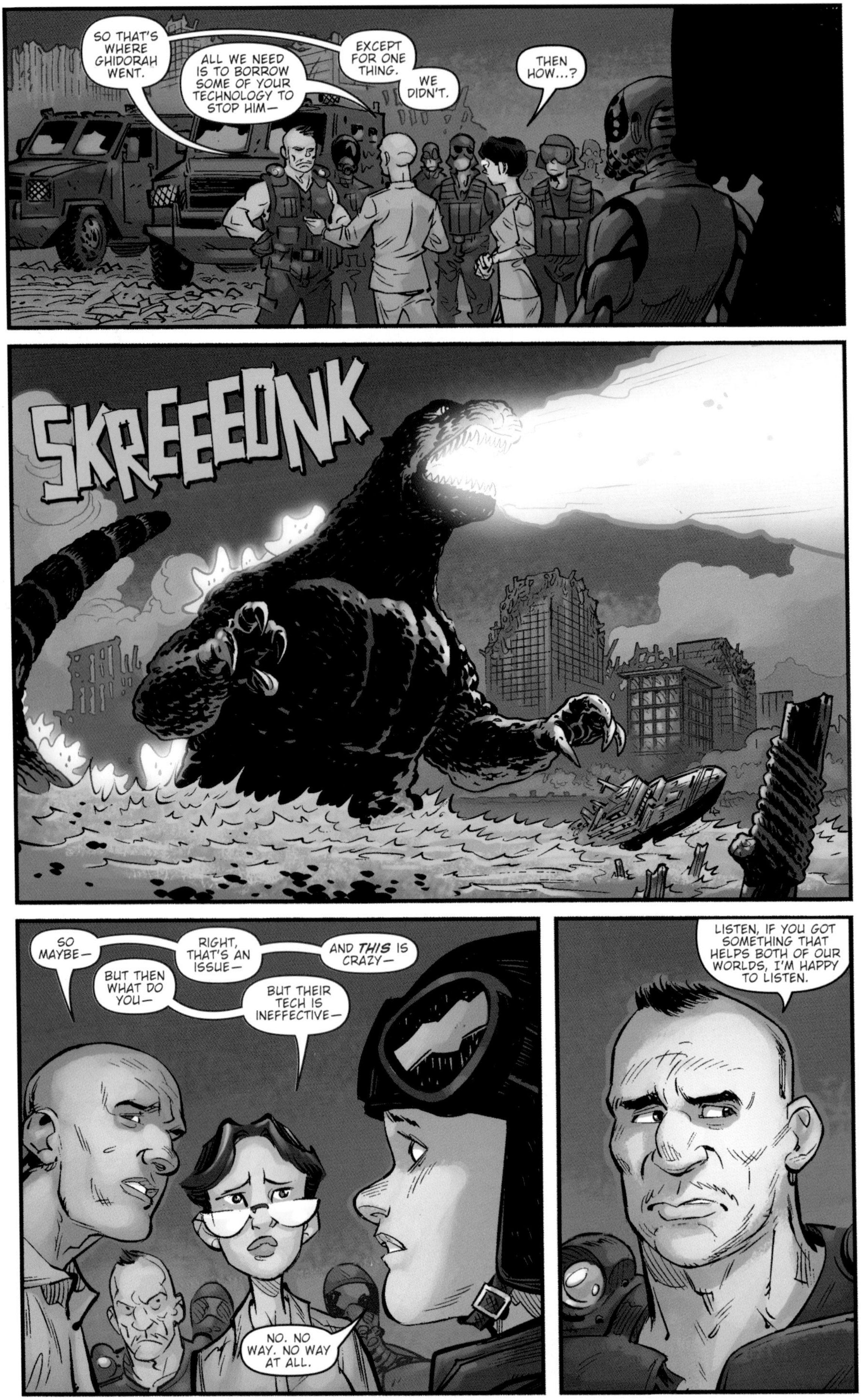
SO THAT'S WHERE GHIDORAH WENT.
ALL WE NEED IS TO BORROW SOME OF YOUR TECHNOLOGY TO STOP HIM—
EXCEPT FOR ONE THING.
WE DIDN'T.
THEN HOW...?
SKREEEONK
SO MAYBE—
BUT THEN WHAT DO YOU—
RIGHT, THAT'S AN ISSUE—
BUT THEIR TECH IS INEFFECTIVE—
AND *THIS* IS CRAZY—
NO. NO WAY. NO WAY AT ALL.
LISTEN, IF YOU GOT SOMETHING THAT HELPS BOTH OF OUR WORLDS, I'M HAPPY TO LISTEN.

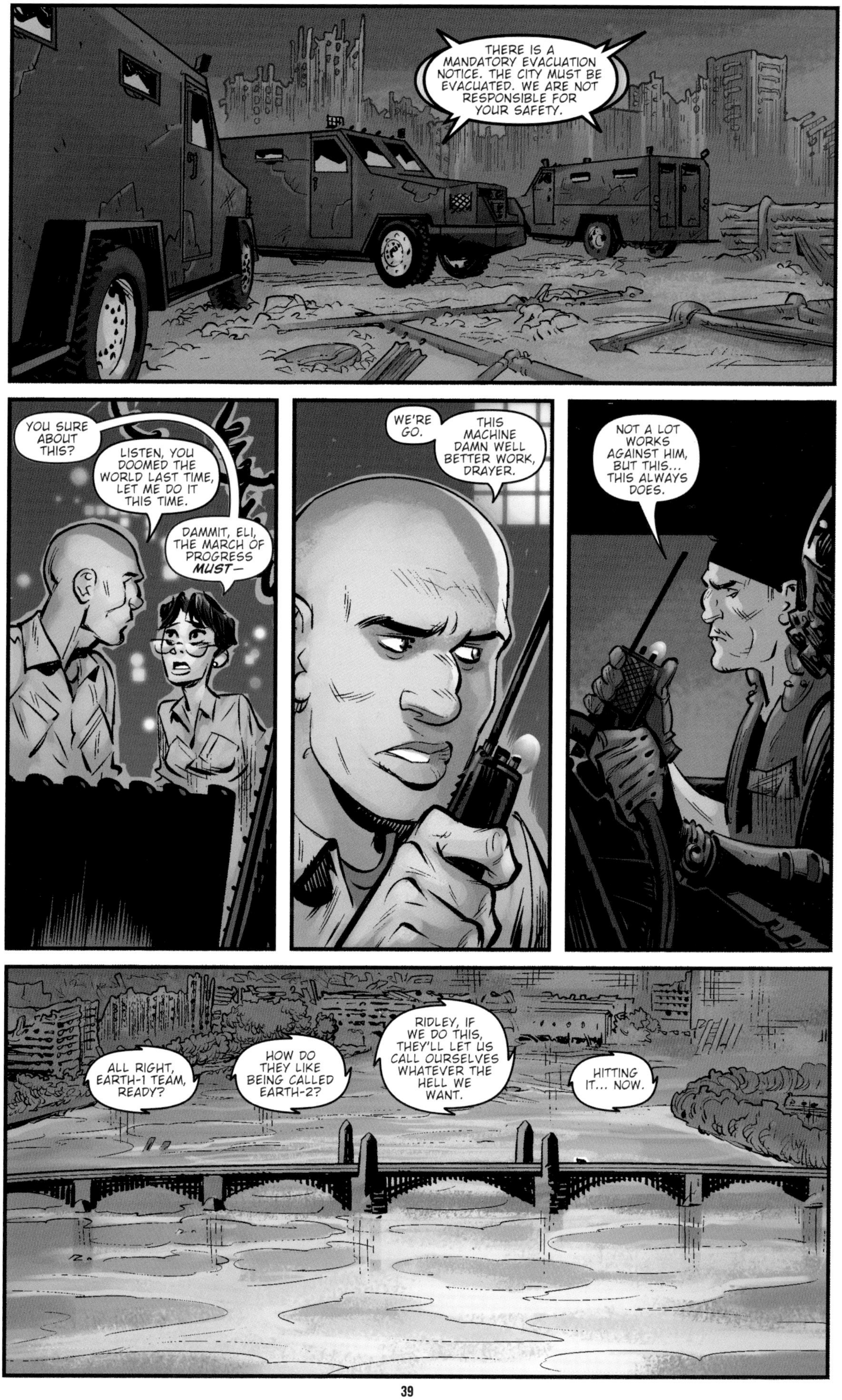
THERE IS A MANDATORY EVACUATION NOTICE. THE CITY MUST BE EVACUATED. WE ARE NOT RESPONSIBLE FOR YOUR SAFETY.
YOU SURE ABOUT THIS?
LISTEN, YOU DOOMED THE WORLD LAST TIME, LET ME DO IT THIS TIME.
DAMMIT, ELI, THE MARCH OF PROGRESS *MUST*—
WE'RE GO.
THIS MACHINE DAMN WELL BETTER WORK, DRAYER.
NOT A LOT WORKS AGAINST HIM, BUT THIS... THIS ALWAYS DOES.
ALL RIGHT, EARTH-1 TEAM, READY?
HOW DO THEY LIKE BEING CALLED EARTH-2?
RIDLEY, IF WE DO THIS, THEY'LL LET US CALL OURSELVES WHATEVER THE HELL WE WANT.
HITTING IT... NOW.

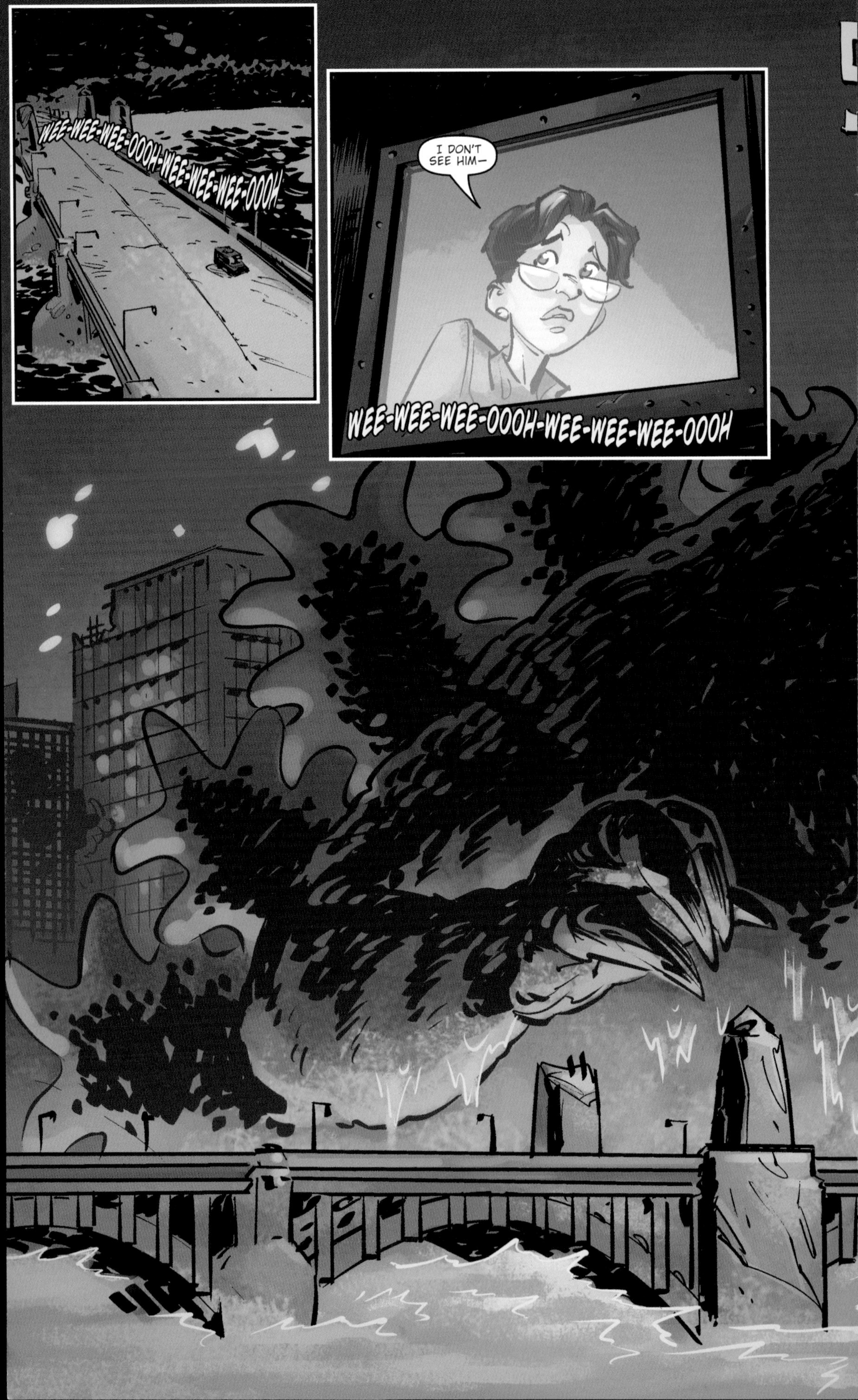
WEE-WEE-WEE-OOOH-WEE-WEE-WEE-OOOH
I DON'T SEE HIM—
WEE-WEE-WEE-OOOH-WEE-WEE-WEE-OOOH

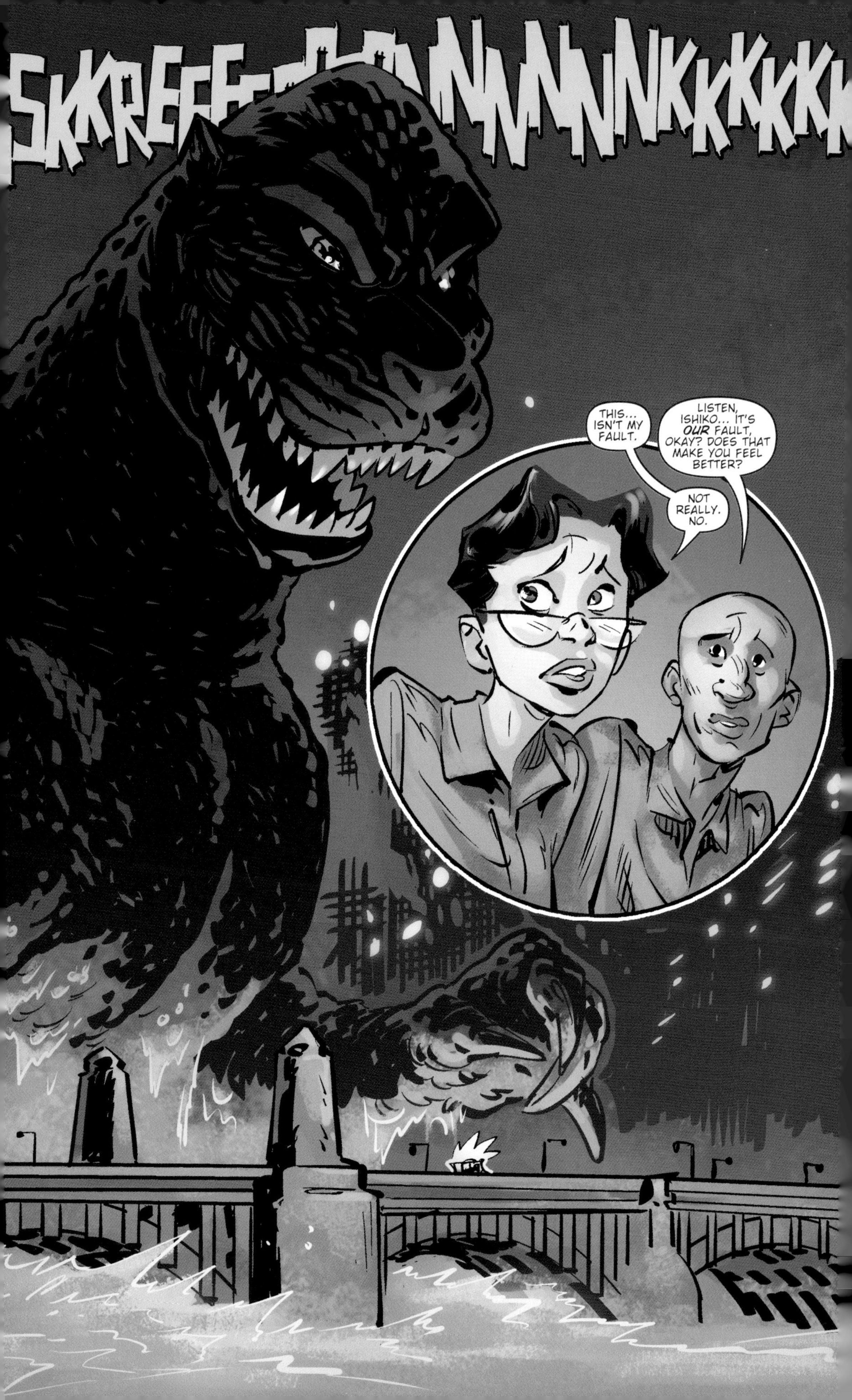
THIS... ISN'T MY FAULT.
LISTEN, ISHIKO... IT'S **OUR** FAULT, OKAY? DOES THAT MAKE YOU FEEL BETTER?
NOT REALLY. NO.

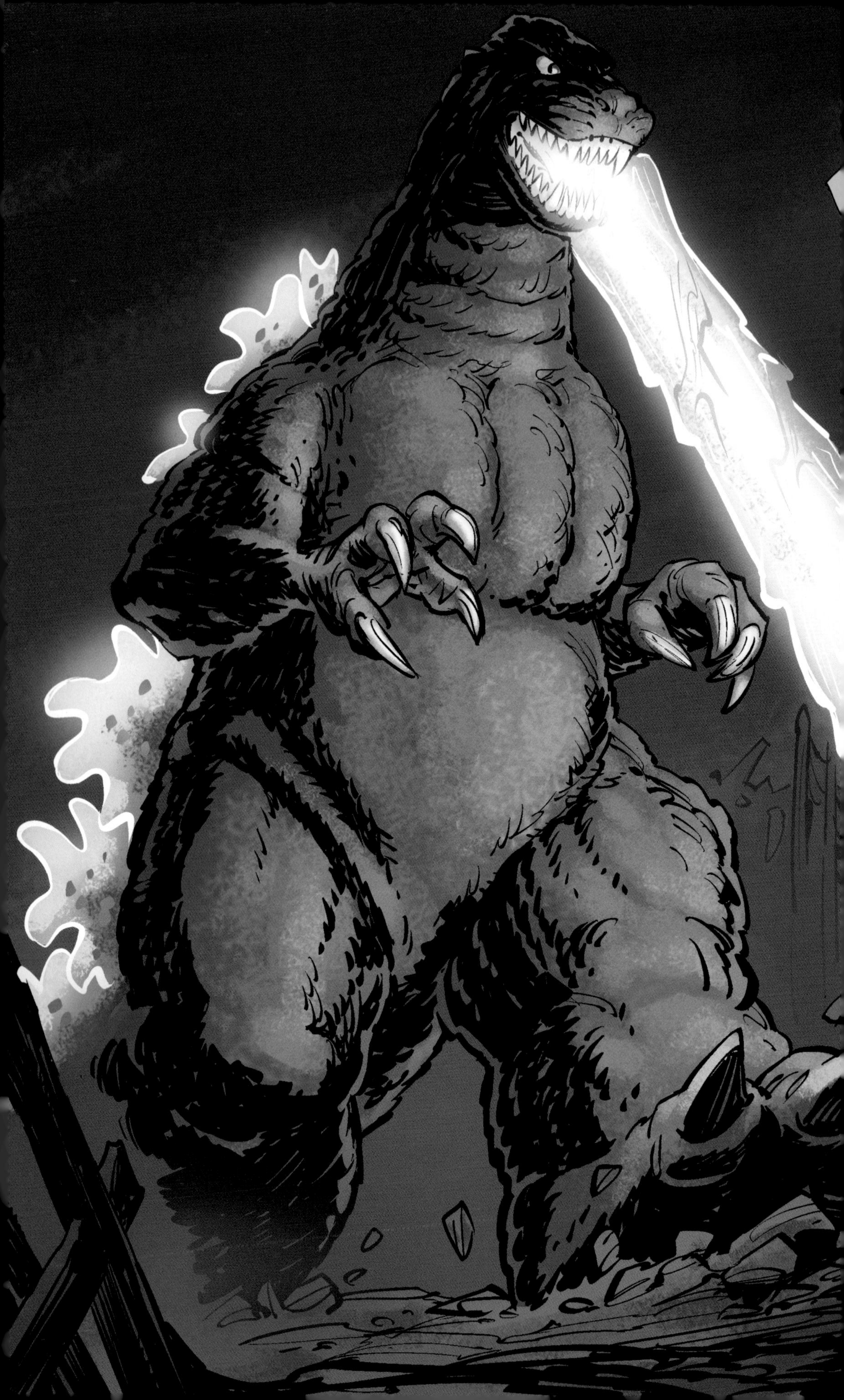

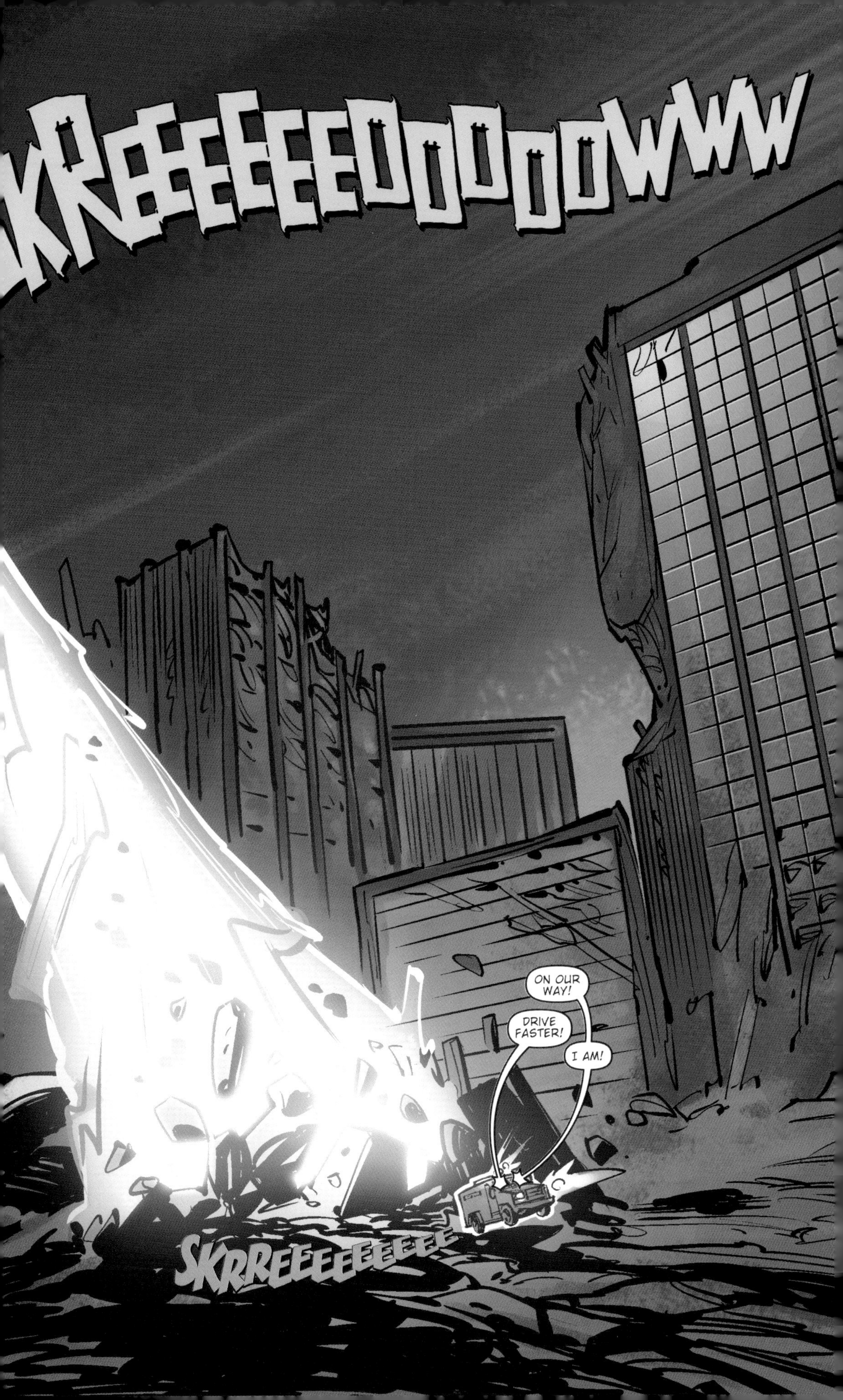
KREEEEEEOOOOOWWW
ON OUR WAY!
DRIVE FASTER!
I AM!
SKRREEEEEEEEE

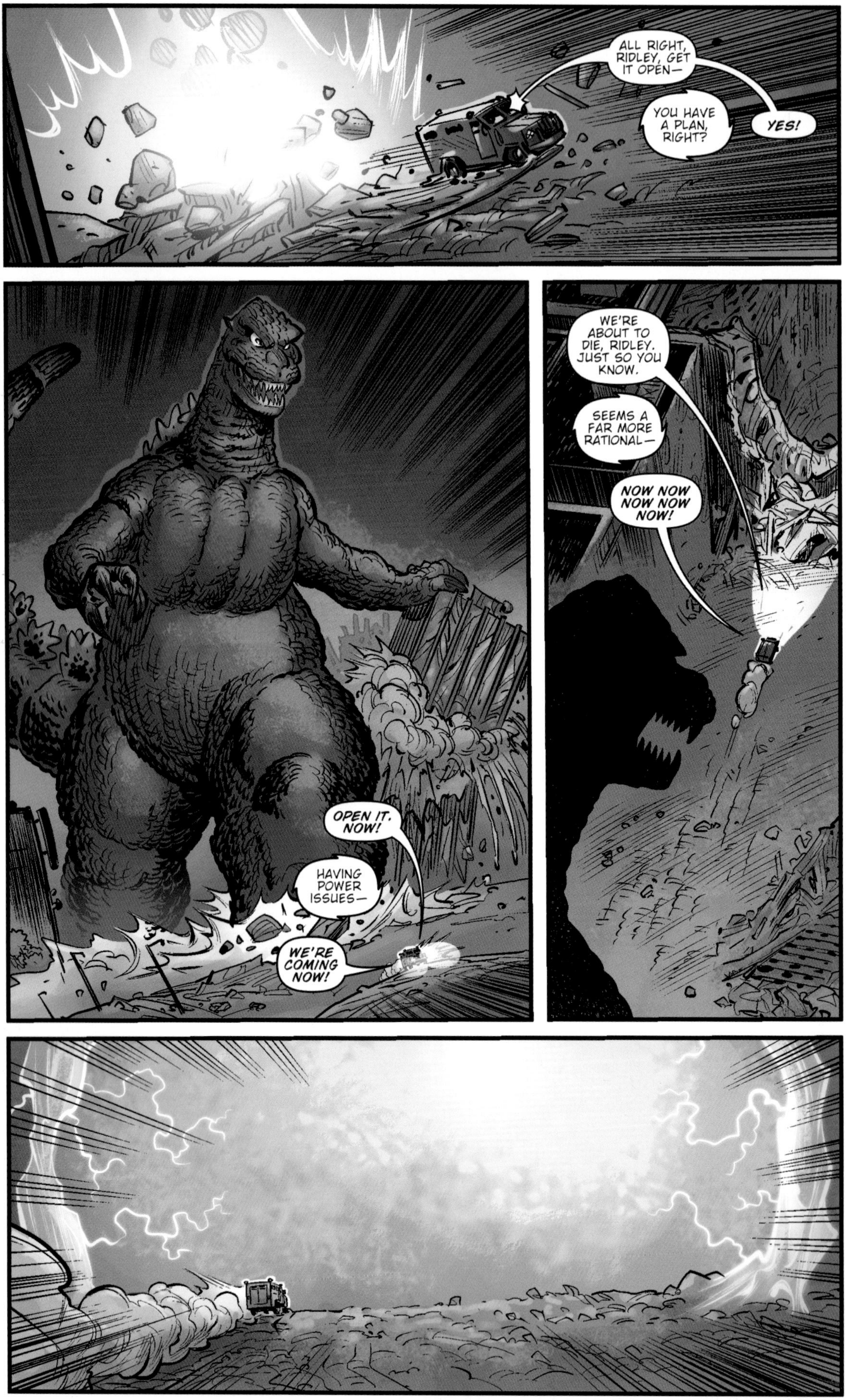
ALL RIGHT, RIDLEY, GET IT OPEN—
YOU HAVE A PLAN, RIGHT?
YES!
OPEN IT. NOW!
HAVING POWER ISSUES—
WE'RE COMING NOW!
WE'RE ABOUT TO DIE, RIDLEY. JUST SO YOU KNOW.
SEEMS A FAR MORE RATIONAL—
NOW NOW NOW NOW NOW!

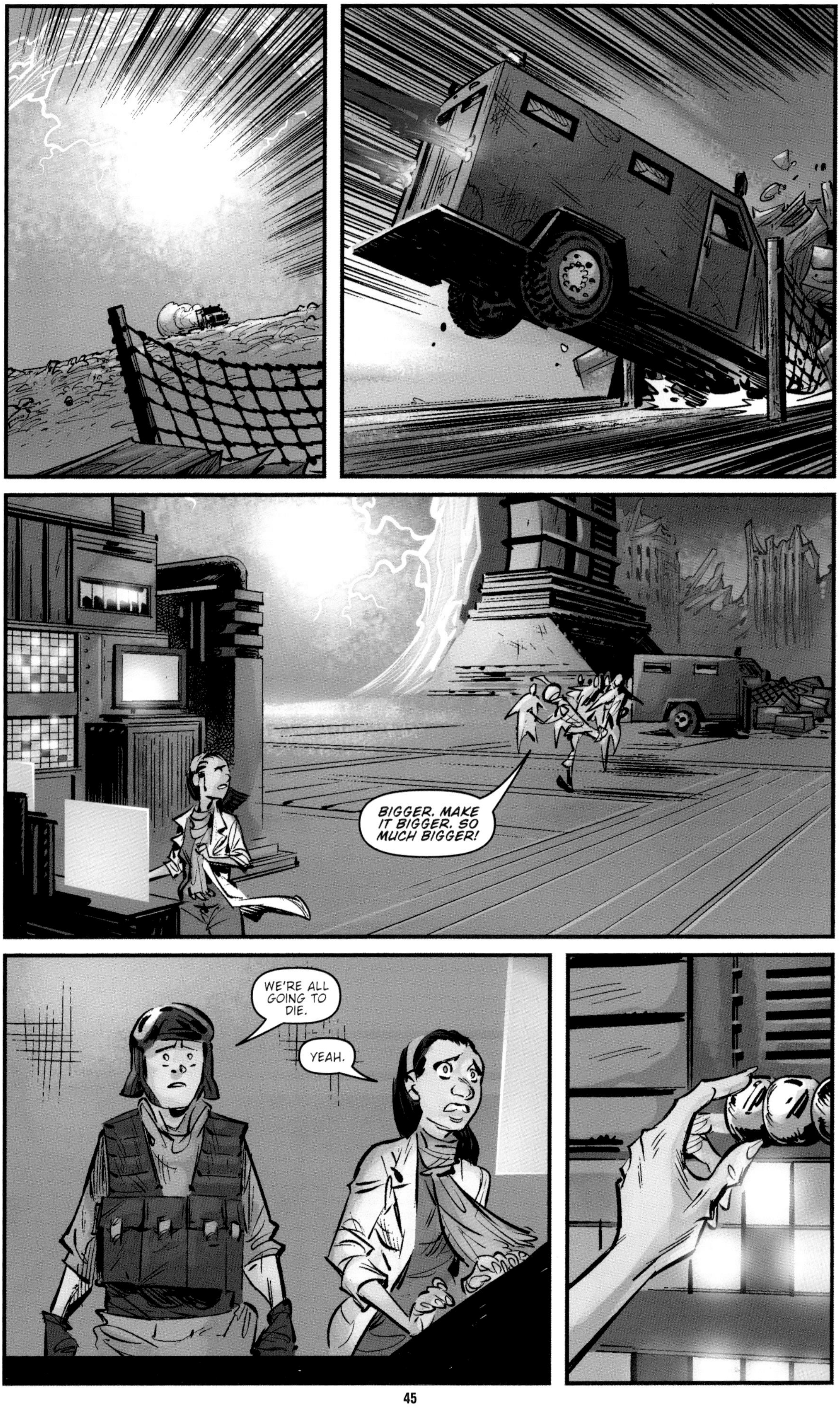
BIGGER. MAKE IT BIGGER. SO MUCH BIGGER!
WE'RE ALL GOING TO DIE.
YEAH.

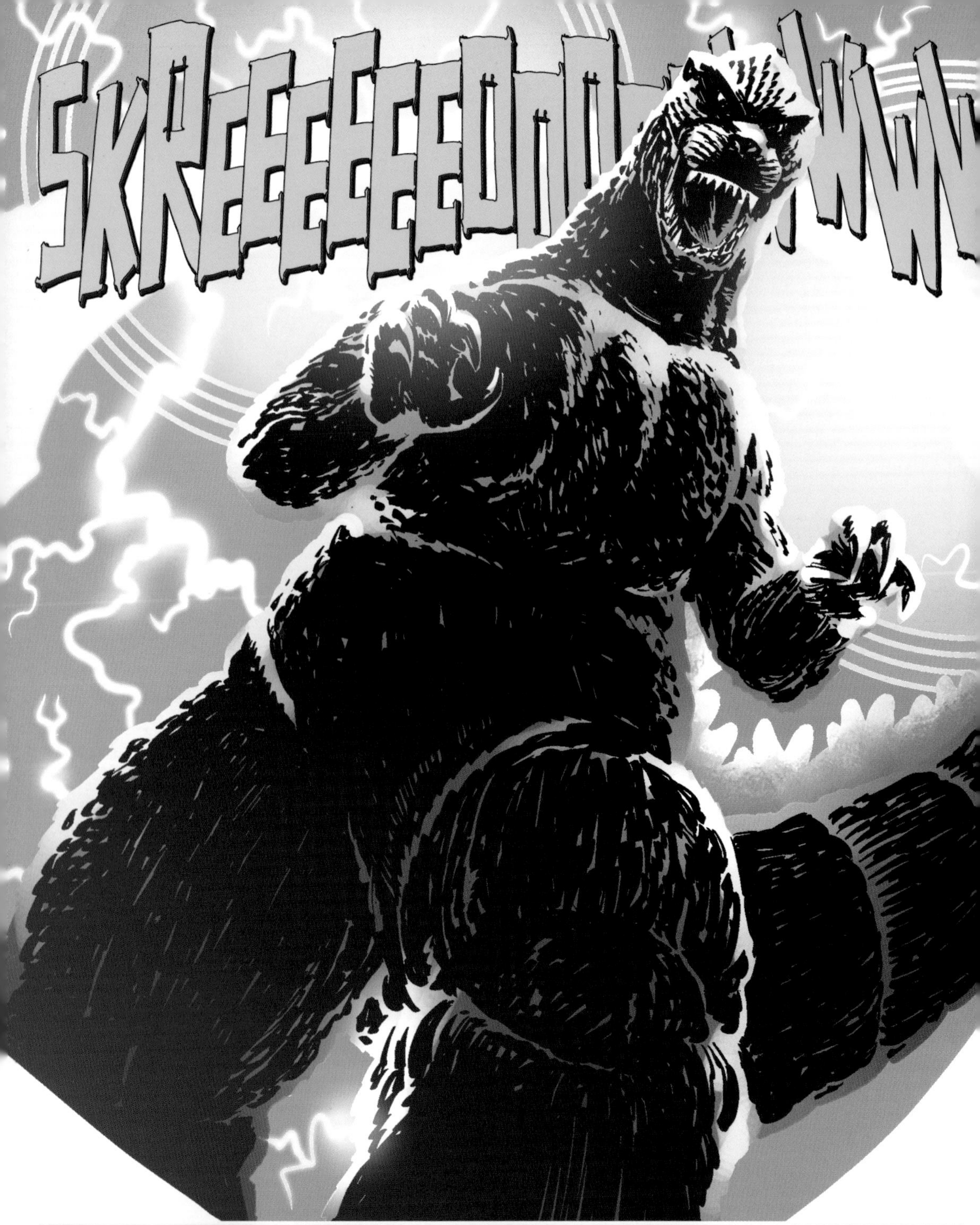
SKREEEEEEOOO...WWN

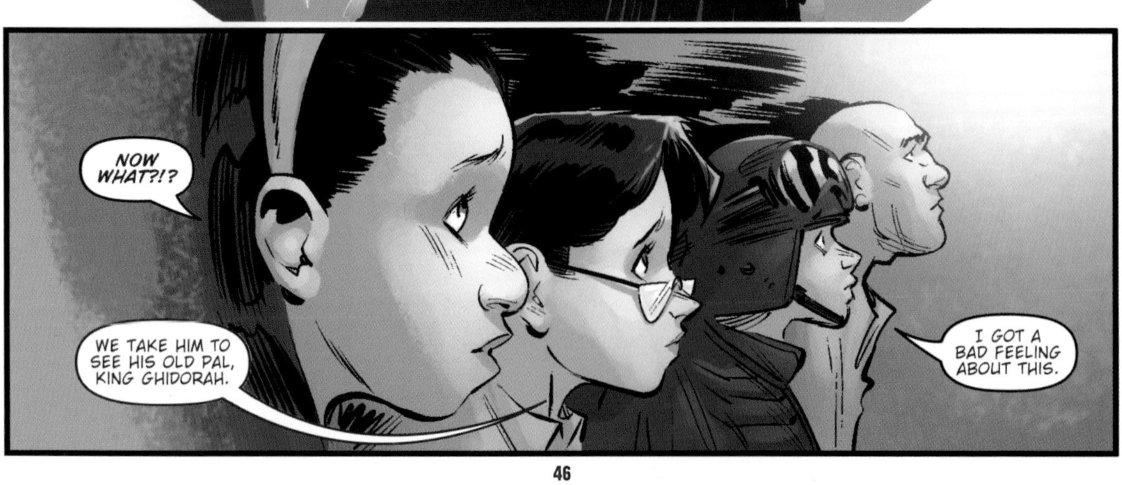
NOW WHAT?!?
WE TAKE HIM TO SEE HIS OLD PAL, KING GHIDORAH.
I GOT A BAD FEELING ABOUT THIS.

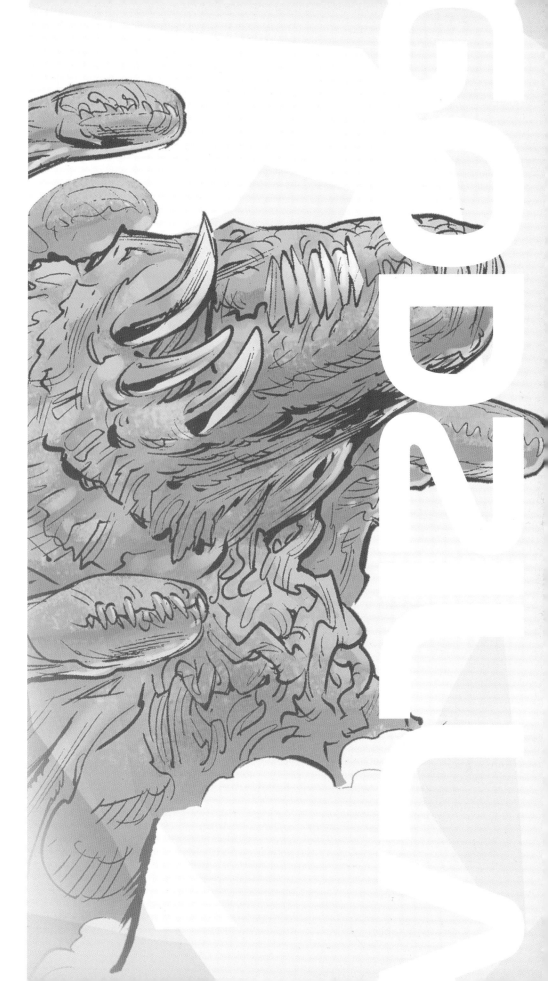

Art by **BRIAN CHURILLA**

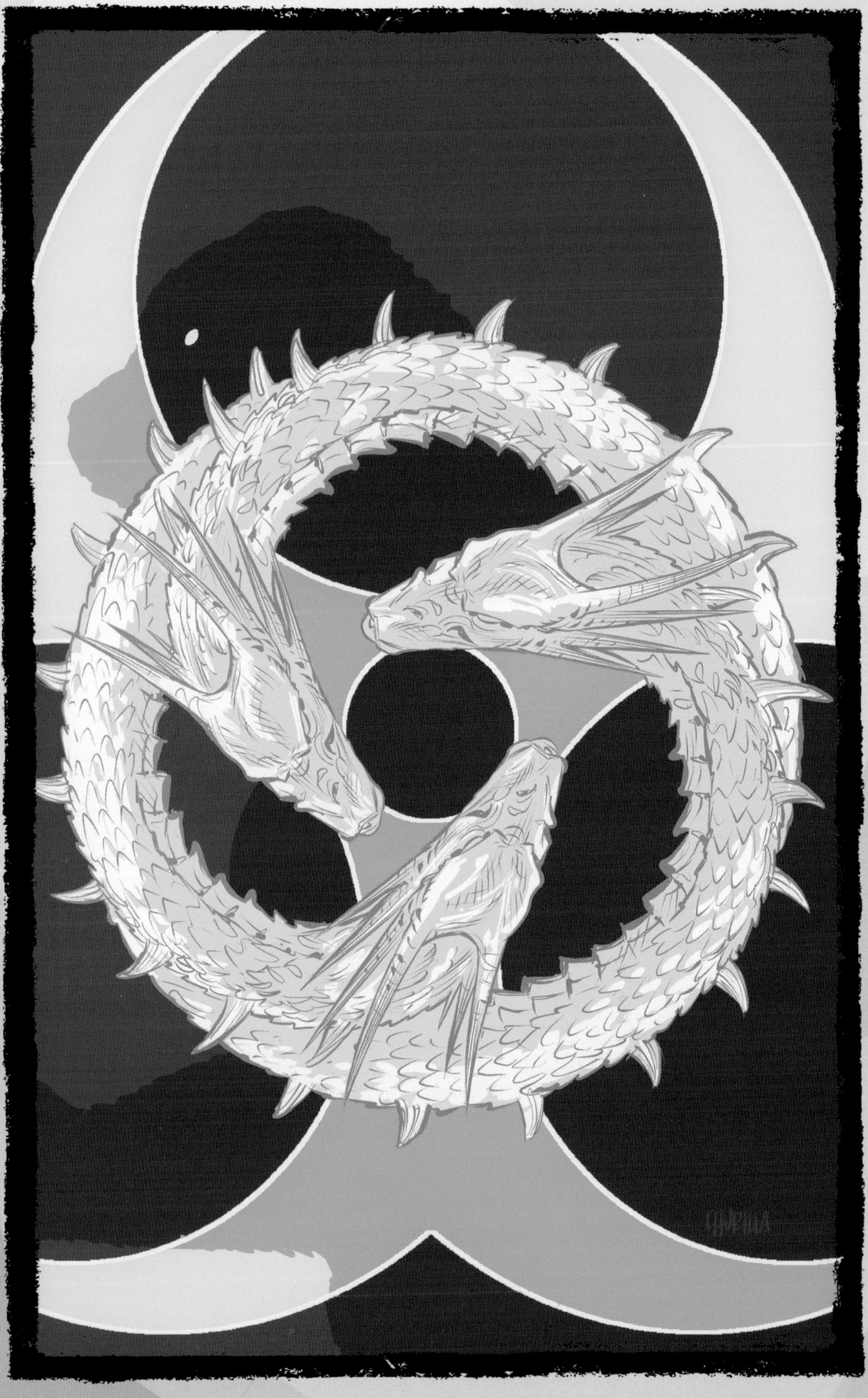

CHURILLA

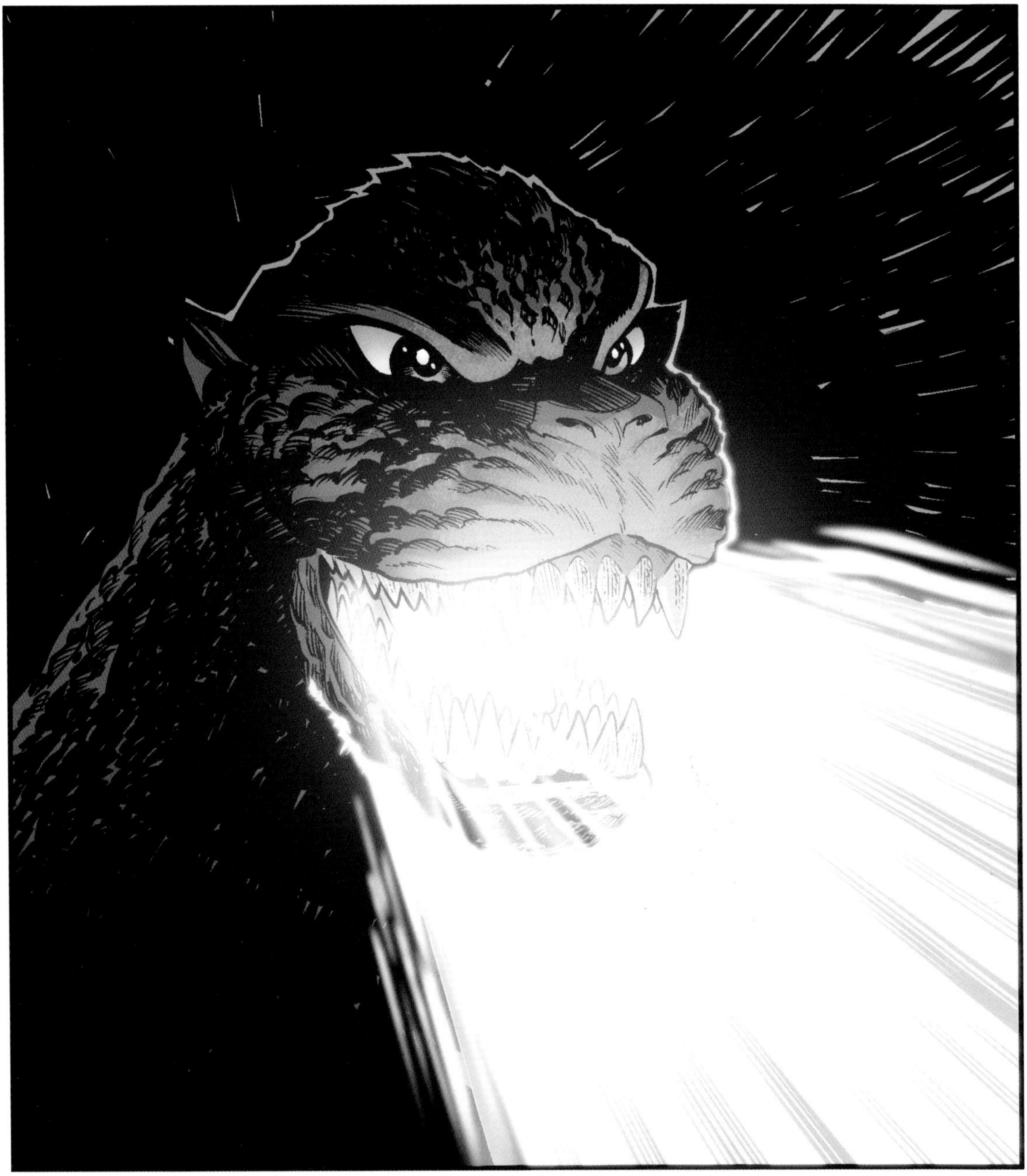

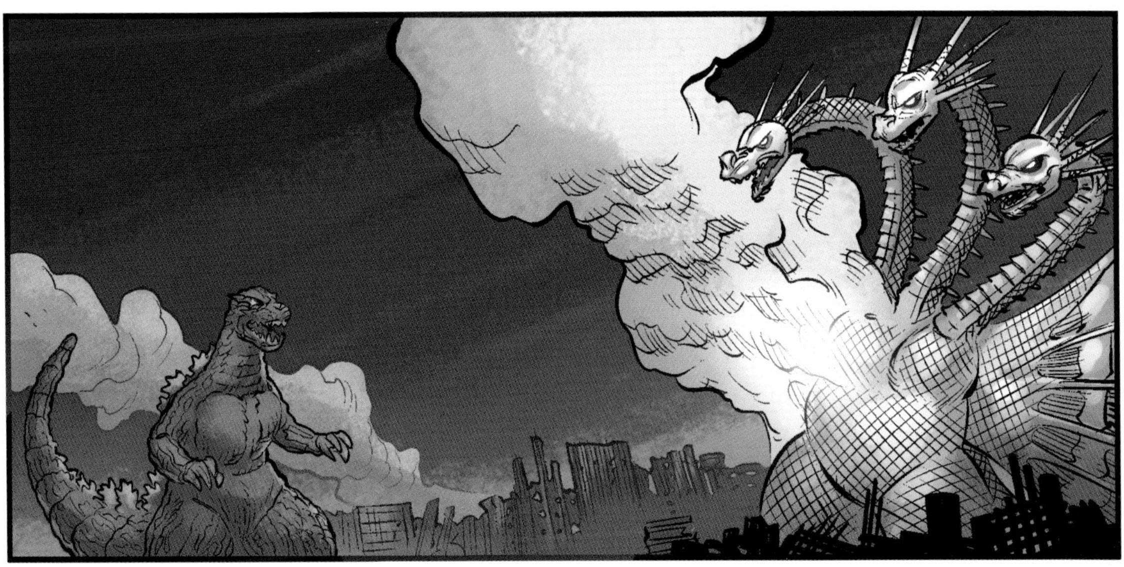

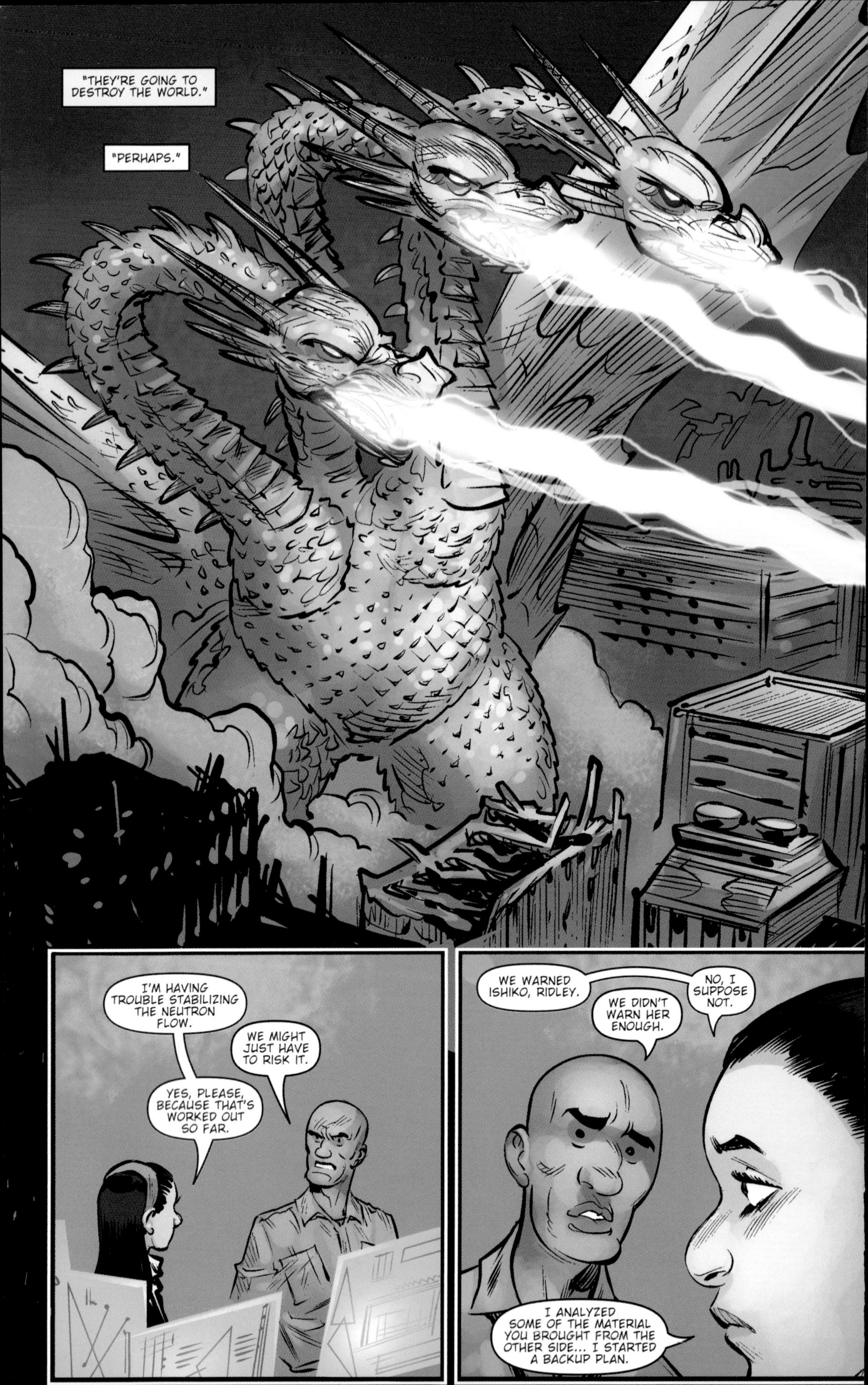
"THEY'RE GOING TO DESTROY THE WORLD."
"PERHAPS."
I'M HAVING TROUBLE STABILIZING THE NEUTRON FLOW.
WE MIGHT JUST HAVE TO RISK IT.
YES, PLEASE, BECAUSE THAT'S WORKED OUT SO FAR.
WE WARNED ISHIKO, RIDLEY.
WE DIDN'T WARN HER ENOUGH.
NO, I SUPPOSE NOT.
I ANALYZED SOME OF THE MATERIAL YOU BROUGHT FROM THE OTHER SIDE... I STARTED A BACKUP PLAN.

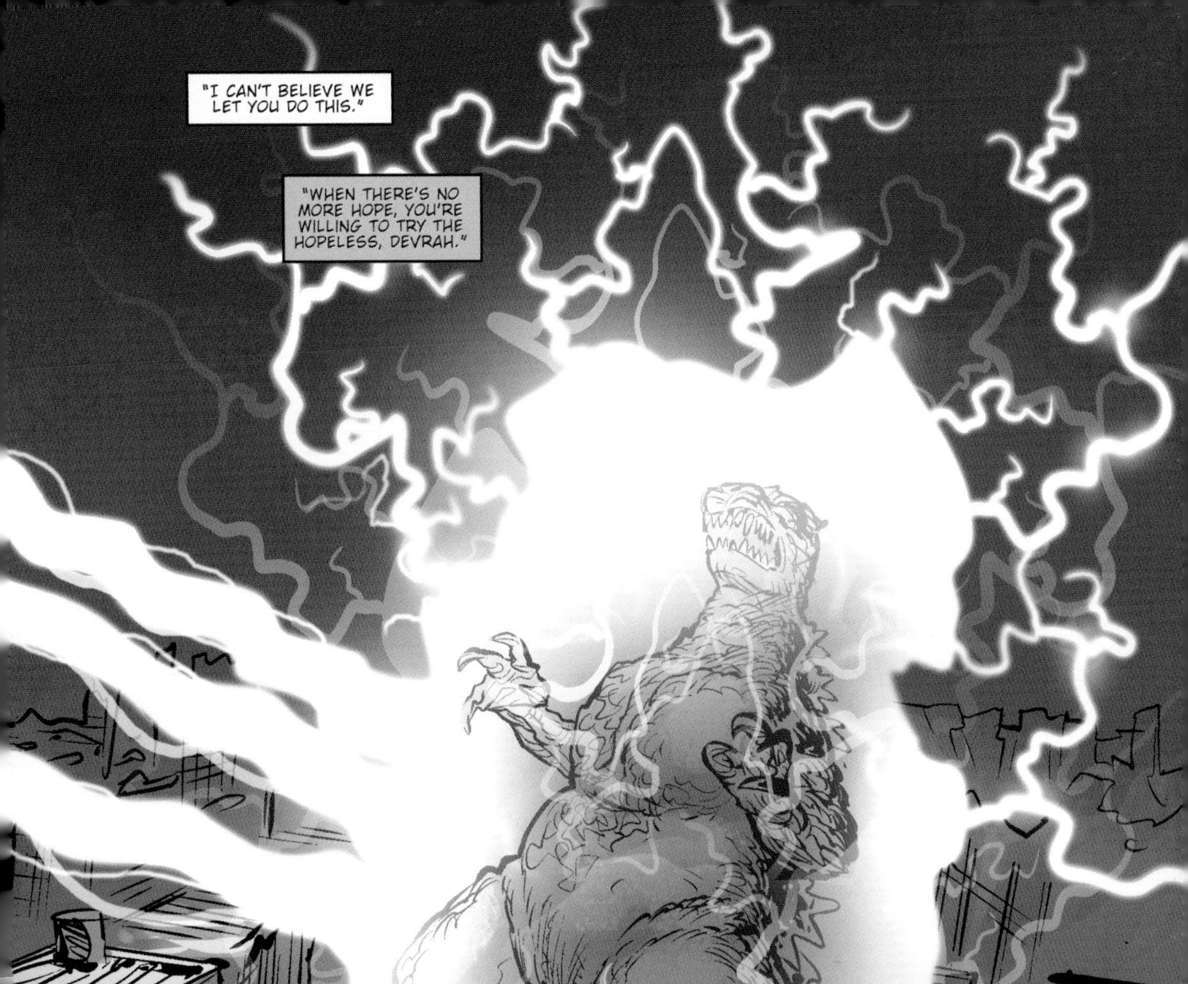
"I CAN'T BELIEVE WE LET YOU DO THIS."
"WHEN THERE'S NO MORE HOPE, YOU'RE WILLING TO TRY THE HOPELESS, DEVRAH."

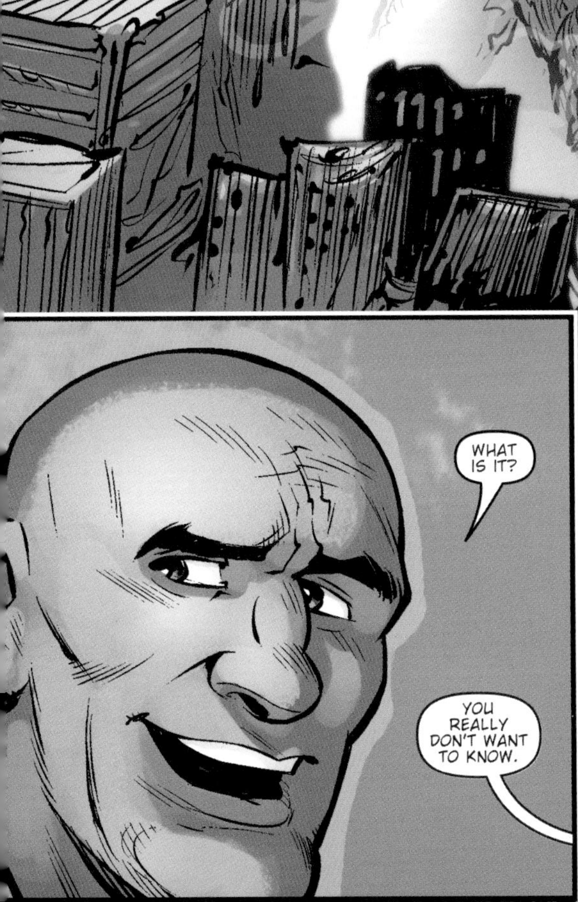
WHAT IS IT?
YOU REALLY DON'T WANT TO KNOW.

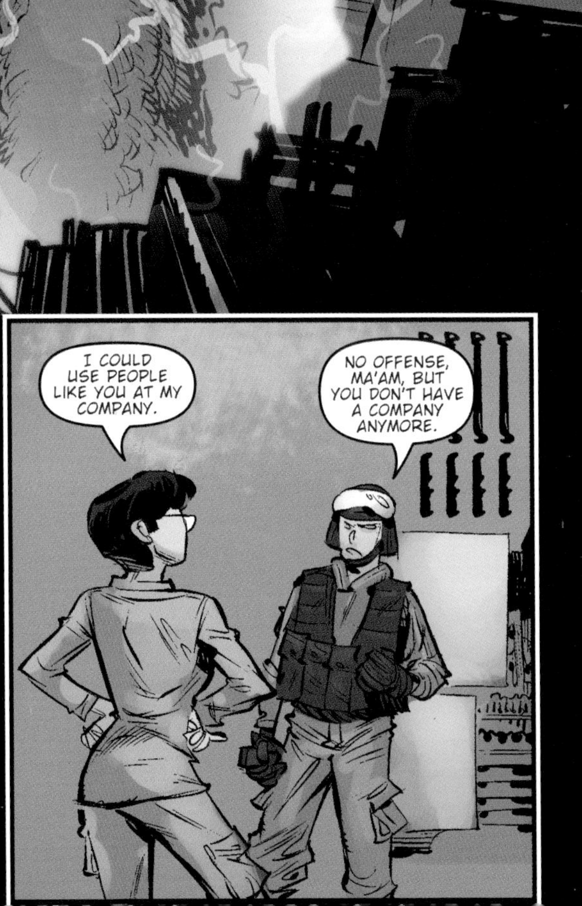
I COULD USE PEOPLE LIKE YOU AT MY COMPANY.
NO OFFENSE, MA'AM, BUT YOU DON'T HAVE A COMPANY ANYMORE.

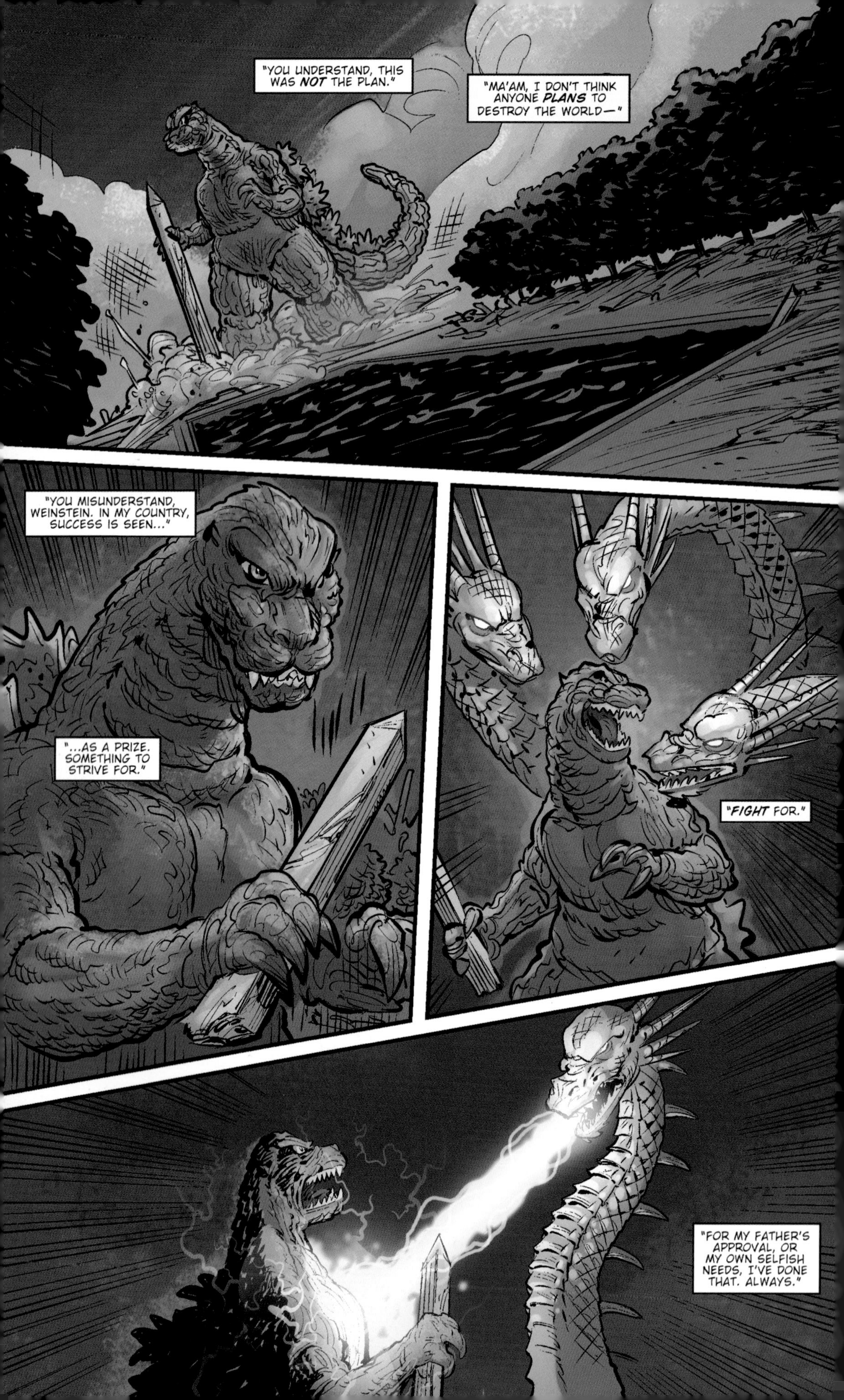
"YOU UNDERSTAND, THIS WAS *NOT* THE PLAN."
"MA'AM, I DON'T THINK ANYONE *PLANS* TO DESTROY THE WORLD—"
"YOU MISUNDERSTAND, WEINSTEIN. IN MY COUNTRY, SUCCESS IS SEEN..."
"...AS A PRIZE. SOMETHING TO STRIVE FOR."
"*FIGHT* FOR."
"FOR MY FATHER'S APPROVAL, OR MY OWN SELFISH NEEDS, I'VE DONE THAT. ALWAYS."

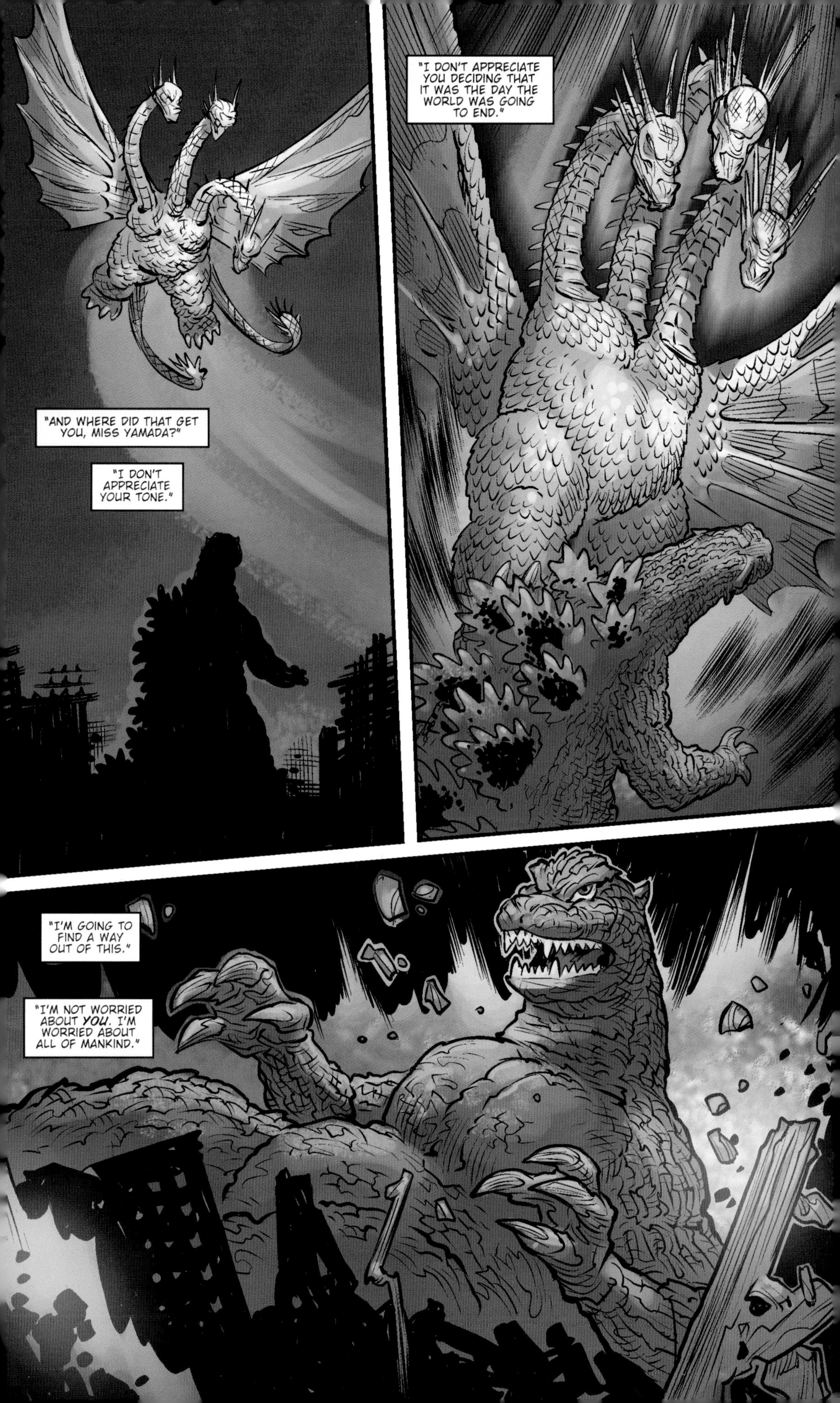
"AND WHERE DID THAT GET YOU, MISS YAMADA?"
"I DON'T APPRECIATE YOUR TONE."
"I DON'T APPRECIATE YOU DECIDING THAT IT WAS THE DAY THE WORLD WAS GOING TO END."
"I'M GOING TO FIND A WAY OUT OF THIS."
"I'M NOT WORRIED ABOUT YOU. I'M WORRIED ABOUT ALL OF MANKIND."

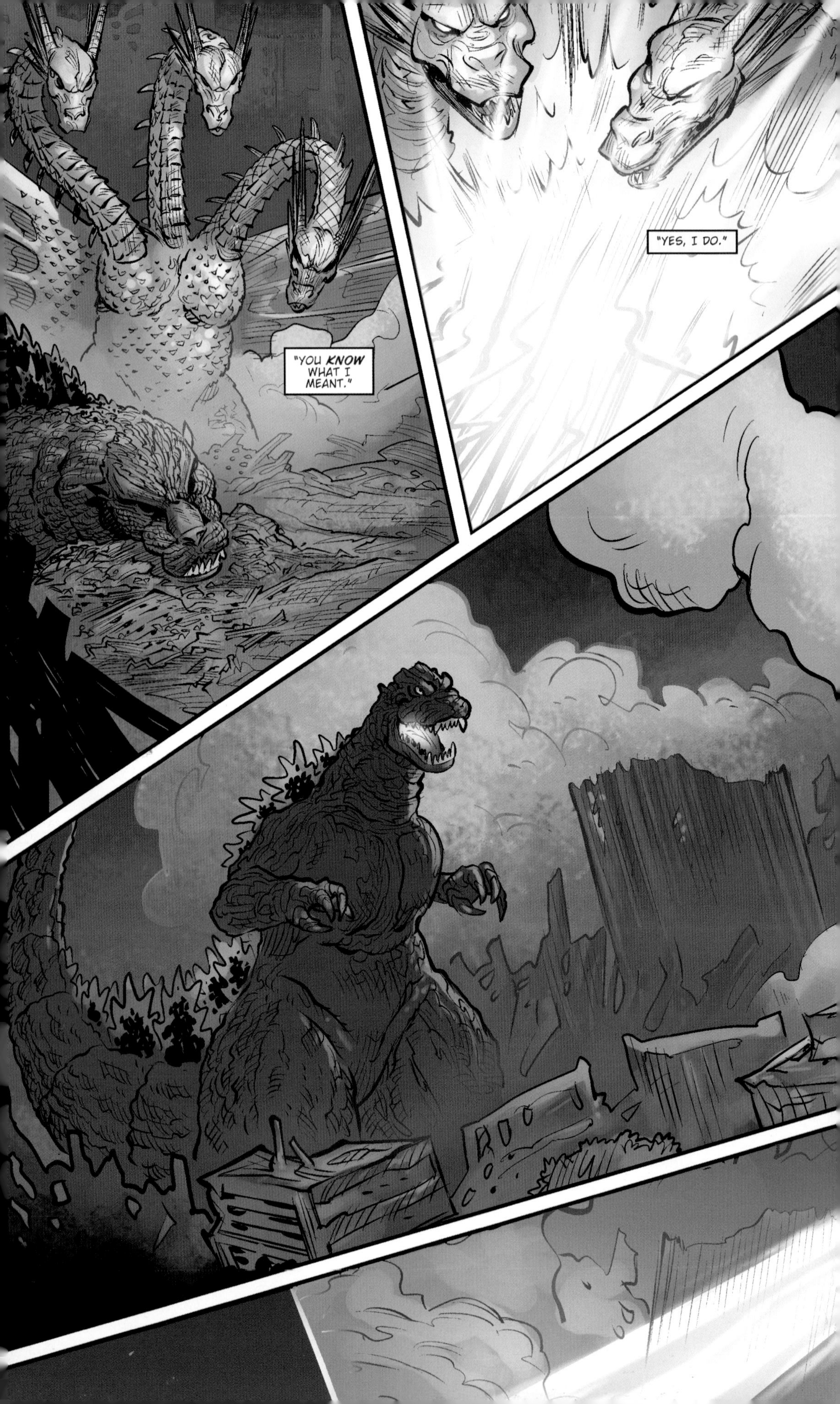
"YOU KNOW WHAT I MEANT."
"YES, I DO."

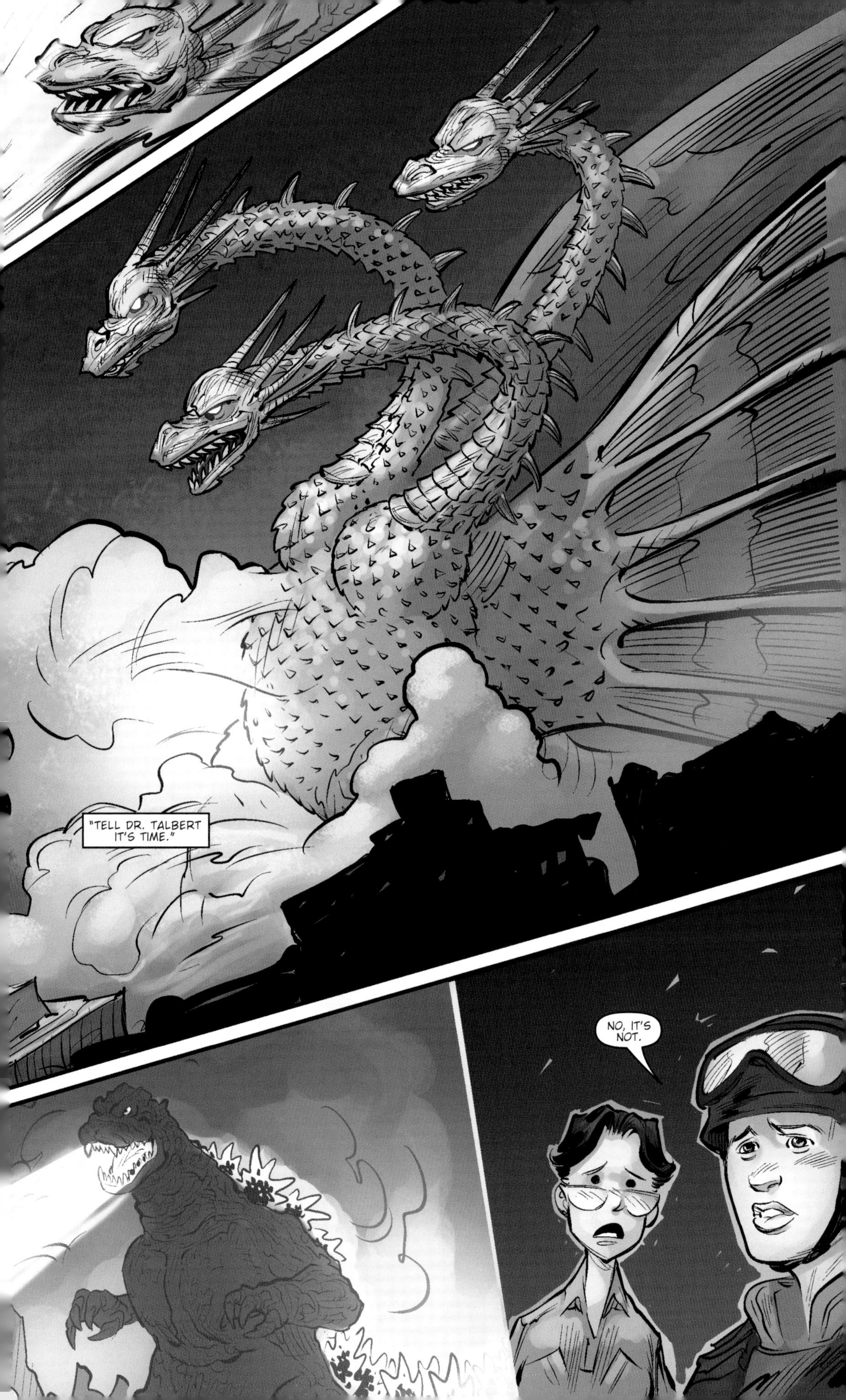
"TELL DR. TALBERT IT'S TIME."
NO, IT'S NOT.

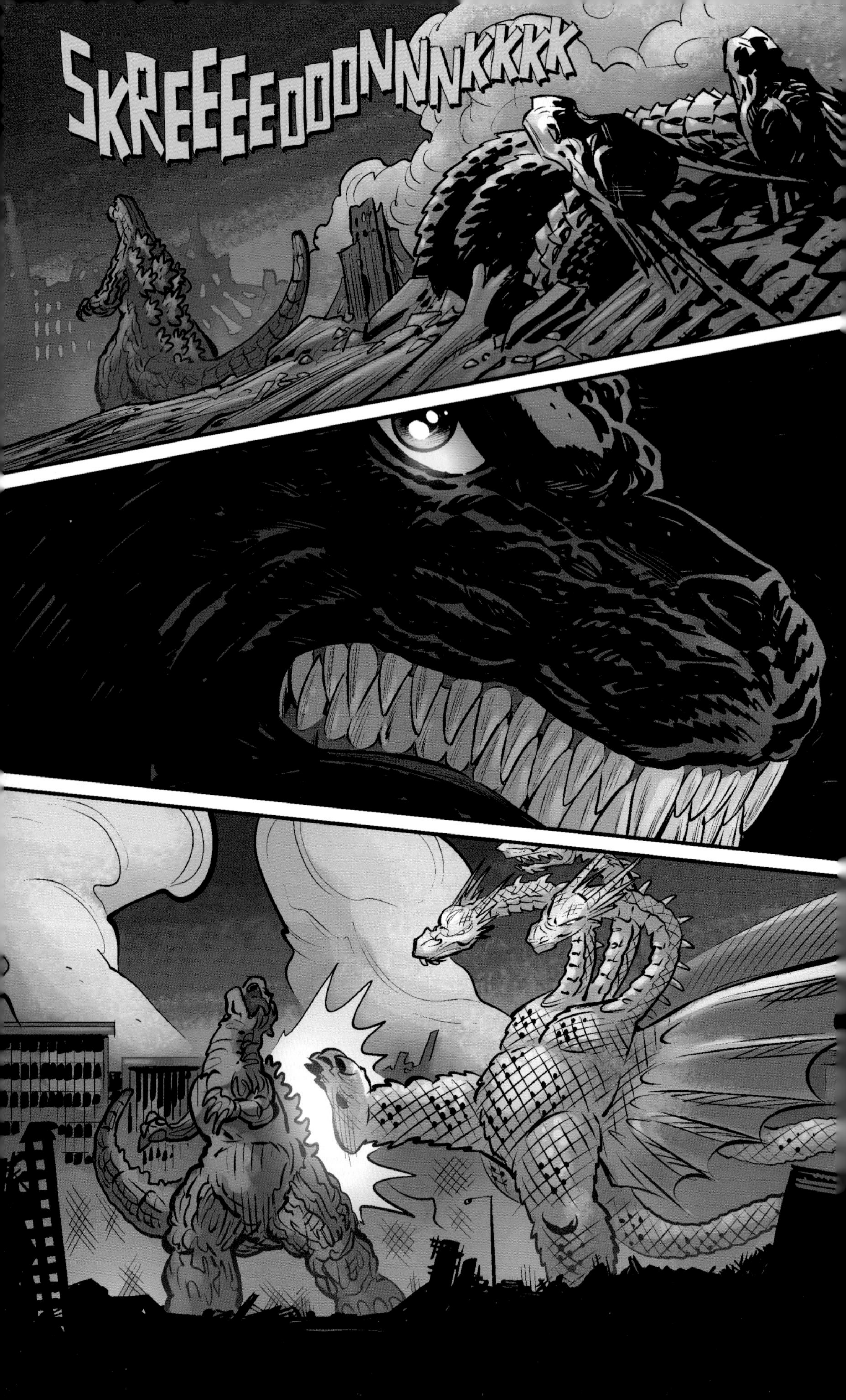
SKREEEEOOONNNKKKK

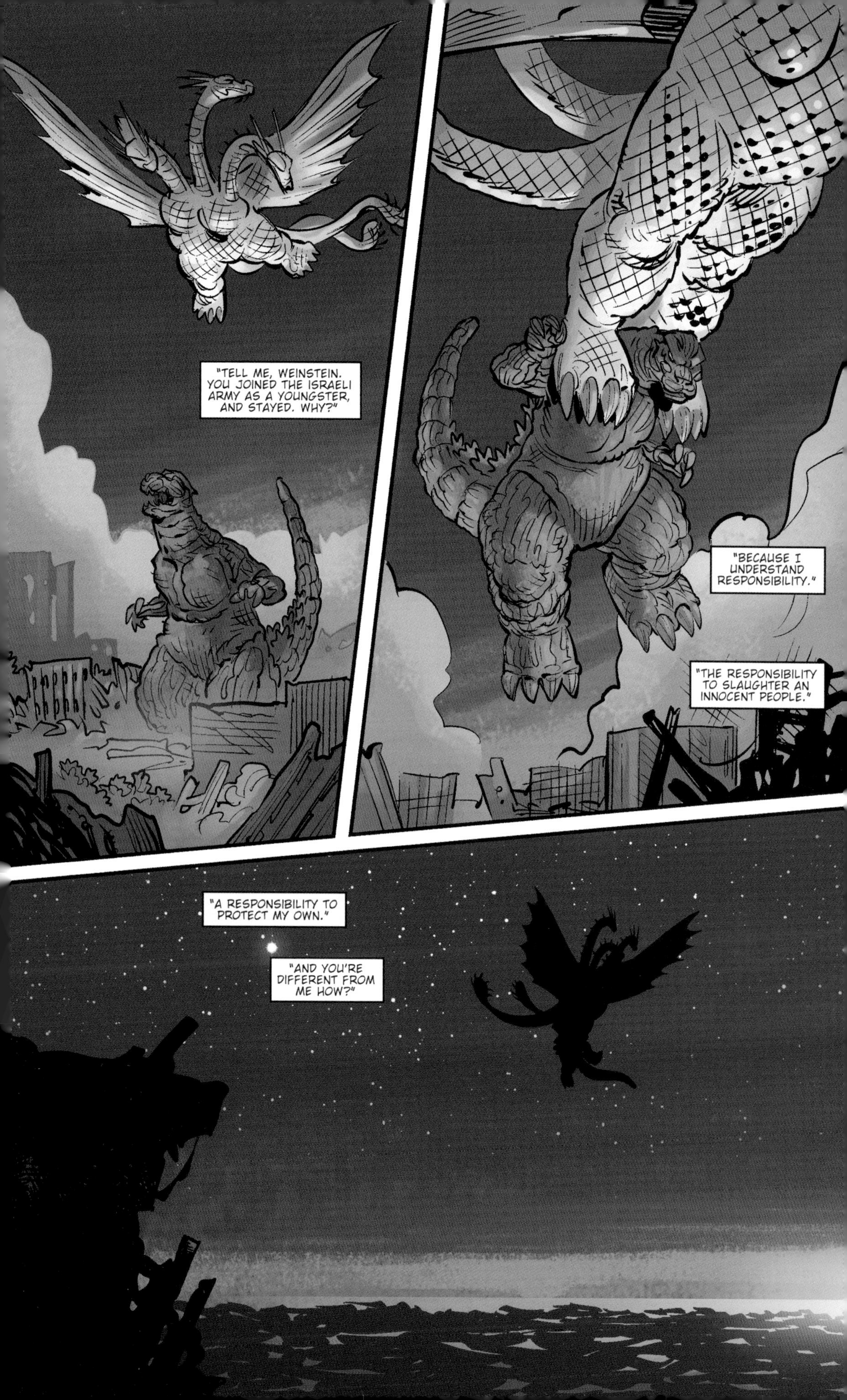
"TELL ME, WEINSTEIN. YOU JOINED THE ISRAELI ARMY AS A YOUNGSTER, AND STAYED. WHY?"
"BECAUSE I UNDERSTAND RESPONSIBILITY."
"THE RESPONSIBILITY TO SLAUGHTER AN INNOCENT PEOPLE."
"A RESPONSIBILITY TO PROTECT MY OWN."
"AND YOU'RE DIFFERENT FROM ME HOW?"

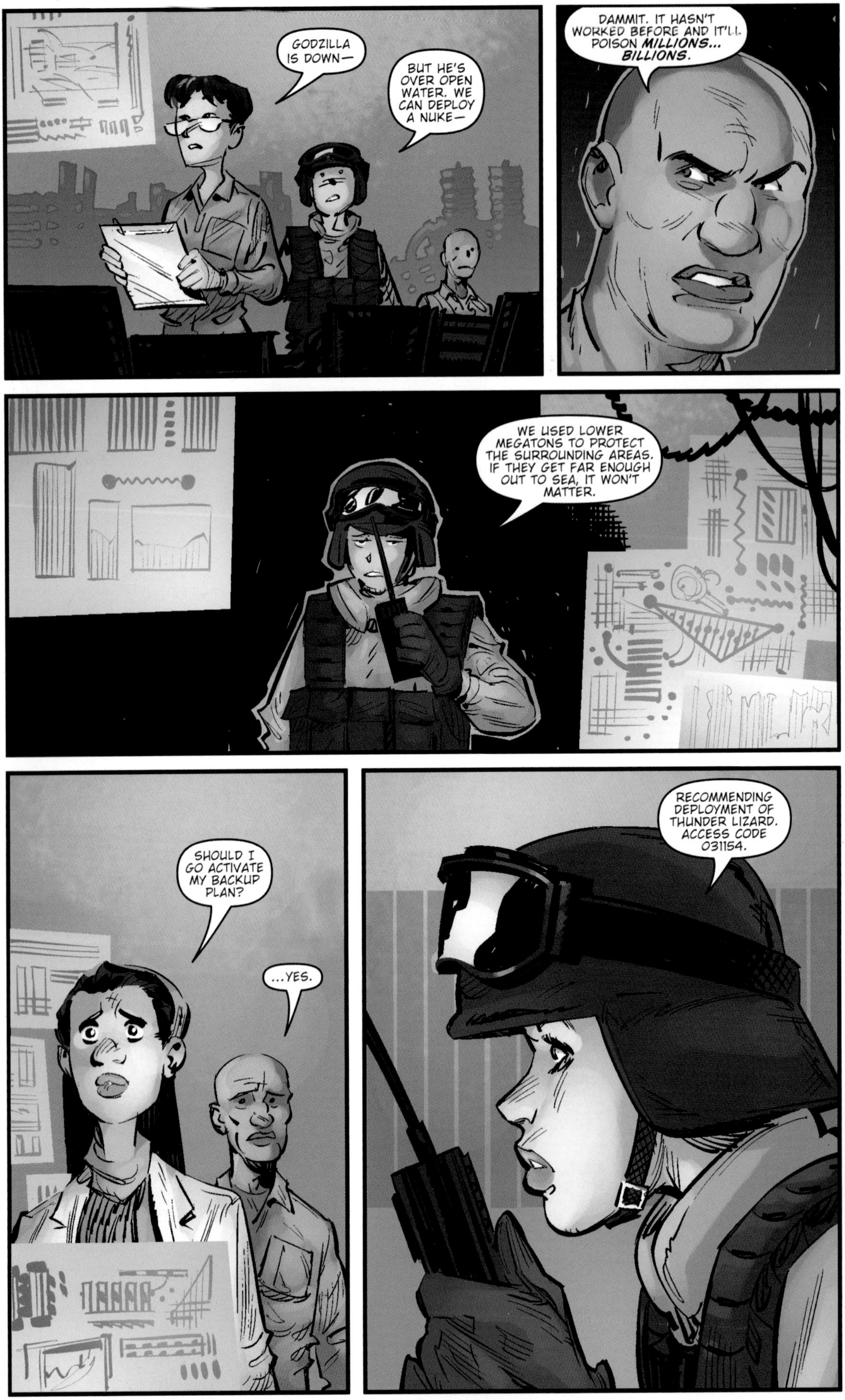
GODZILLA IS DOWN—
BUT HE'S OVER OPEN WATER. WE CAN DEPLOY A NUKE—
DAMMIT. IT HASN'T WORKED BEFORE AND IT'LL POISON MILLIONS... BILLIONS.
WE USED LOWER MEGATONS TO PROTECT THE SURROUNDING AREAS. IF THEY GET FAR ENOUGH OUT TO SEA, IT WON'T MATTER.
SHOULD I GO ACTIVATE MY BACKUP PLAN?
...YES.
RECOMMENDING DEPLOYMENT OF THUNDER LIZARD. ACCESS CODE 031154.

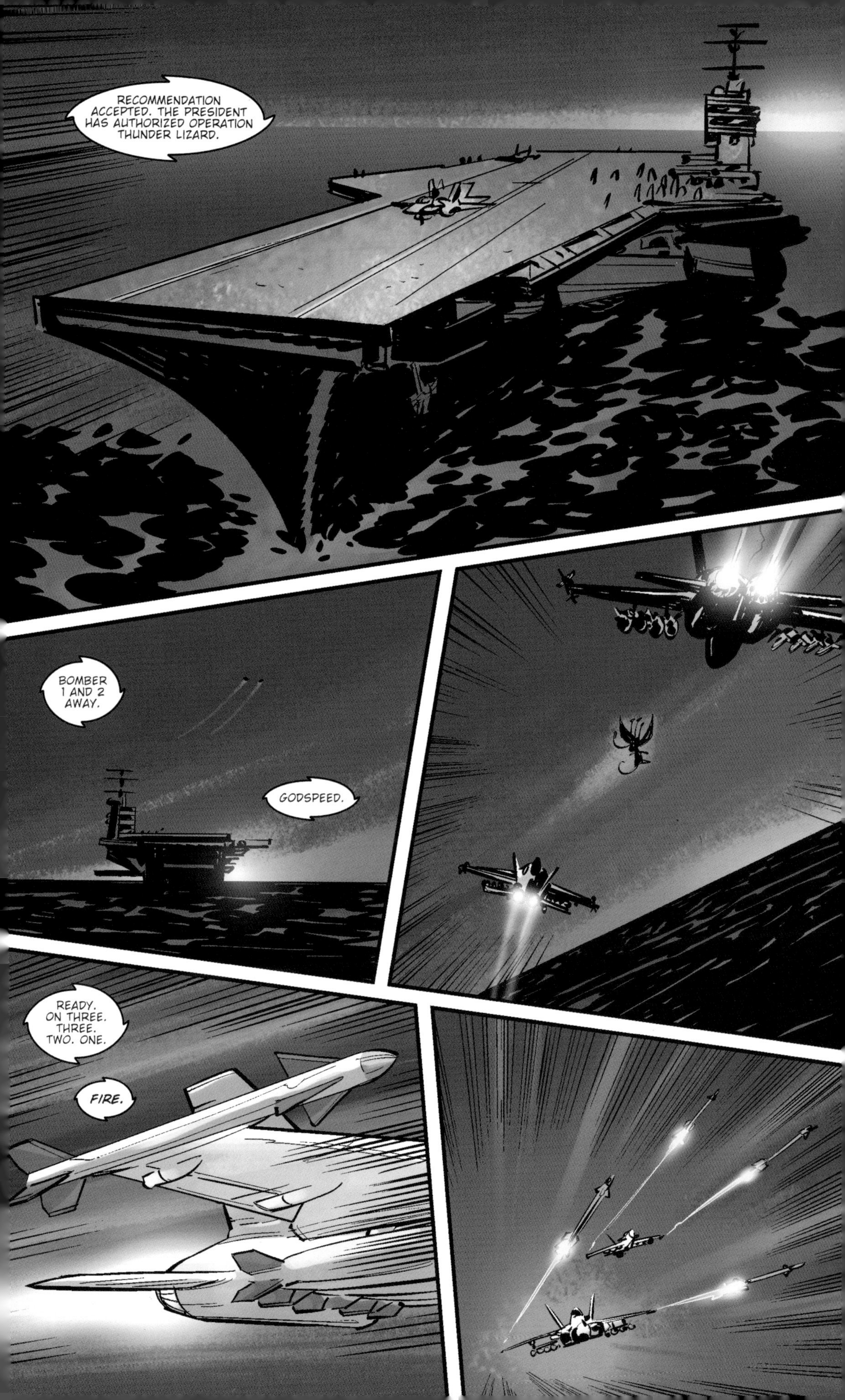
RECOMMENDATION ACCEPTED. THE PRESIDENT HAS AUTHORIZED OPERATION THUNDER LIZARD.
BOMBER 1 AND 2 AWAY.
GODSPEED.
READY. ON THREE. THREE. TWO. ONE.
FIRE.

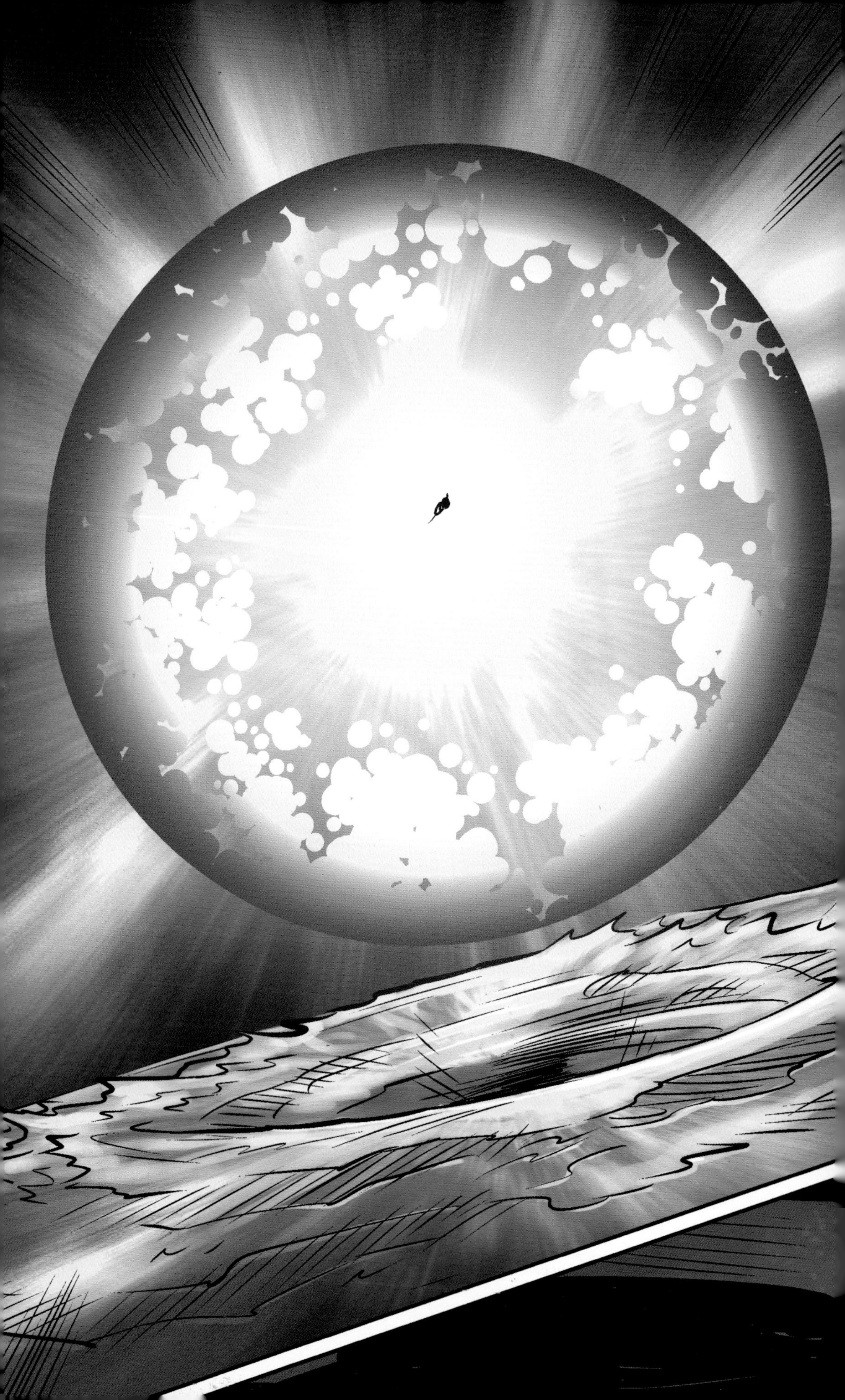

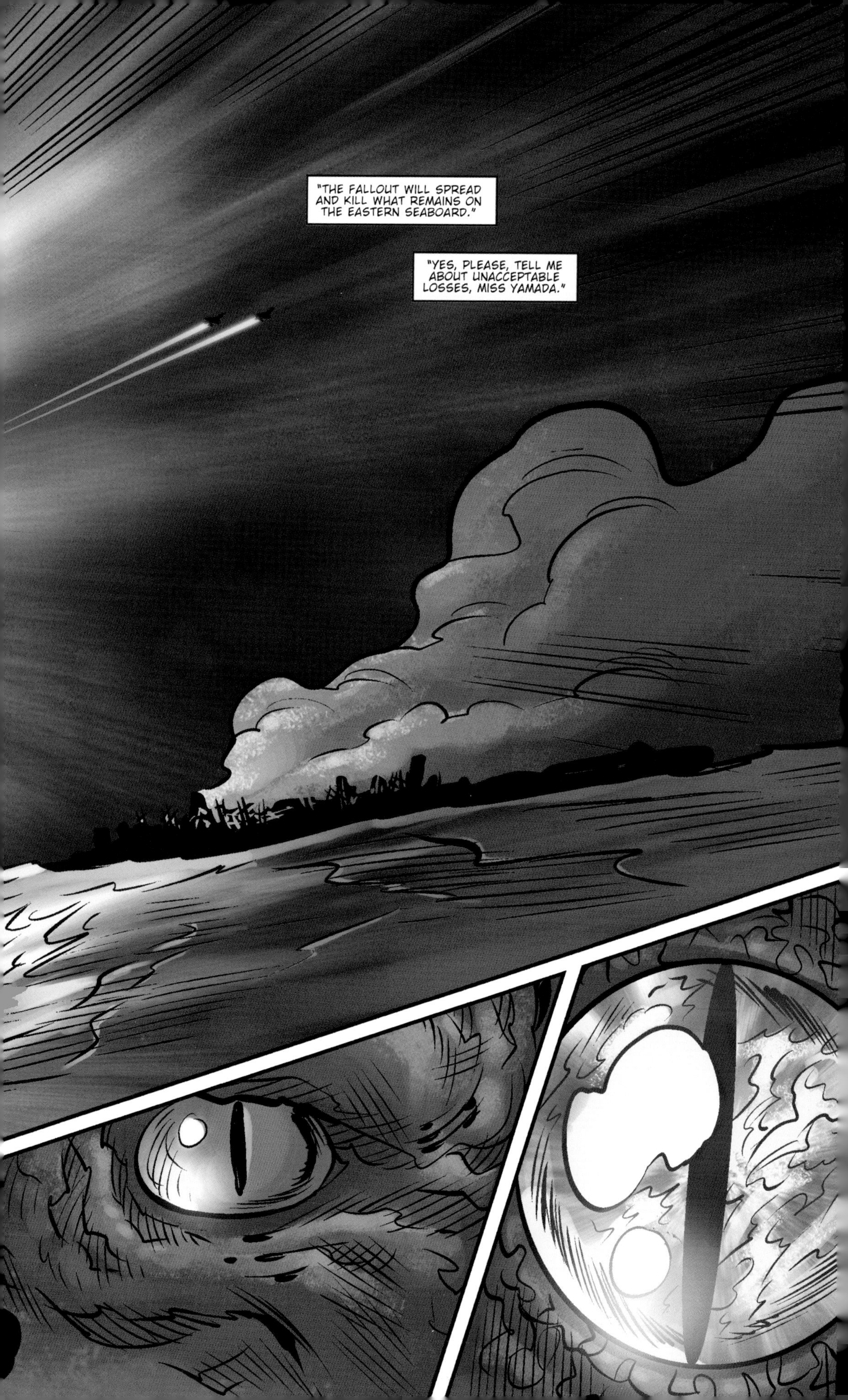
"THE FALLOUT WILL SPREAD AND KILL WHAT REMAINS ON THE EASTERN SEABOARD."
"YES, PLEASE, TELL ME ABOUT UNACCEPTABLE LOSSES, MISS YAMADA."

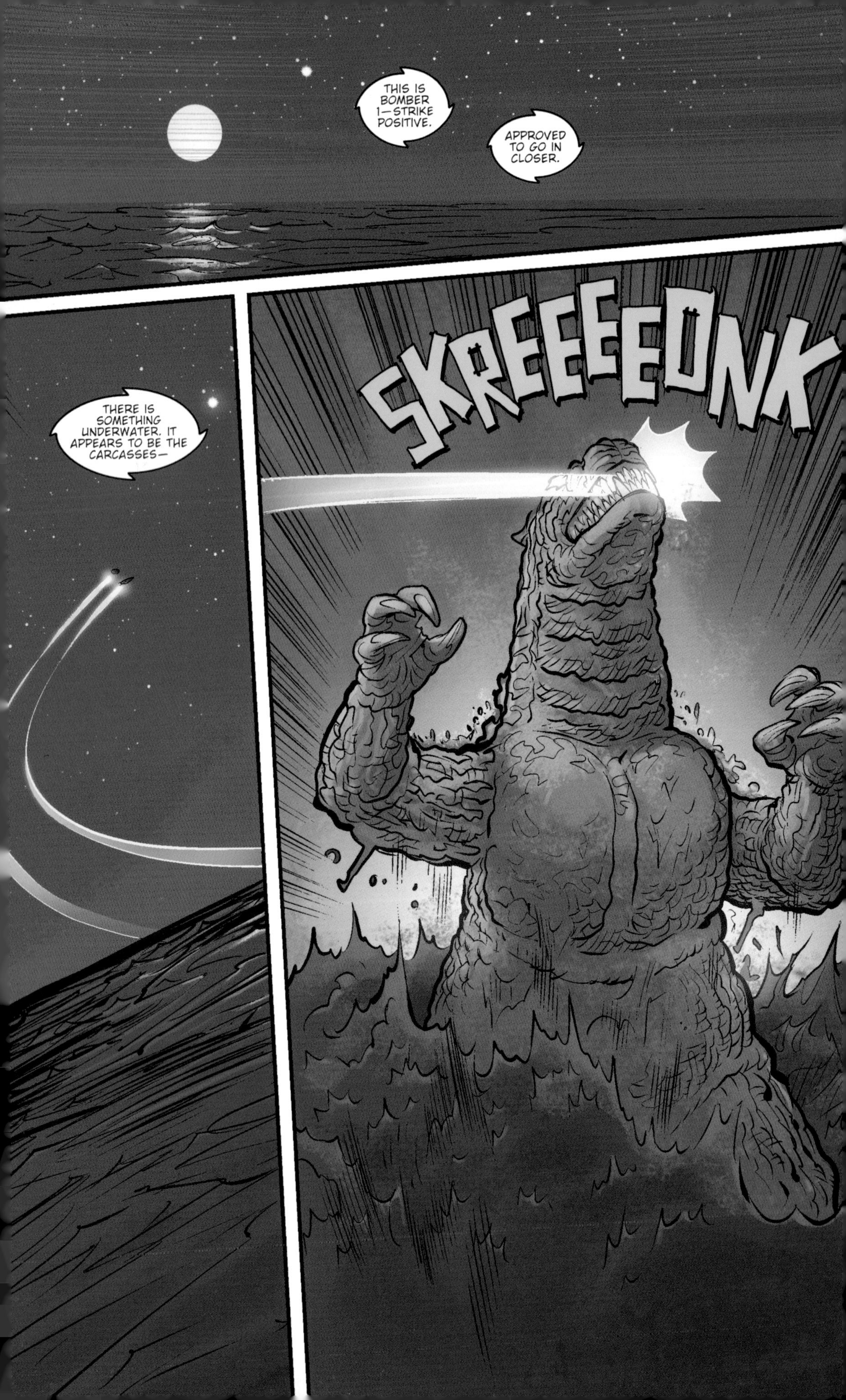
THIS IS BOMBER 1—STRIKE POSITIVE.
APPROVED TO GO IN CLOSER.
THERE IS SOMETHING UNDERWATER. IT APPEARS TO BE THE CARCASSES—
SKREEEEONK

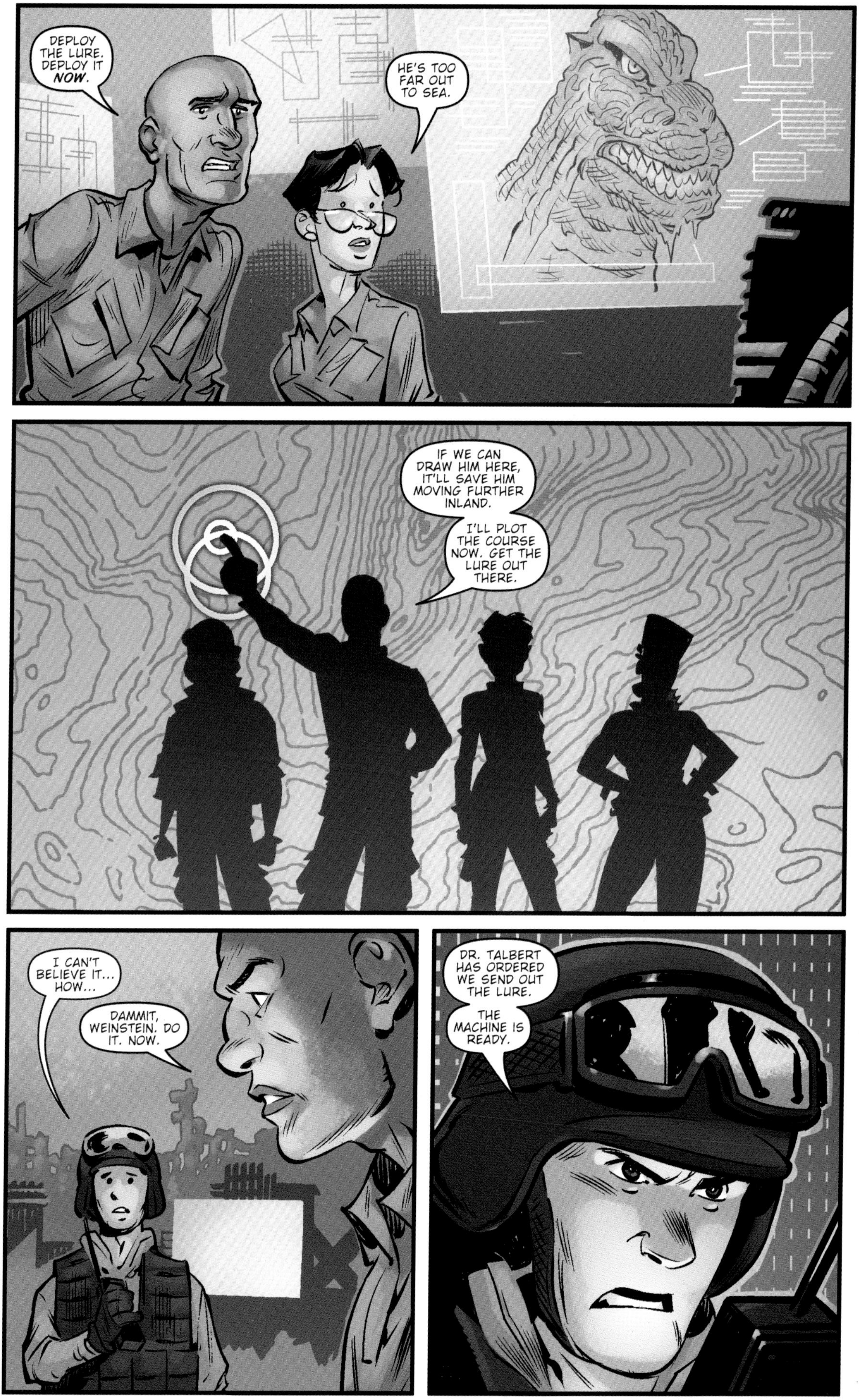
DEPLOY THE LURE. DEPLOY IT NOW.
HE'S TOO FAR OUT TO SEA.
IF WE CAN DRAW HIM HERE, IT'LL SAVE HIM MOVING FURTHER INLAND.
I'LL PLOT THE COURSE NOW. GET THE LURE OUT THERE.
I CAN'T BELIEVE IT... HOW...
DAMMIT, WEINSTEIN. DO IT. NOW.
DR. TALBERT HAS ORDERED WE SEND OUT THE LURE.
THE MACHINE IS READY.

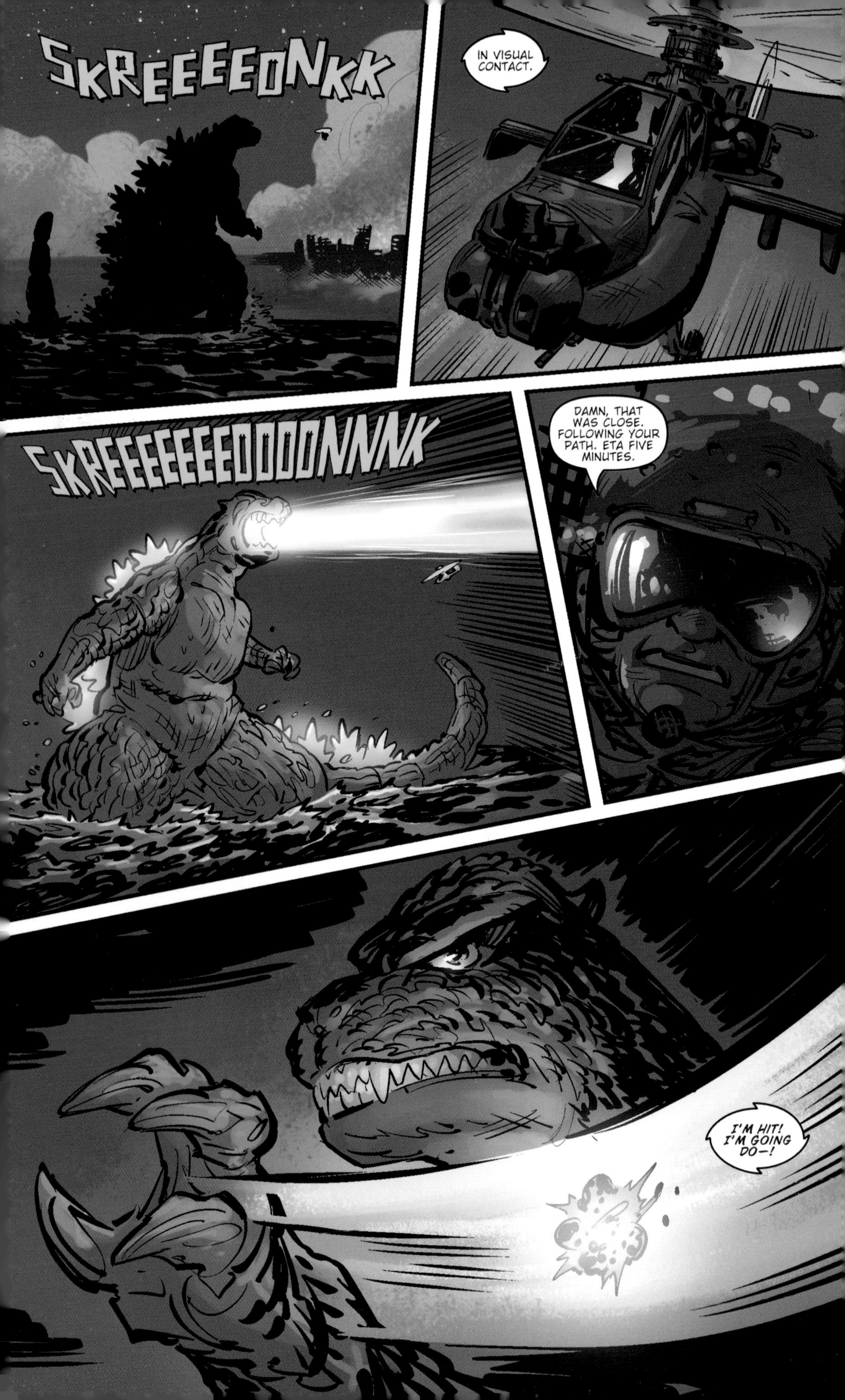
SKREEEEEONKK
IN VISUAL CONTACT.
SKREEEEEEEOOOONNNK
DAMN, THAT WAS CLOSE. FOLLOWING YOUR PATH. ETA FIVE MINUTES.
I'M HIT! I'M GOING DO--!

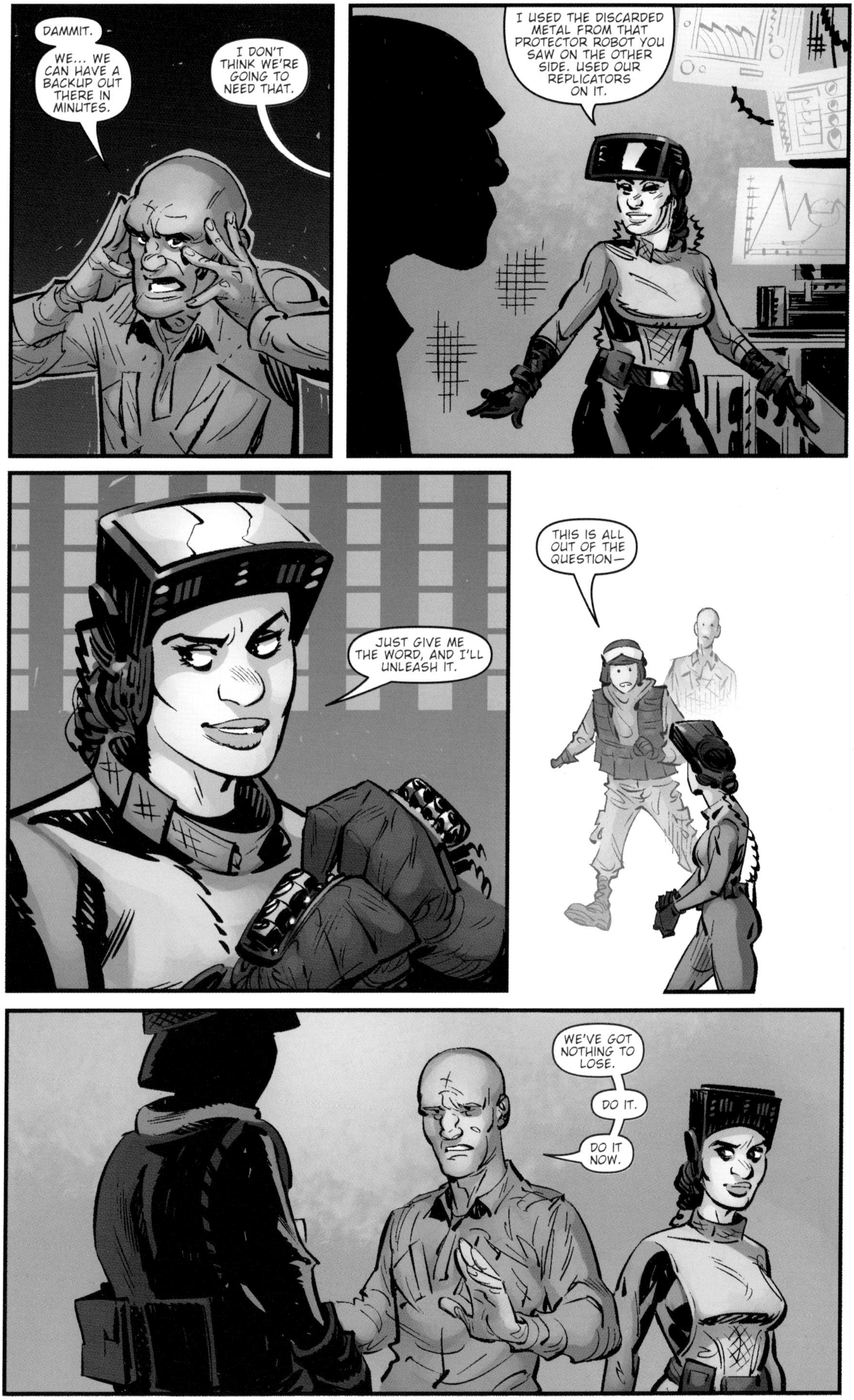
DAMMIT.
WE... WE CAN HAVE A BACKUP OUT THERE IN MINUTES.
I DON'T THINK WE'RE GOING TO NEED THAT.
I USED THE DISCARDED METAL FROM THAT PROTECTOR ROBOT YOU SAW ON THE OTHER SIDE. USED OUR REPLICATORS ON IT.
JUST GIVE ME THE WORD, AND I'LL UNLEASH IT.
THIS IS ALL OUT OF THE QUESTION—
WE'VE GOT NOTHING TO LOSE.
DO IT.
DO IT NOW.

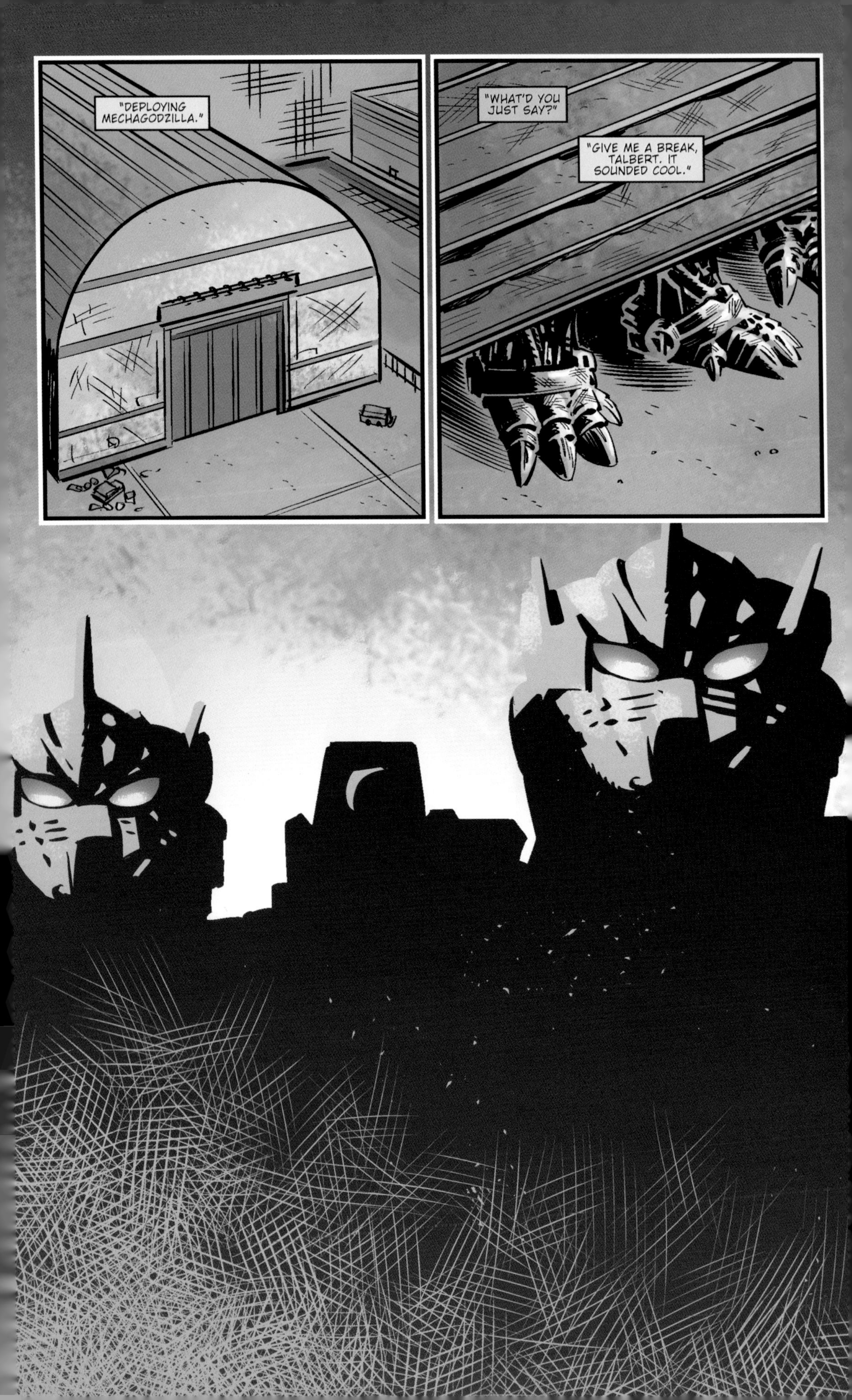
"DEPLOYING MECHAGODZILLA."
"WHAT'D YOU JUST SAY?"
"GIVE ME A BREAK, TALBERT. IT SOUNDED COOL."

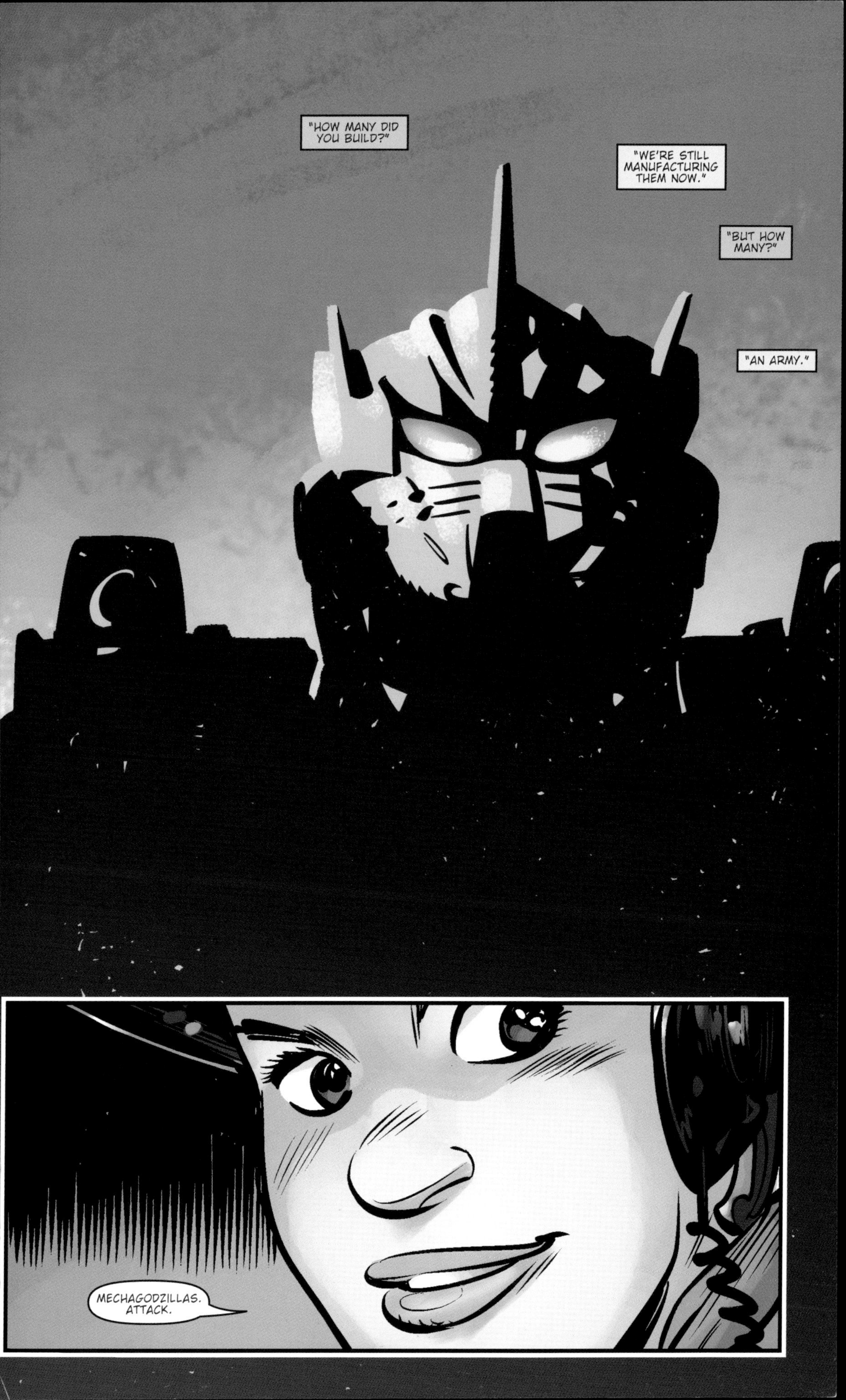
"HOW MANY DID YOU BUILD?"
"WE'RE STILL MANUFACTURING THEM NOW."
"BUT HOW MANY?"
"AN ARMY."
MECHAGODZILLAS. ATTACK.

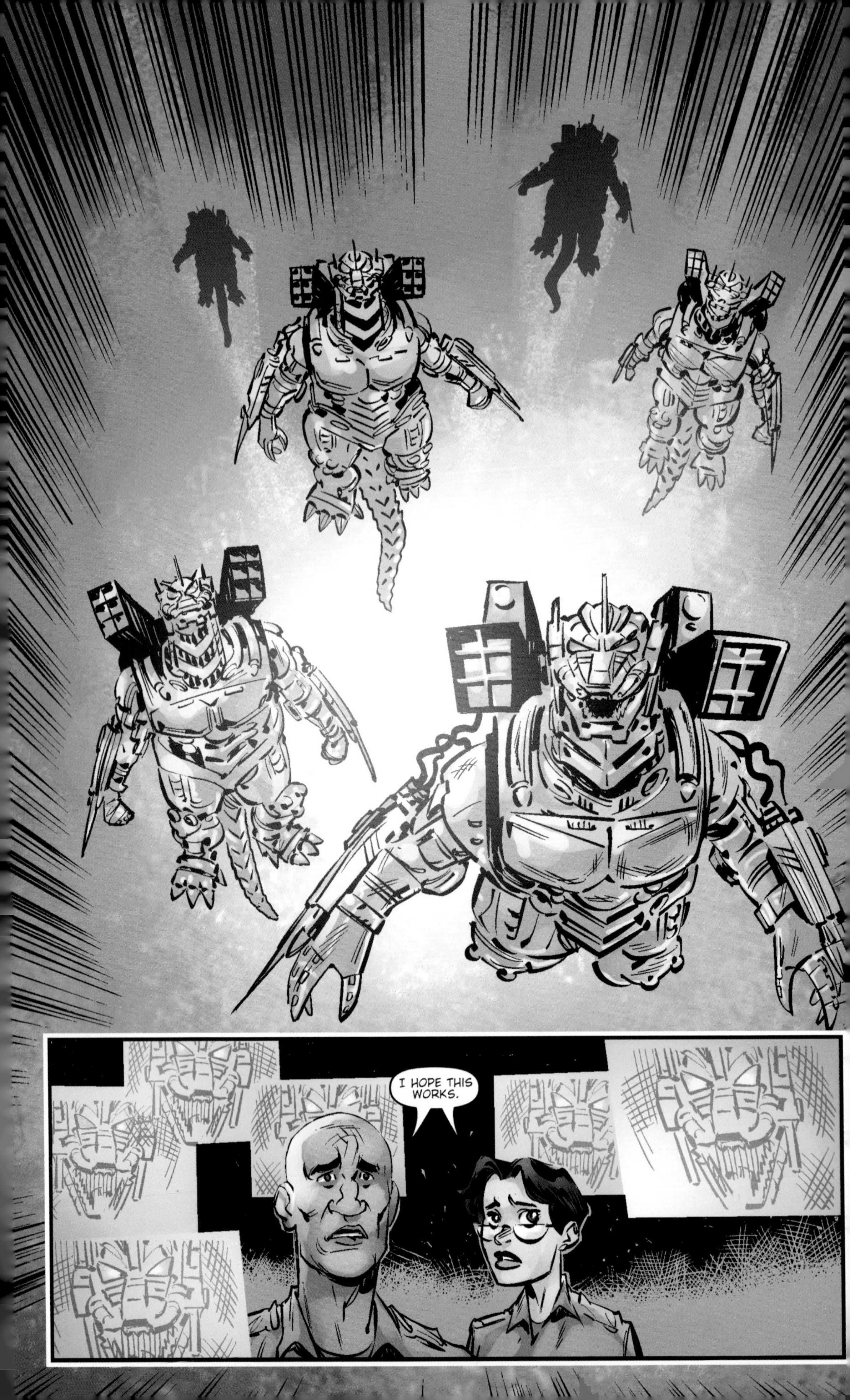
I HOPE THIS WORKS.

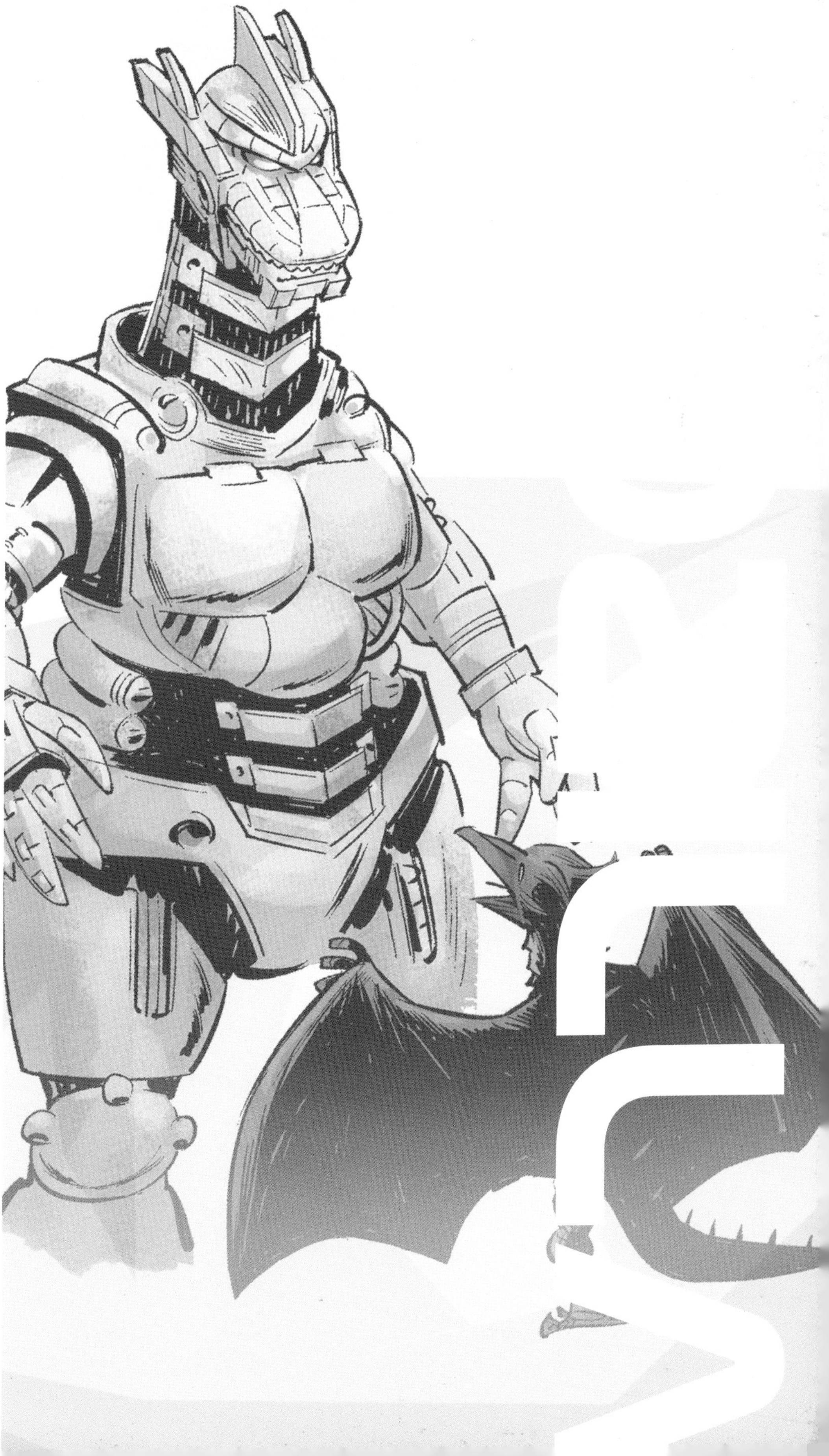

Art by BRIAN CHURILLA

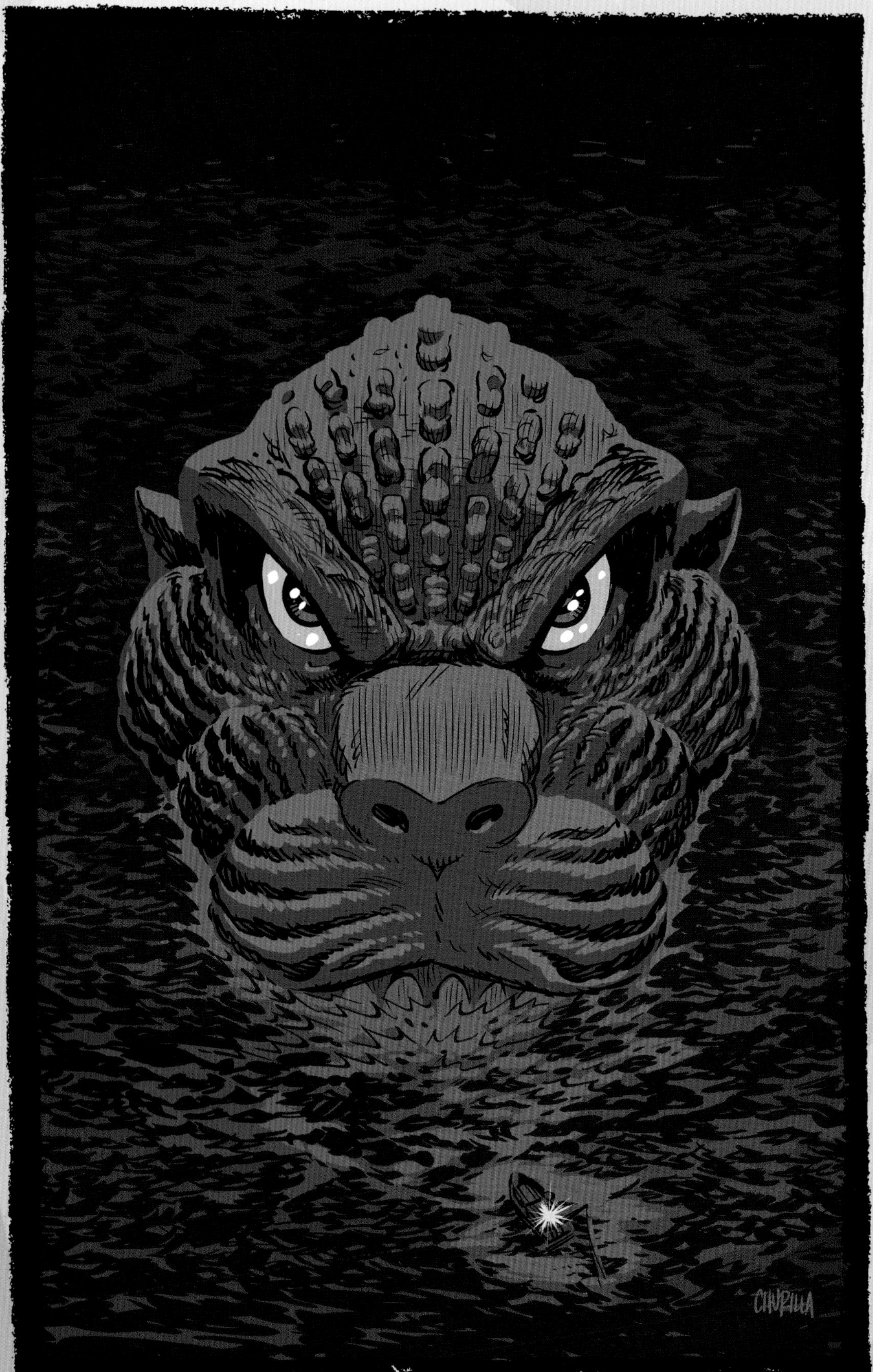
CHURILLA

"WHY DIDN'T YOU JUST BUILD ONE GIANT ONE?"
"YOU CAN'T JUST SAY 'GOOD JOB,' CAN YOU?"
"HE'S GOING TO SWAT THEM DOWN LIKE FLIES, RIDLEY."
"Y'KNOW, ELI, YOU'VE GOT A REAL NEGATIVE STREAK LATELY."
"WELL, WHEN YOU ACCIDENTALLY CAUSE THE APOCALYPSE THAT'LL HAPPEN."
"TO BE FAIR, THE APOCALYPSE ISN'T QUITE OVER YET."

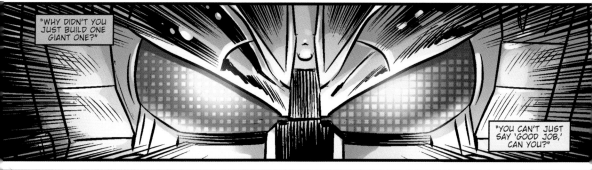

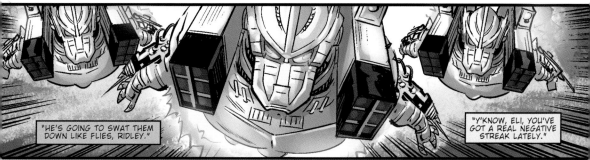

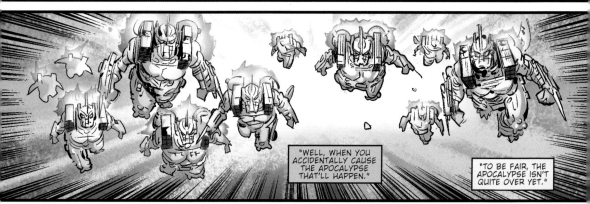

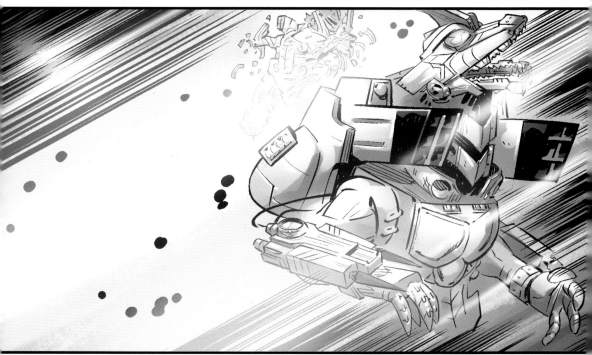

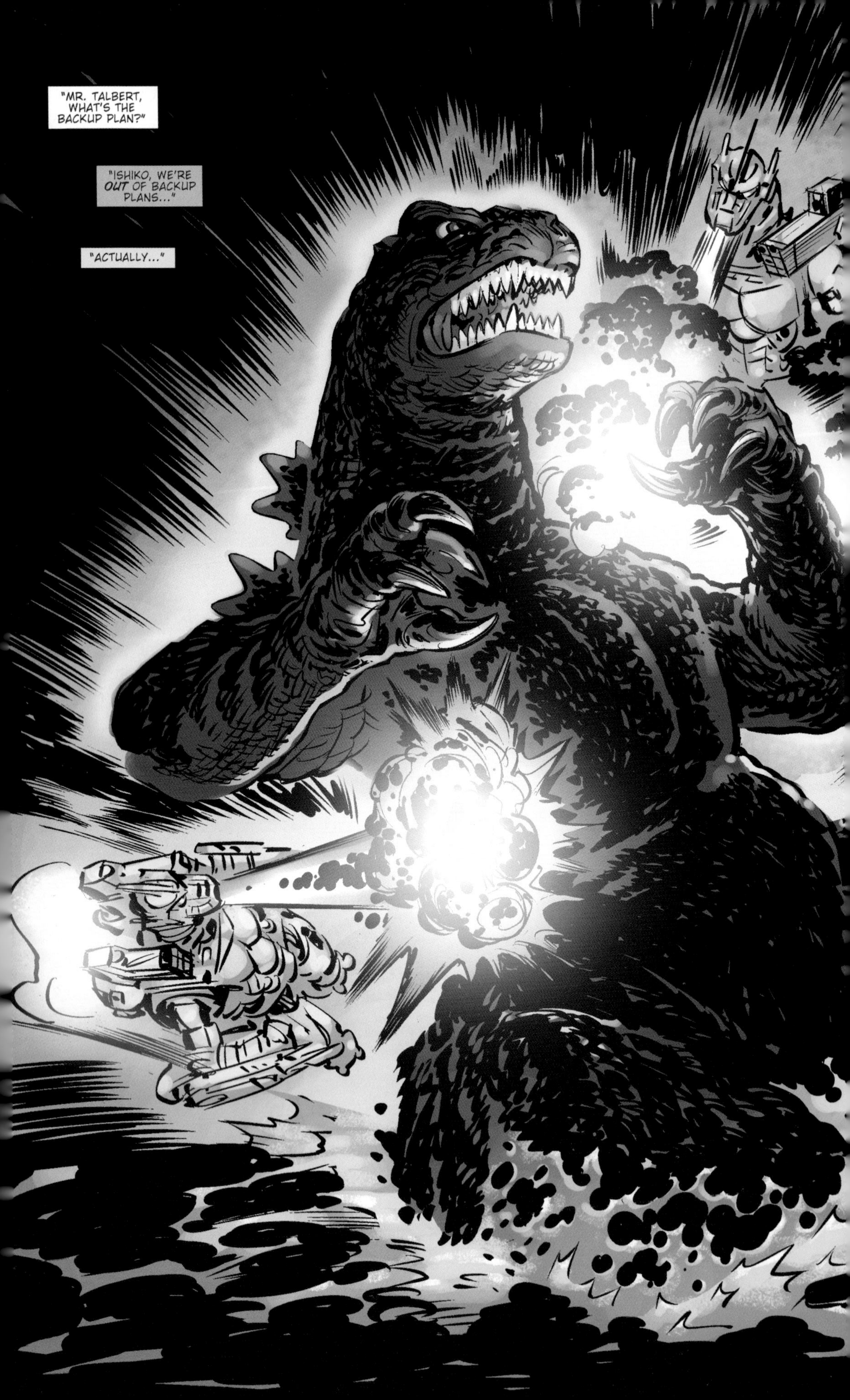
"MR. TALBERT, WHAT'S THE BACKUP PLAN?"
"ISHIKO, WE'RE OUT OF BACKUP PLANS..."
"ACTUALLY..."

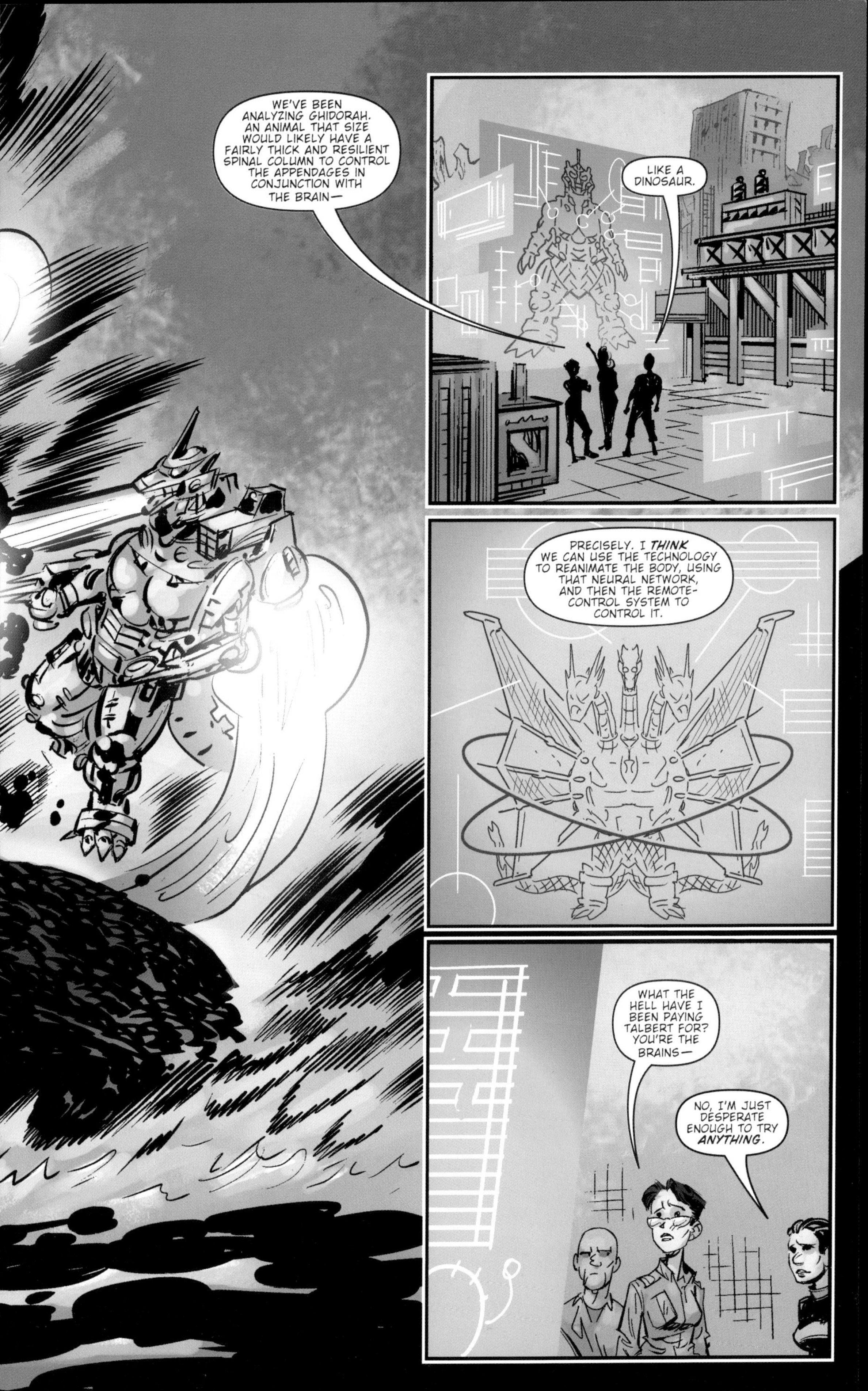
WE'VE BEEN ANALYZING GHIDORAH. AN ANIMAL THAT SIZE WOULD LIKELY HAVE A FAIRLY THICK AND RESILIENT SPINAL COLUMN TO CONTROL THE APPENDAGES IN CONJUNCTION WITH THE BRAIN—
LIKE A DINOSAUR.
PRECISELY. I *THINK* WE CAN USE THE TECHNOLOGY TO REANIMATE THE BODY, USING THAT NEURAL NETWORK, AND THEN THE REMOTE-CONTROL SYSTEM TO CONTROL IT.
WHAT THE HELL HAVE I BEEN PAYING TALBERT FOR? YOU'RE THE BRAINS—
NO, I'M JUST DESPERATE ENOUGH TO TRY *ANYTHING*.

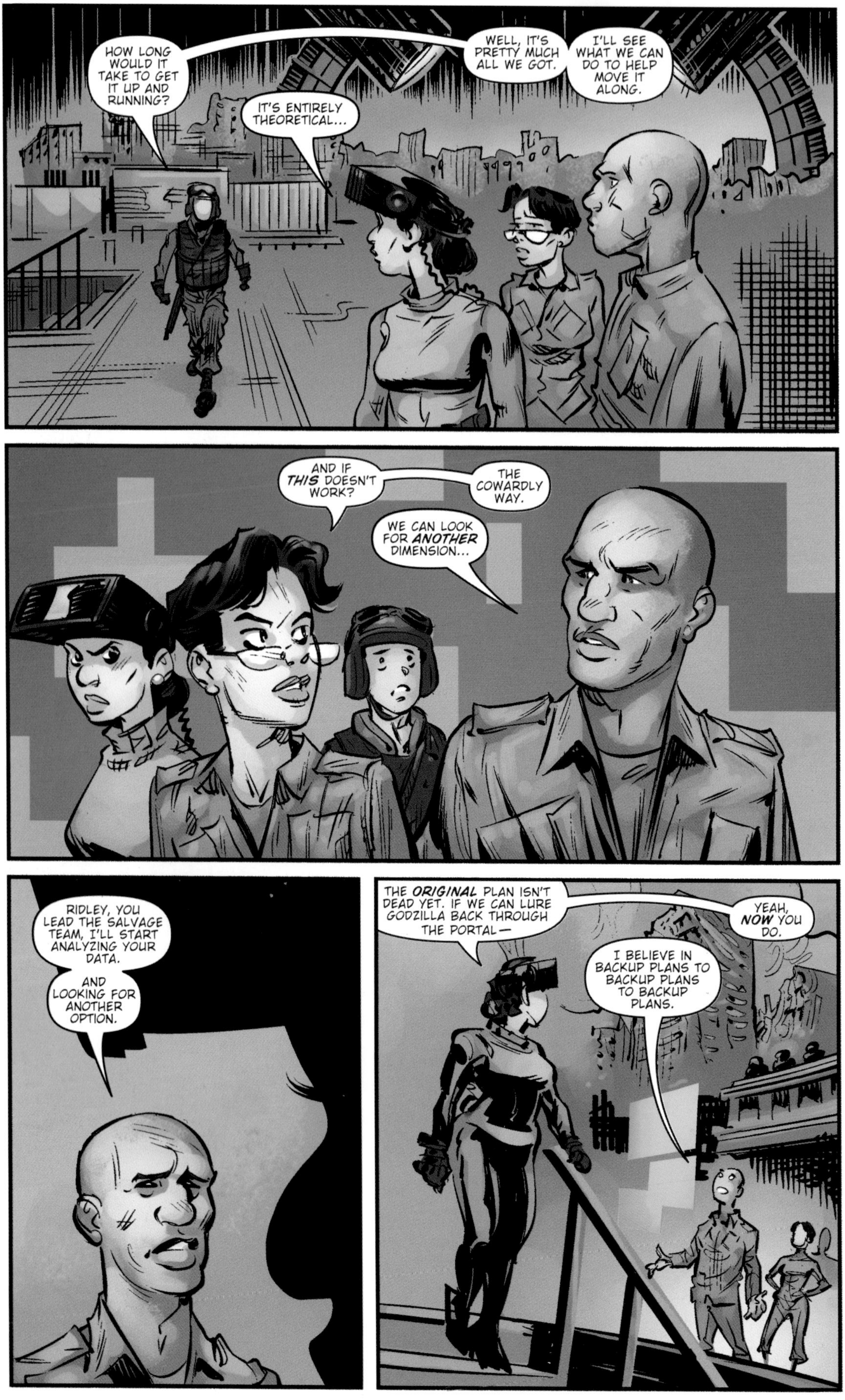
HOW LONG WOULD IT TAKE TO GET IT UP AND RUNNING?
IT'S ENTIRELY THEORETICAL...
WELL, IT'S PRETTY MUCH ALL WE GOT.
I'LL SEE WHAT WE CAN DO TO HELP MOVE IT ALONG.
AND IF THIS DOESN'T WORK?
THE COWARDLY WAY.
WE CAN LOOK FOR ANOTHER DIMENSION...
RIDLEY, YOU LEAD THE SALVAGE TEAM, I'LL START ANALYZING YOUR DATA.
AND LOOKING FOR ANOTHER OPTION.
THE ORIGINAL PLAN ISN'T DEAD YET. IF WE CAN LURE GODZILLA BACK THROUGH THE PORTAL—
YEAH, NOW YOU DO.
I BELIEVE IN BACKUP PLANS TO BACKUP PLANS TO BACKUP PLANS.

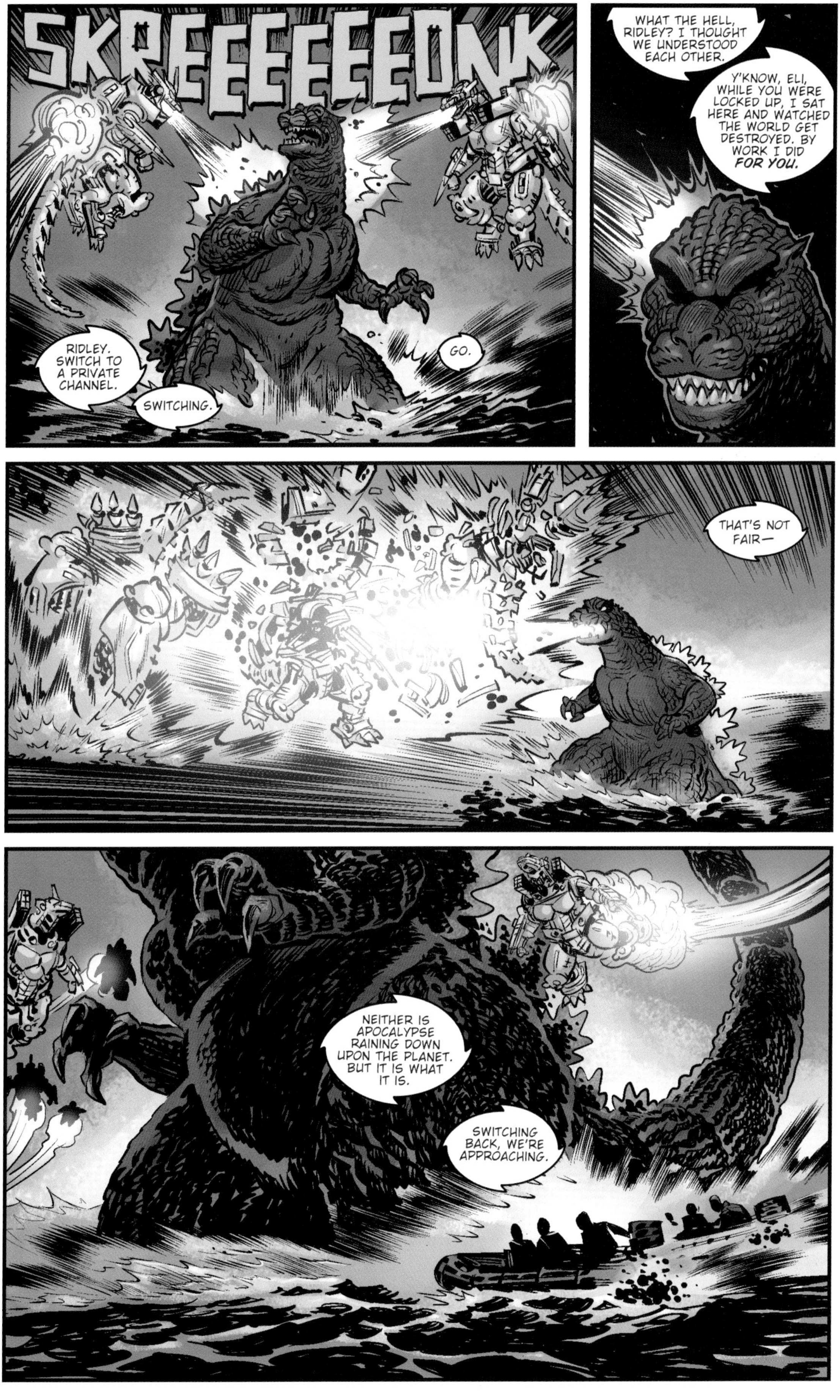
SKREEEEEEEONK
RIDLEY. SWITCH TO A PRIVATE CHANNEL.
SWITCHING.
GO.
WHAT THE HELL, RIDLEY? I THOUGHT WE UNDERSTOOD EACH OTHER.
Y'KNOW, ELI, WHILE YOU WERE LOCKED UP, I SAT HERE AND WATCHED THE WORLD GET DESTROYED. BY WORK I DID FOR YOU.
THAT'S NOT FAIR—
NEITHER IS APOCALYPSE RAINING DOWN UPON THE PLANET. BUT IT IS WHAT IT IS.
SWITCHING BACK, WE'RE APPROACHING.

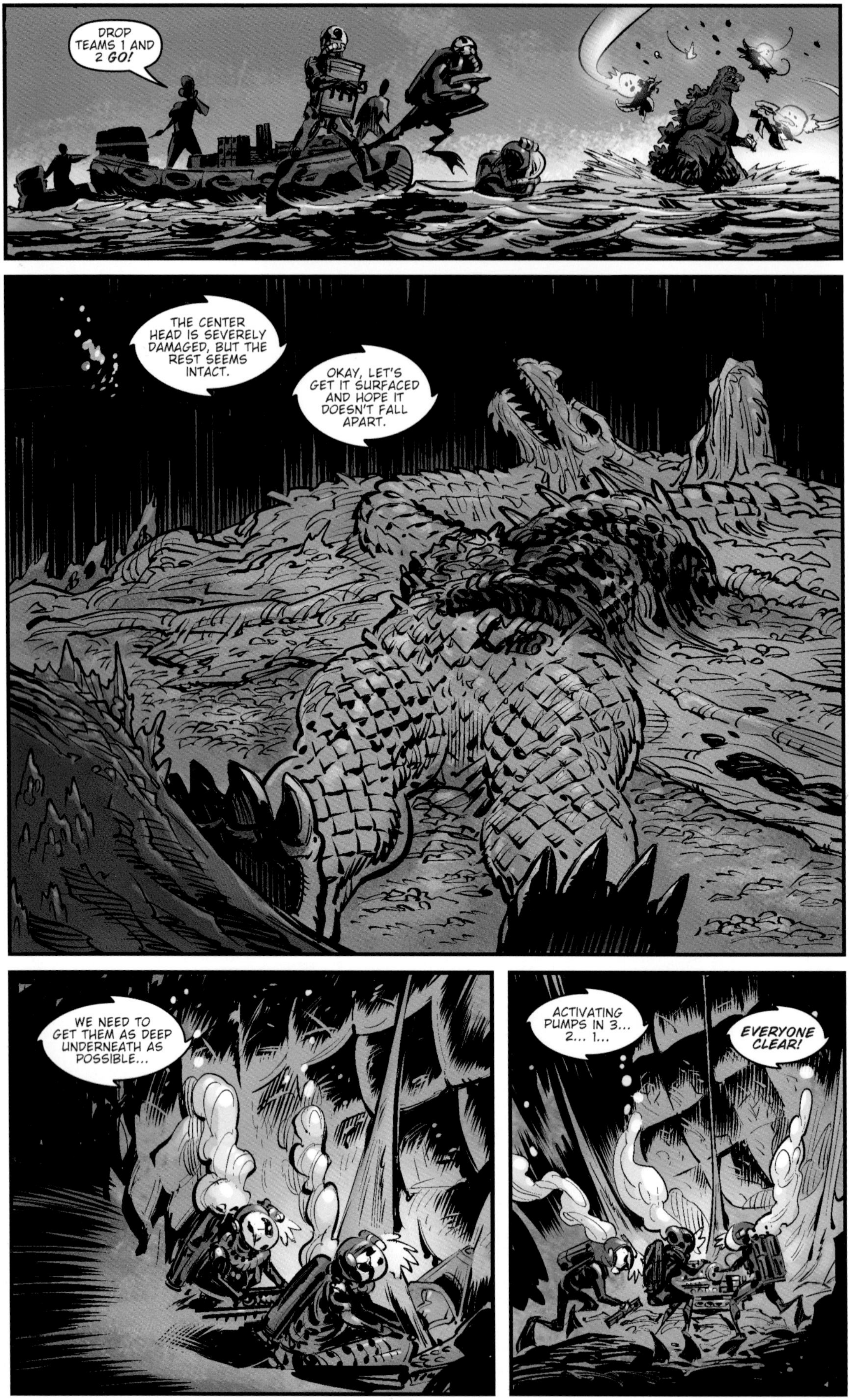
DROP TEAMS 1 AND 2 GO!
THE CENTER HEAD IS SEVERELY DAMAGED, BUT THE REST SEEMS INTACT.
OKAY, LET'S GET IT SURFACED AND HOPE IT DOESN'T FALL APART.
WE NEED TO GET THEM AS DEEP UNDERNEATH AS POSSIBLE...
ACTIVATING PUMPS IN 3... 2... 1...
EVERYONE CLEAR!

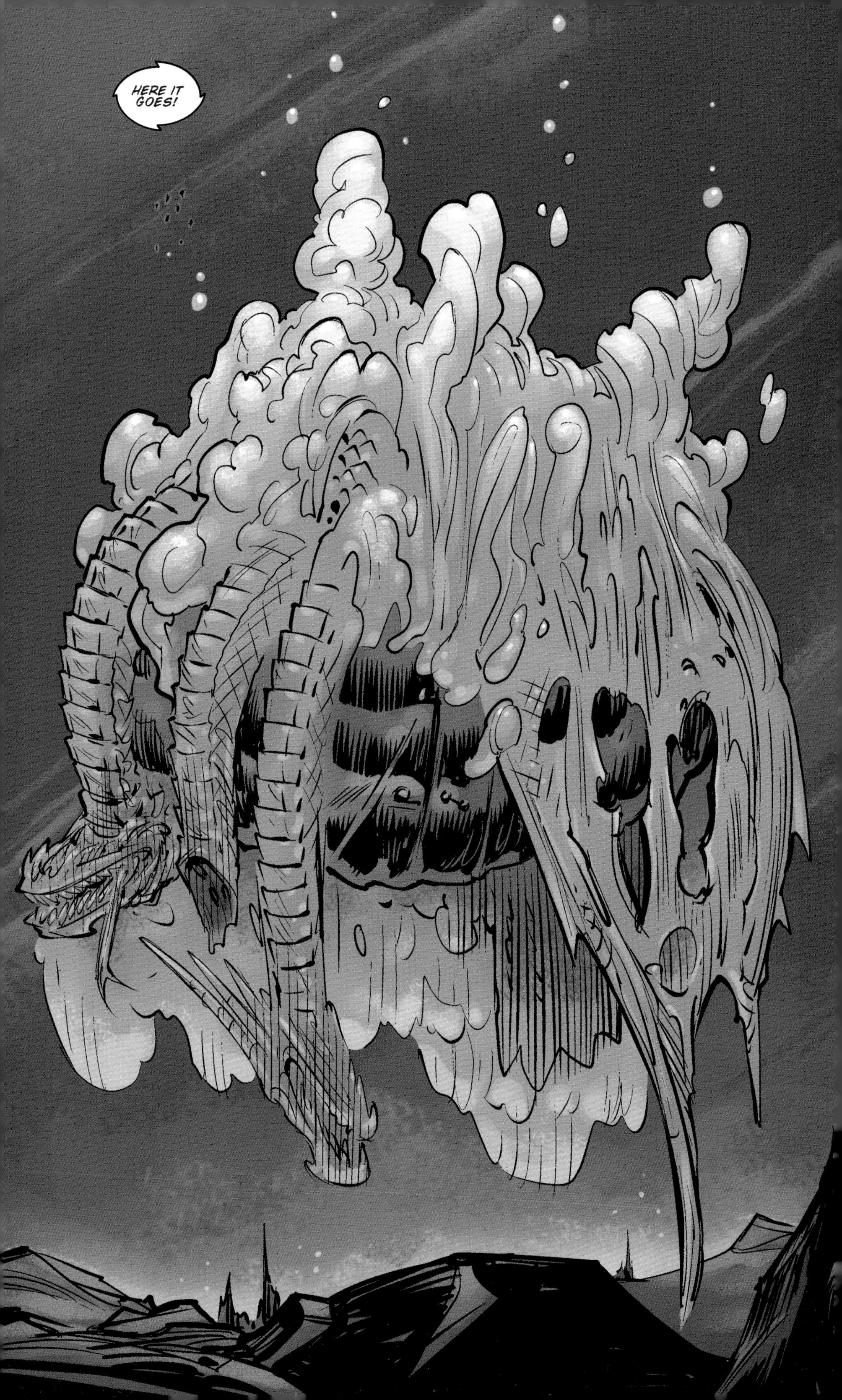
HERE IT GOES!

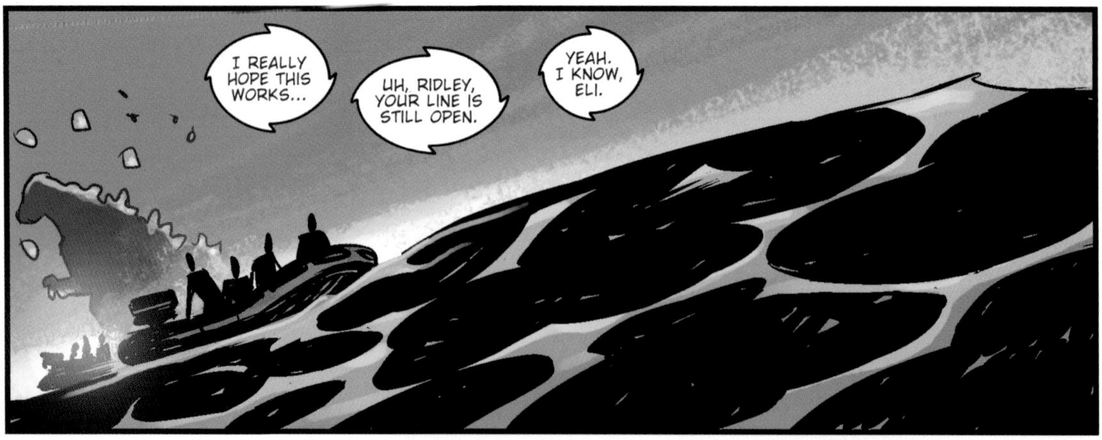
I REALLY HOPE THIS WORKS...
UH, RIDLEY, YOUR LINE IS STILL OPEN.
YEAH. I KNOW, ELI.

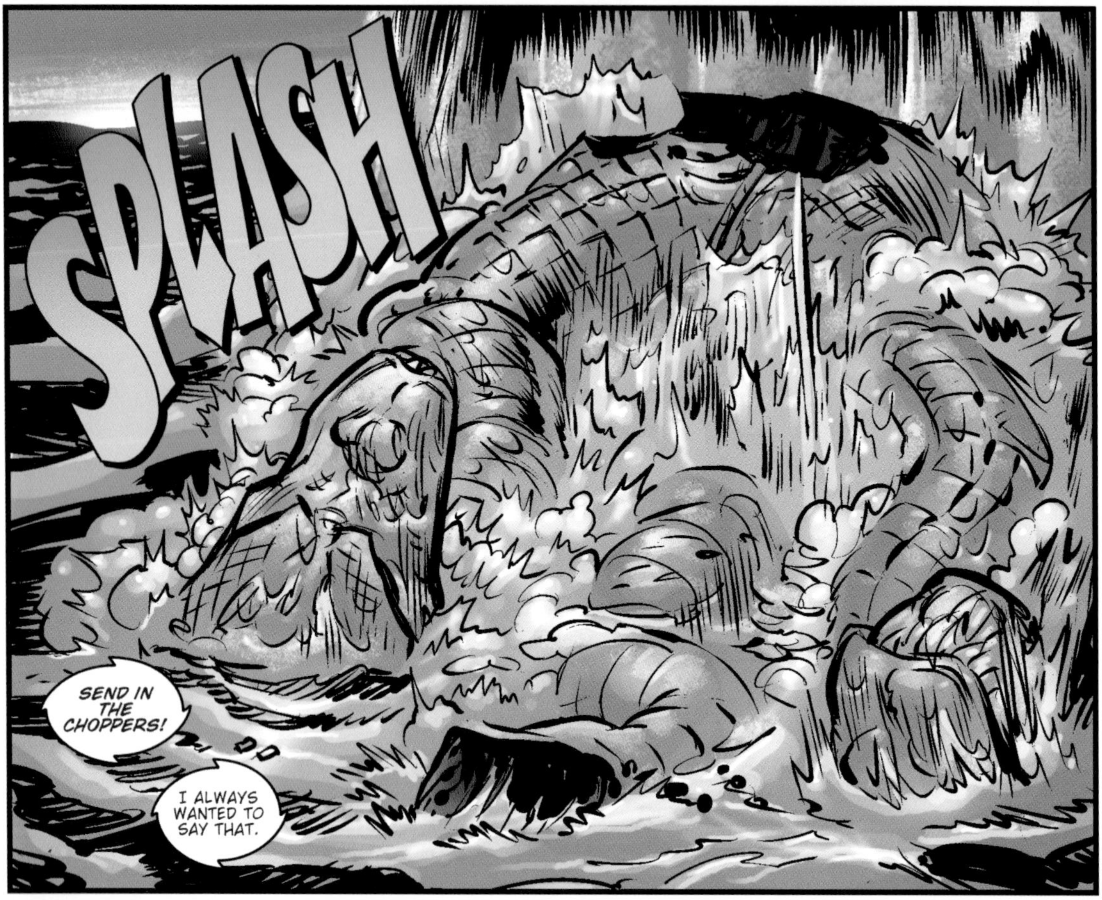
SPLASH
SEND IN THE CHOPPERS!
I ALWAYS WANTED TO SAY THAT.

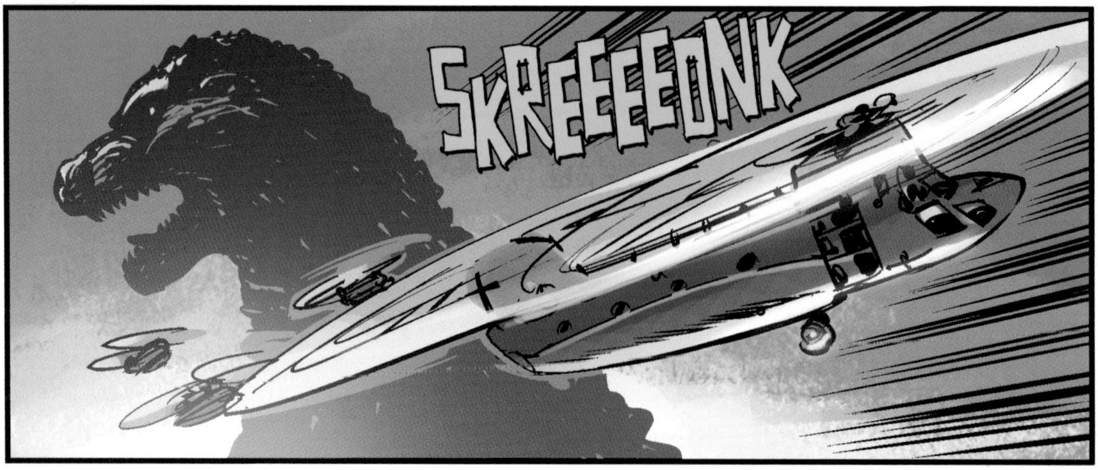
SKREEEEONK

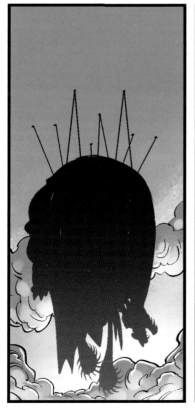

THIS IS WAY GROSSER UP CLOSE.

WAIT'LL WE HAVE TO SHOVE A ROBOT ON TOP OF IT...

I'LL LET YOU HANDLE THAT PART.

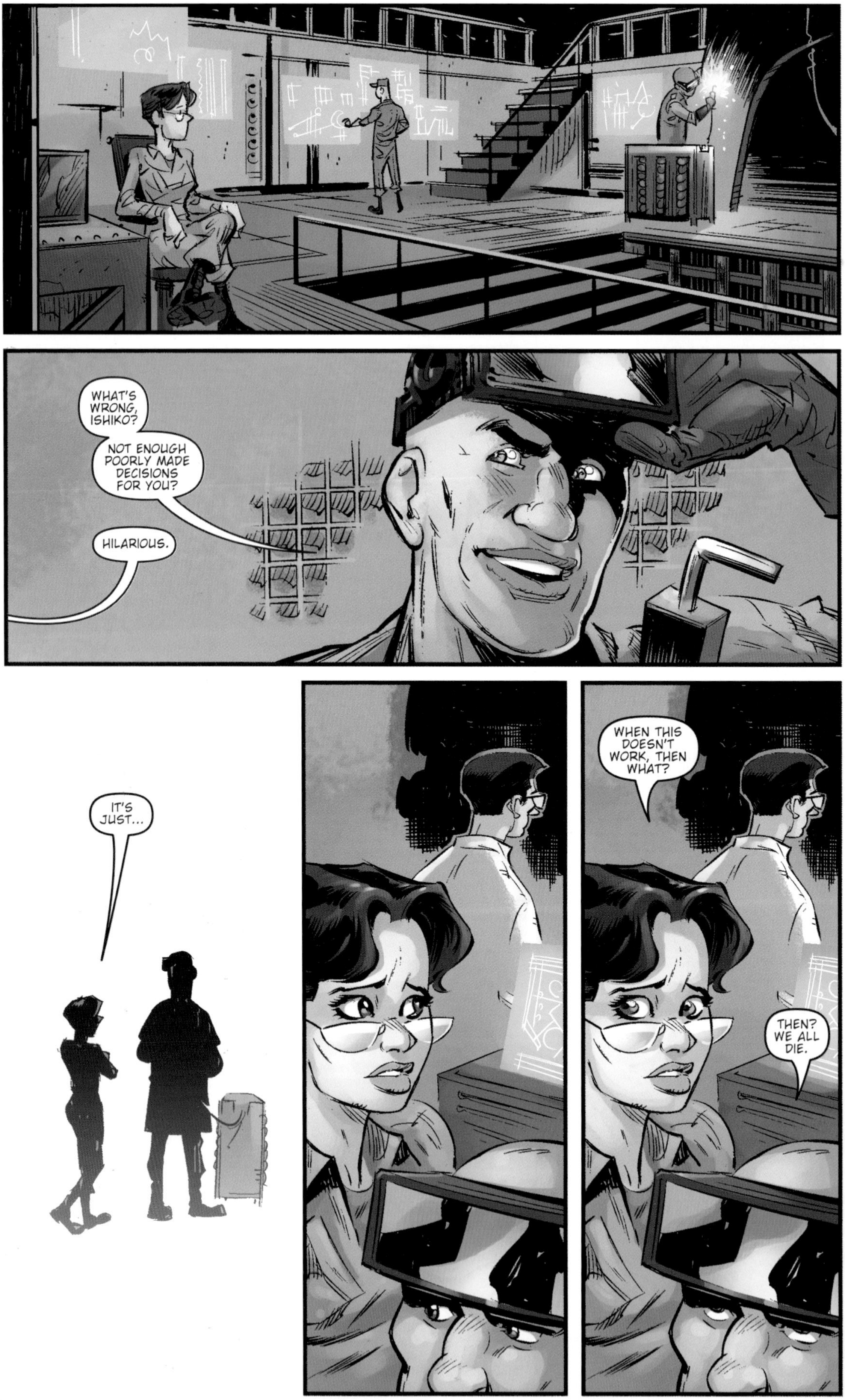
WHAT'S WRONG, ISHIKO?
NOT ENOUGH POORLY MADE DECISIONS FOR YOU?
HILARIOUS.
IT'S JUST...
WHEN THIS DOESN'T WORK, THEN WHAT?
THEN? WE ALL DIE.

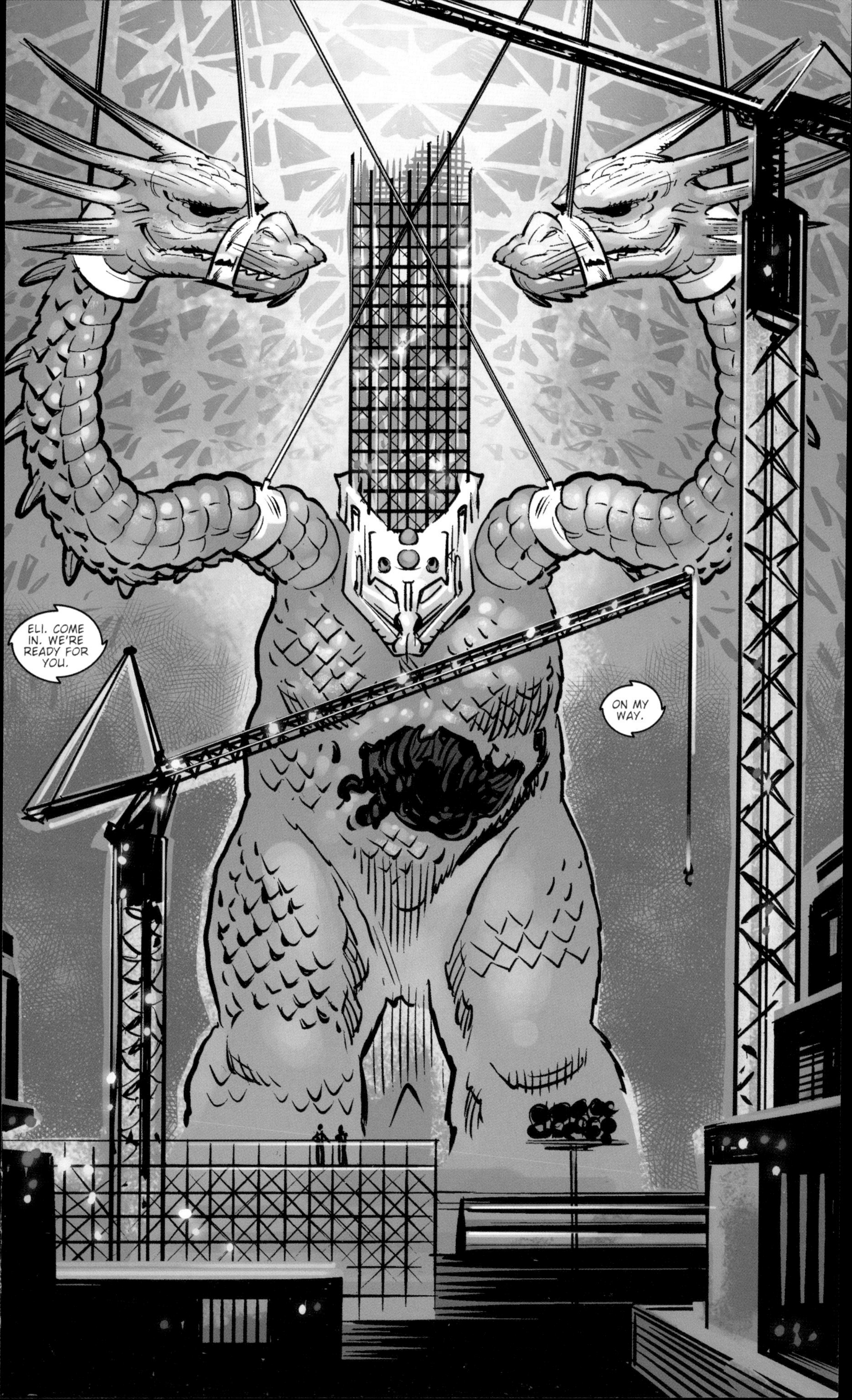
ELI. COME IN. WE'RE READY FOR YOU.
ON MY WAY.

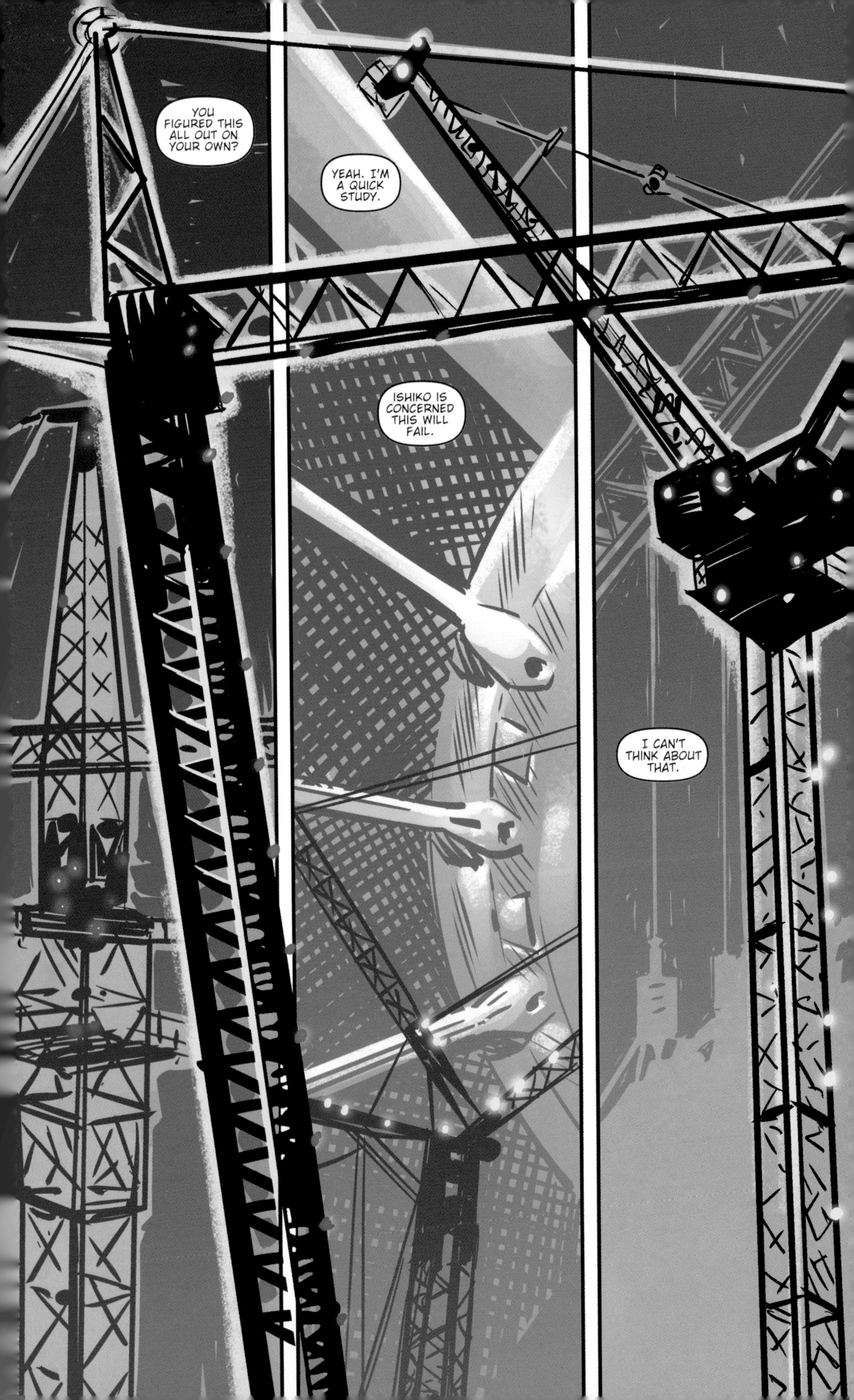
YOU FIGURED THIS ALL OUT ON YOUR OWN?
YEAH. I'M A QUICK STUDY.
ISHIKO IS CONCERNED THIS WILL FAIL.
I CAN'T THINK ABOUT THAT.

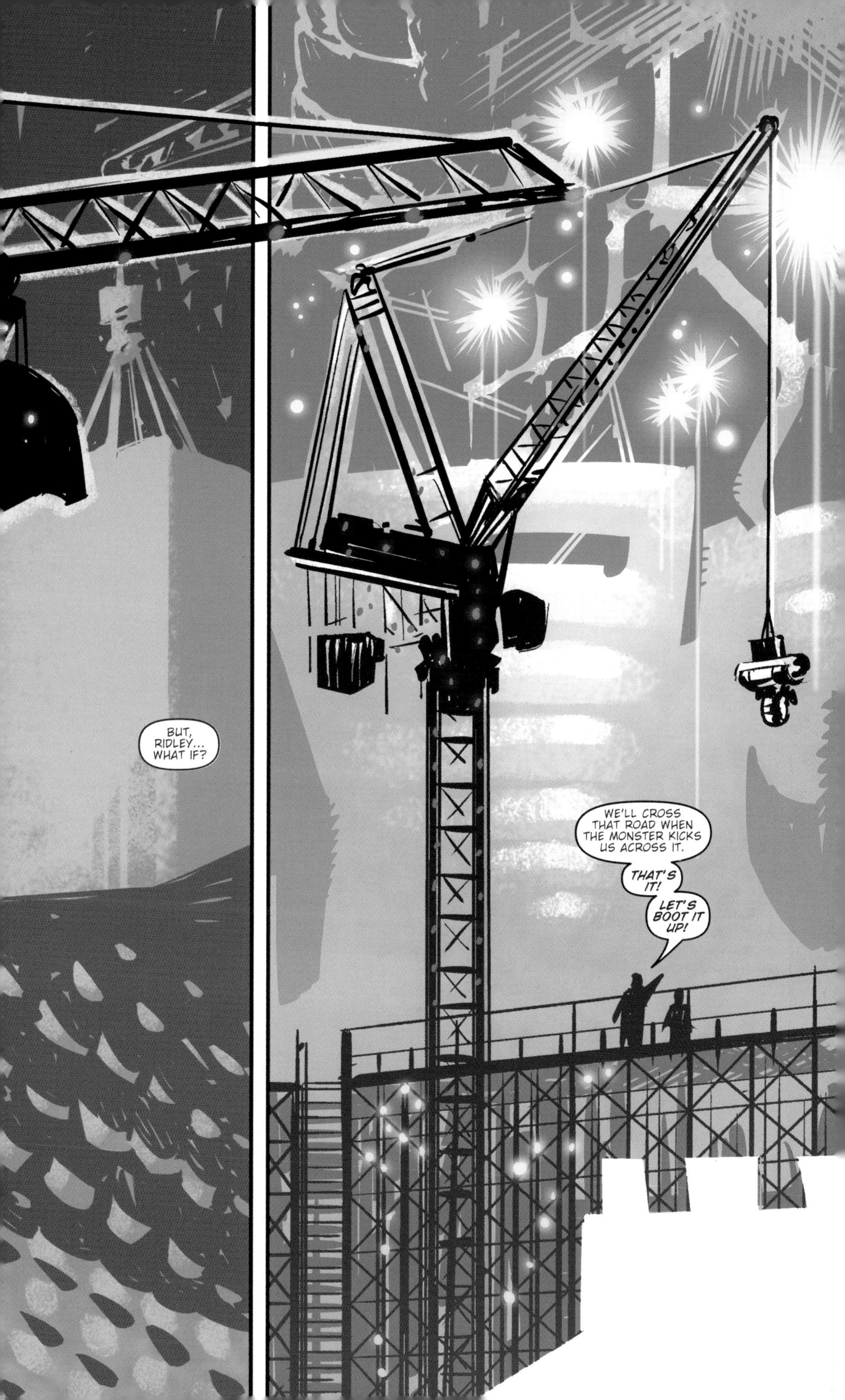
BUT, RIDLEY... WHAT IF?
WE'LL CROSS THAT ROAD WHEN THE MONSTER KICKS US ACROSS IT.
THAT'S IT!
LET'S BOOT IT UP!

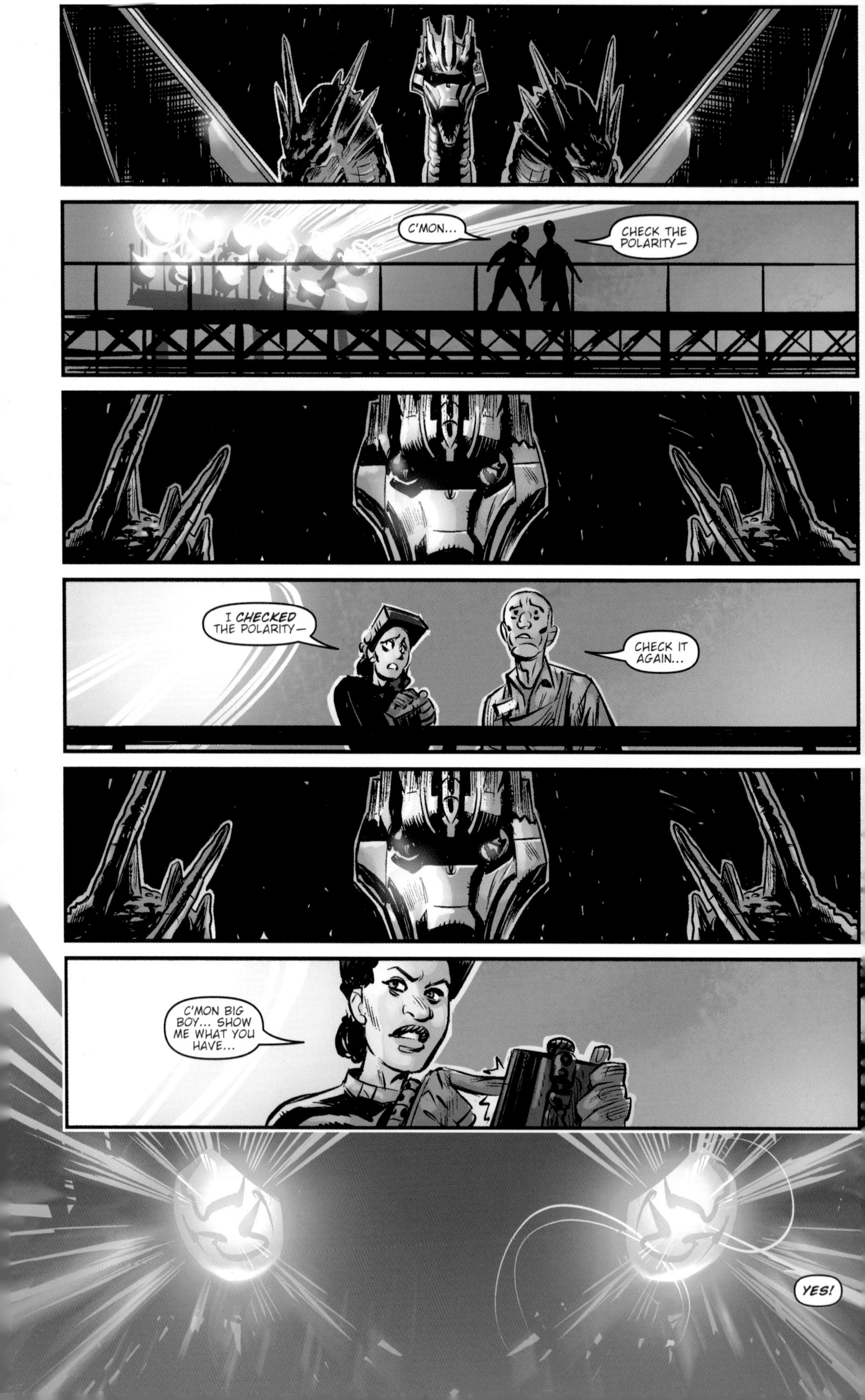
C'MON...
CHECK THE POLARITY—
I CHECKED THE POLARITY—
CHECK IT AGAIN...
C'MON BIG BOY... SHOW ME WHAT YOU HAVE...
YES!

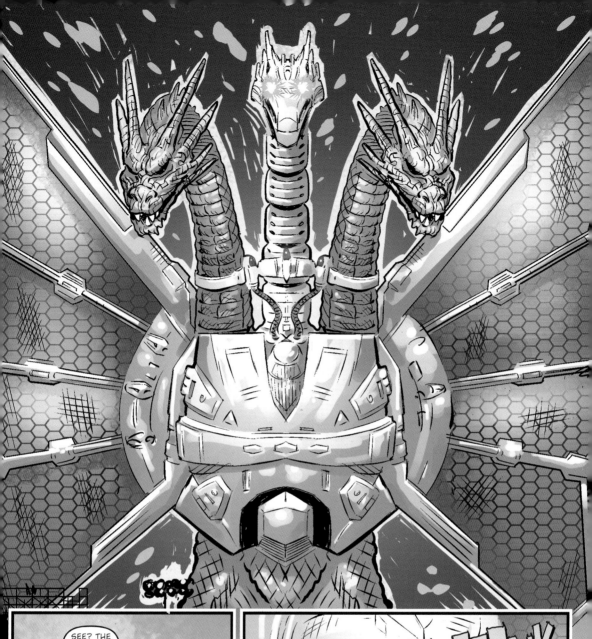

SEE? THE POWER OF POSITIVE THINKING.

SKREEEEEEONK

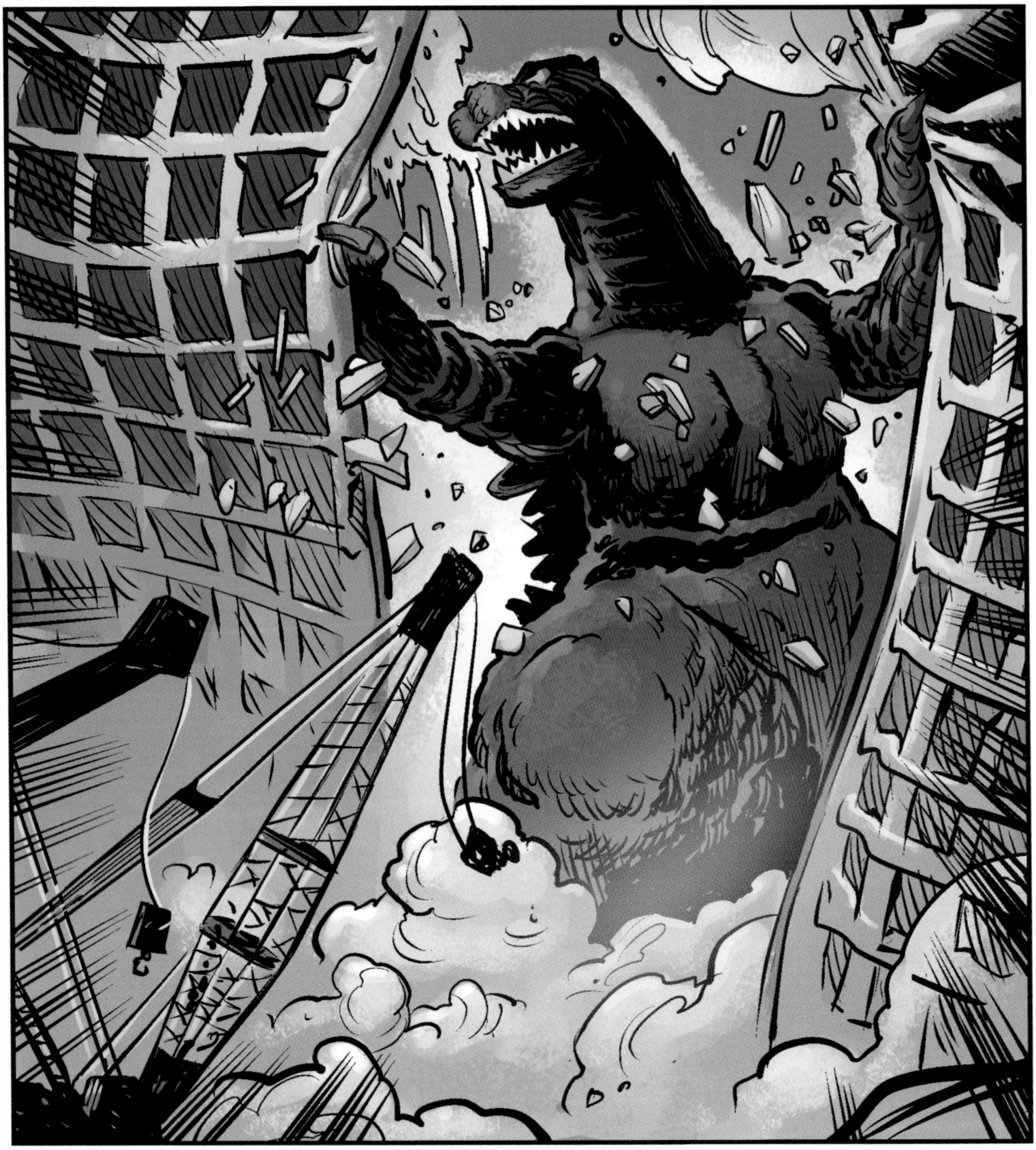

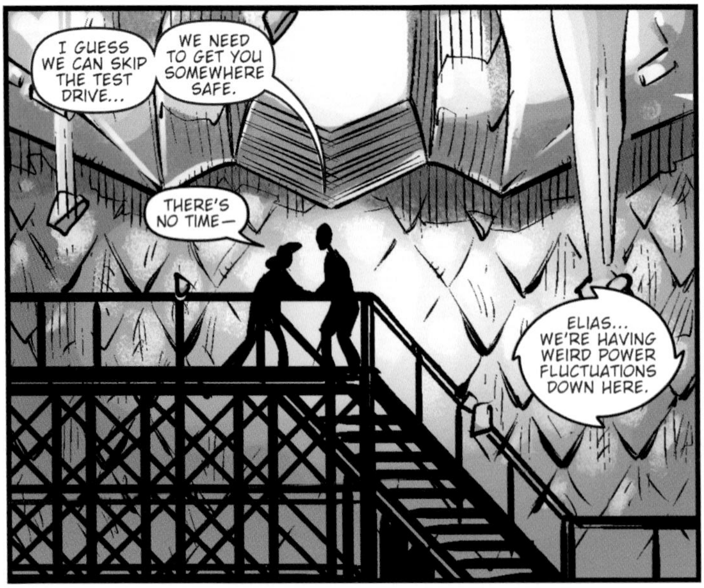

I GUESS WE CAN SKIP THE TEST DRIVE...
WE NEED TO GET YOU SOMEWHERE SAFE.
THERE'S NO TIME—
ELIAS... WE'RE HAVING WEIRD POWER FLUCTUATIONS DOWN HERE.

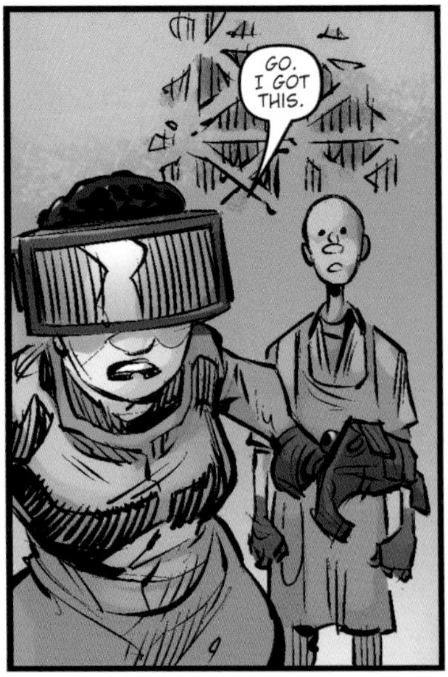

GO. I GOT THIS.

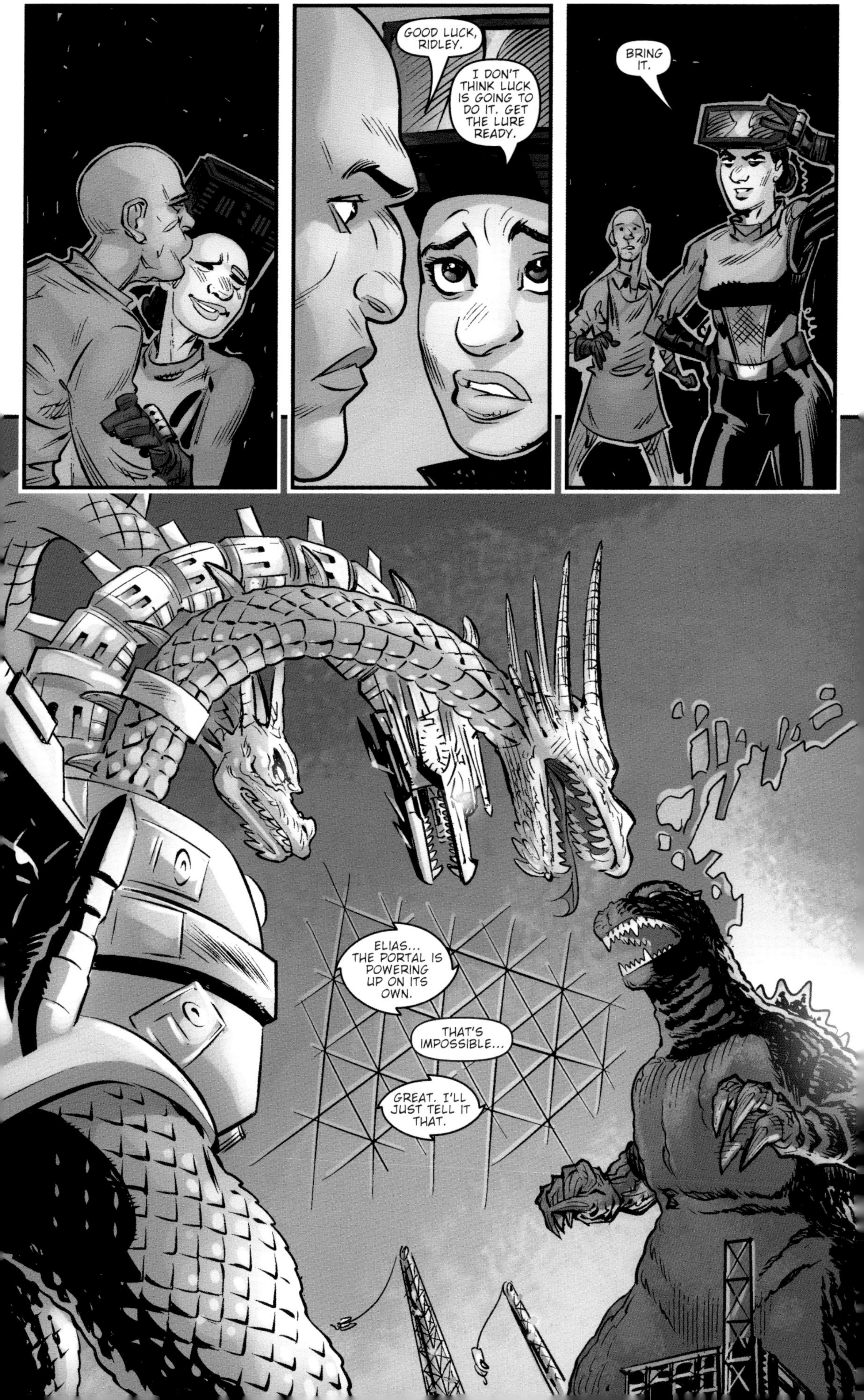
GOOD LUCK, RIDLEY.
I DON'T THINK LUCK IS GOING TO DO IT. GET THE LURE READY.
BRING IT.
ELIAS... THE PORTAL IS POWERING UP ON ITS OWN.
THAT'S IMPOSSIBLE...
GREAT. I'LL JUST TELL IT THAT.

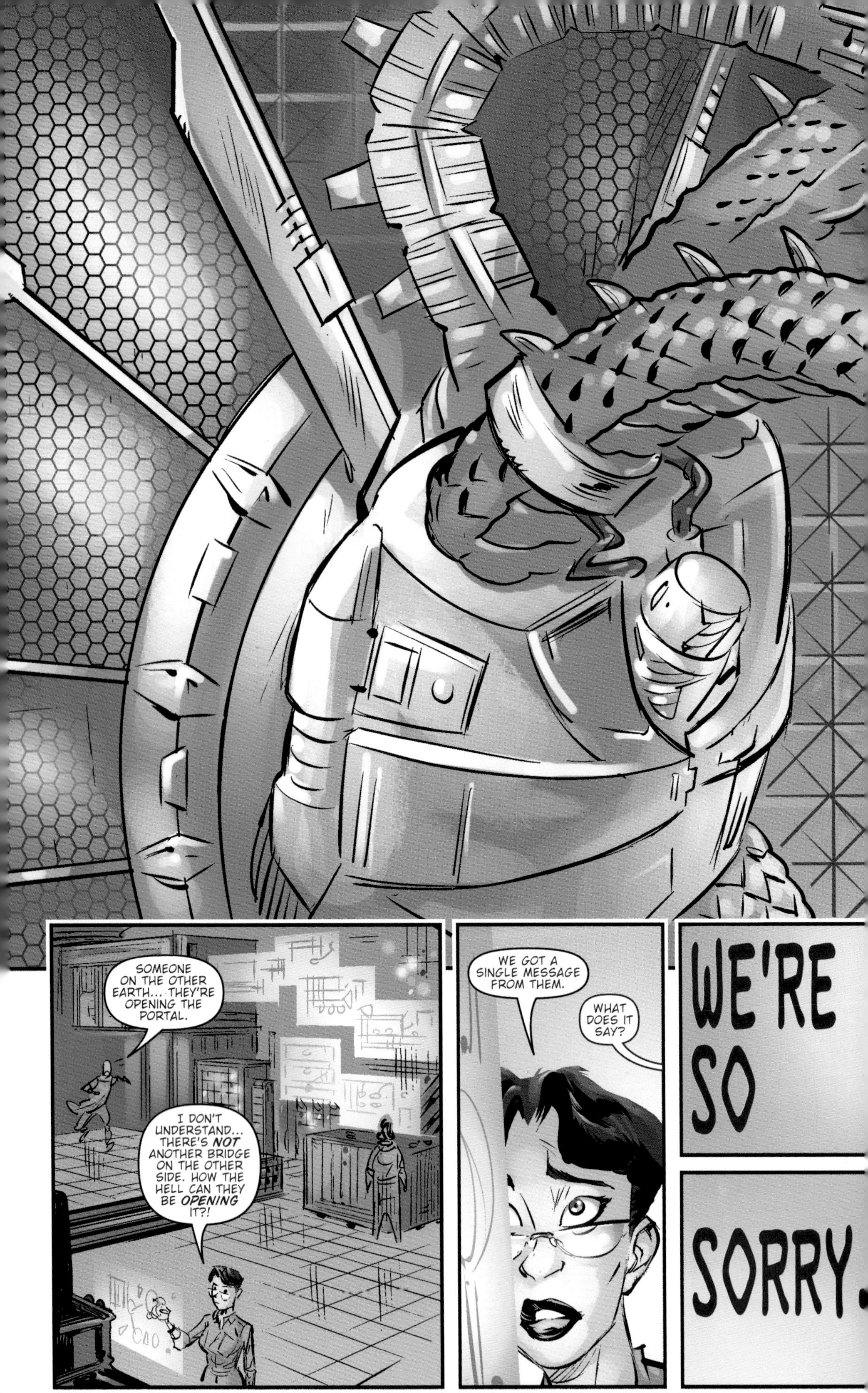
SOMEONE ON THE OTHER EARTH... THEY'RE OPENING THE PORTAL.
I DON'T UNDERSTAND... THERE'S **NOT** ANOTHER BRIDGE ON THE OTHER SIDE. HOW THE HELL CAN THEY BE **OPENING** IT?!
WE GOT A SINGLE MESSAGE FROM THEM.
WHAT DOES IT SAY?
WE'RE SO
SORRY.

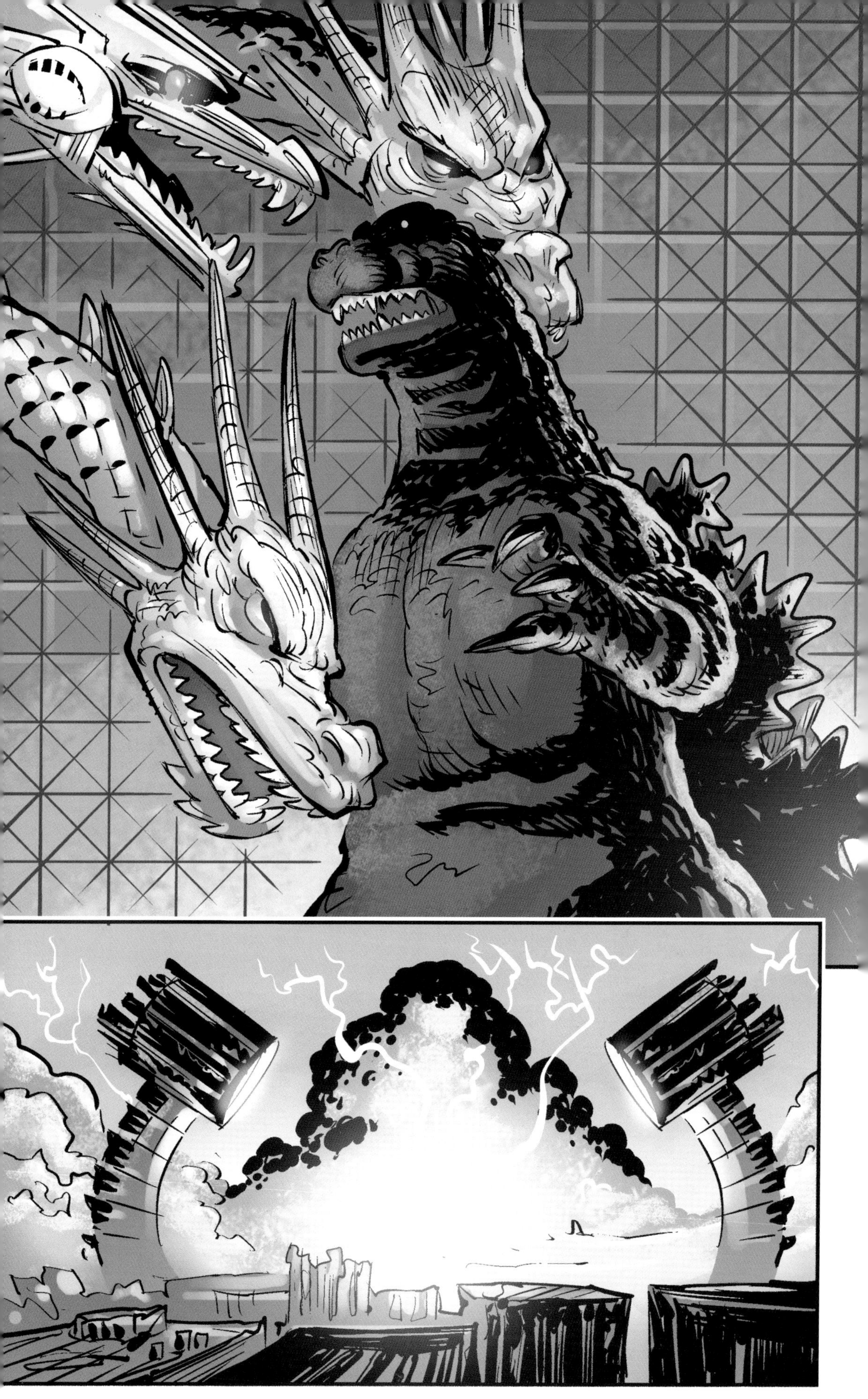

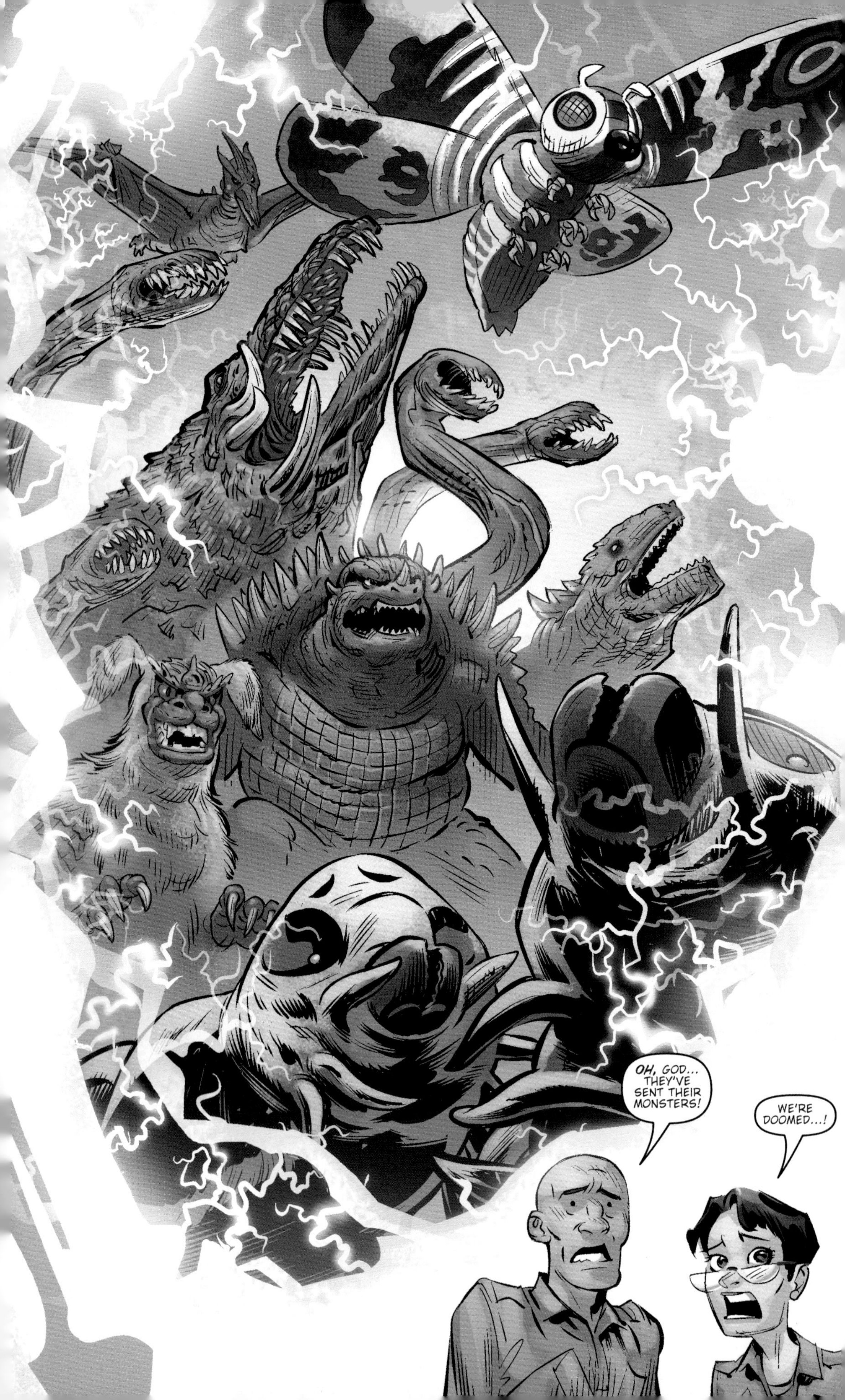
OH, GOD... THEY'VE SENT THEIR MONSTERS!
WE'RE DOOMED...!

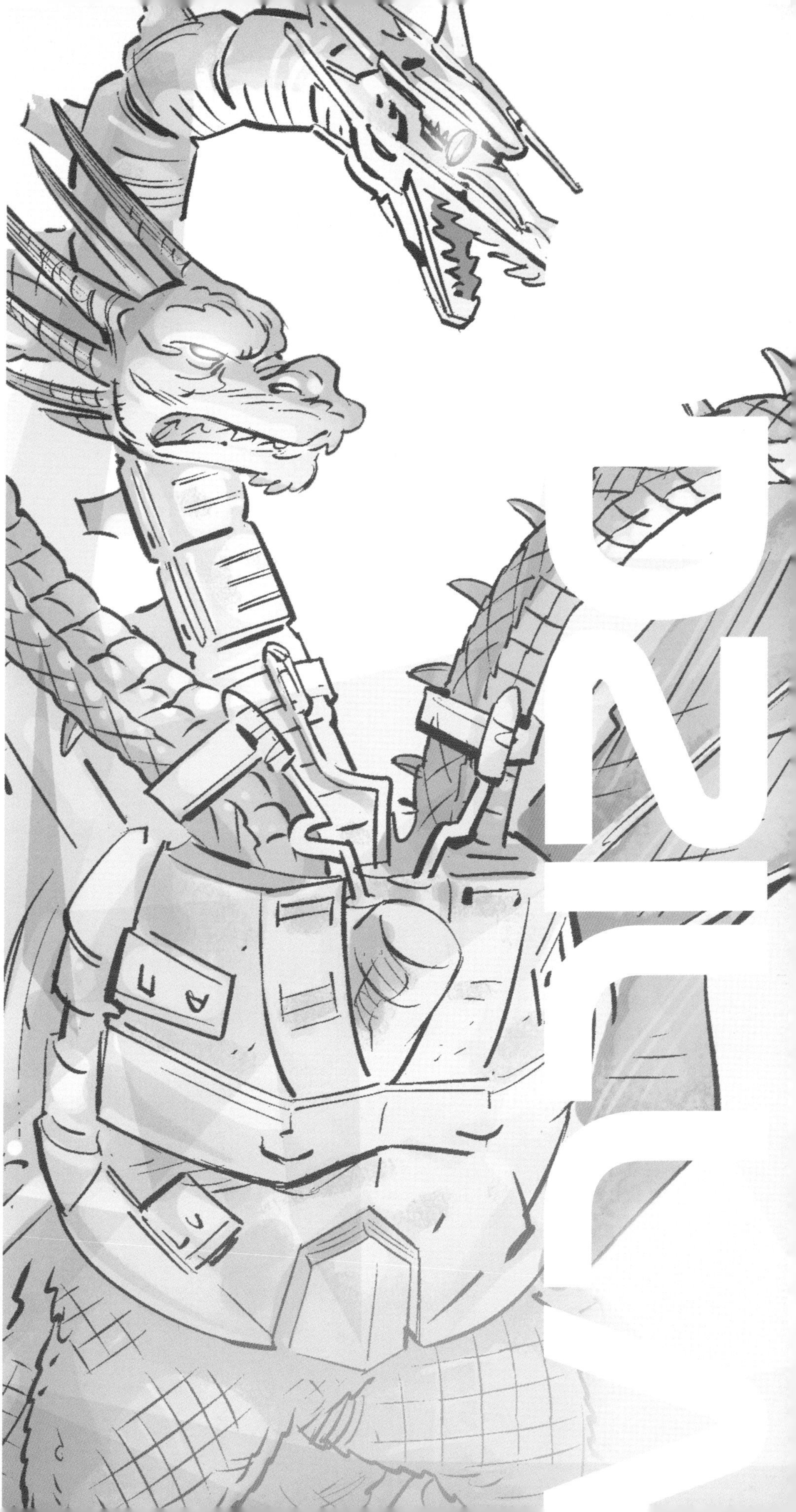

Art by **BRIAN CHURILLA**

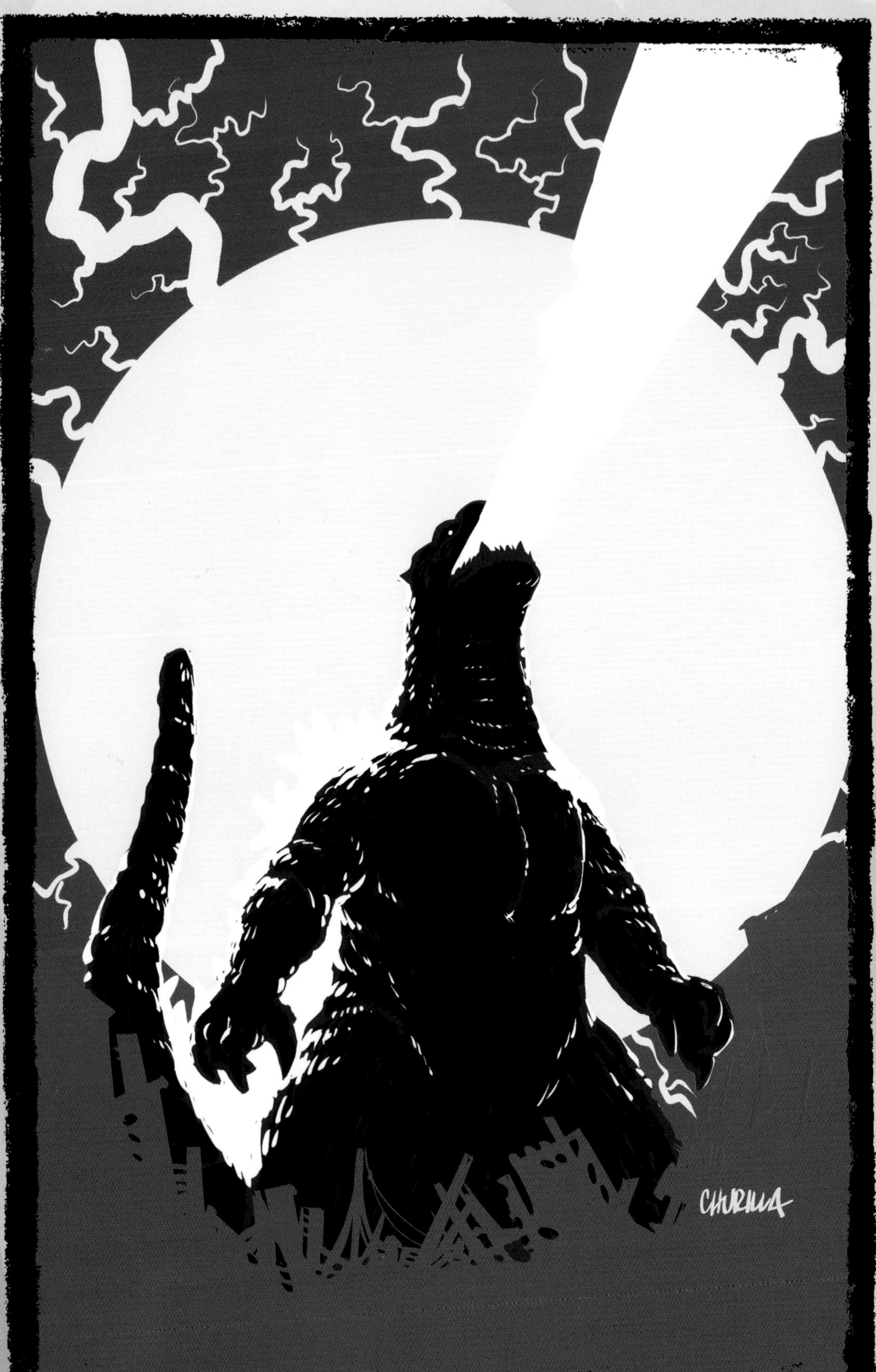
CHURILLA

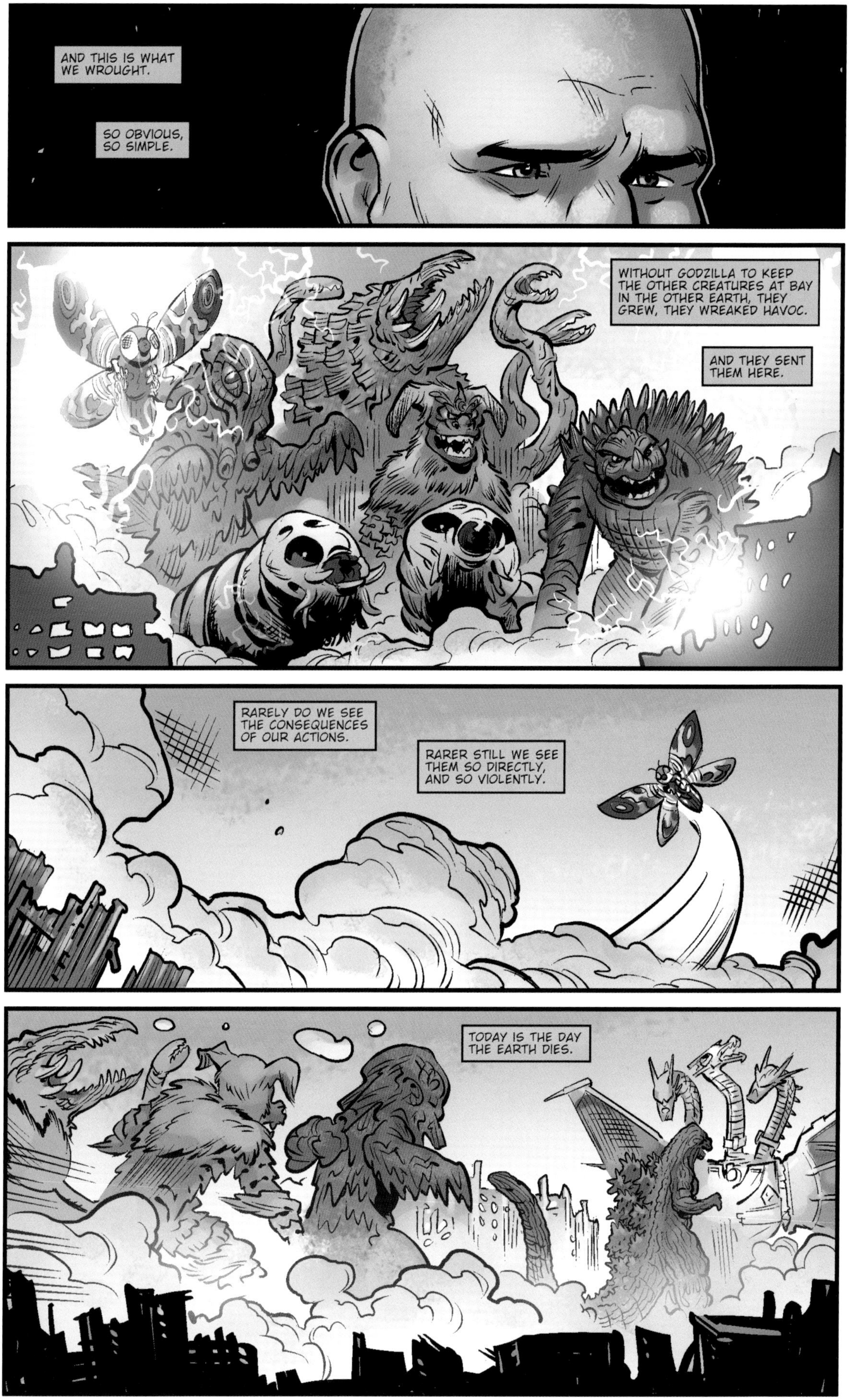
AND THIS IS WHAT WE WROUGHT.
SO OBVIOUS, SO SIMPLE.
WITHOUT GODZILLA TO KEEP THE OTHER CREATURES AT BAY IN THE OTHER EARTH, THEY GREW, THEY WREAKED HAVOC.
AND THEY SENT THEM HERE.
RARELY DO WE SEE THE CONSEQUENCES OF OUR ACTIONS.
RARER STILL WE SEE THEM SO DIRECTLY, AND SO VIOLENTLY.
TODAY IS THE DAY THE EARTH DIES.

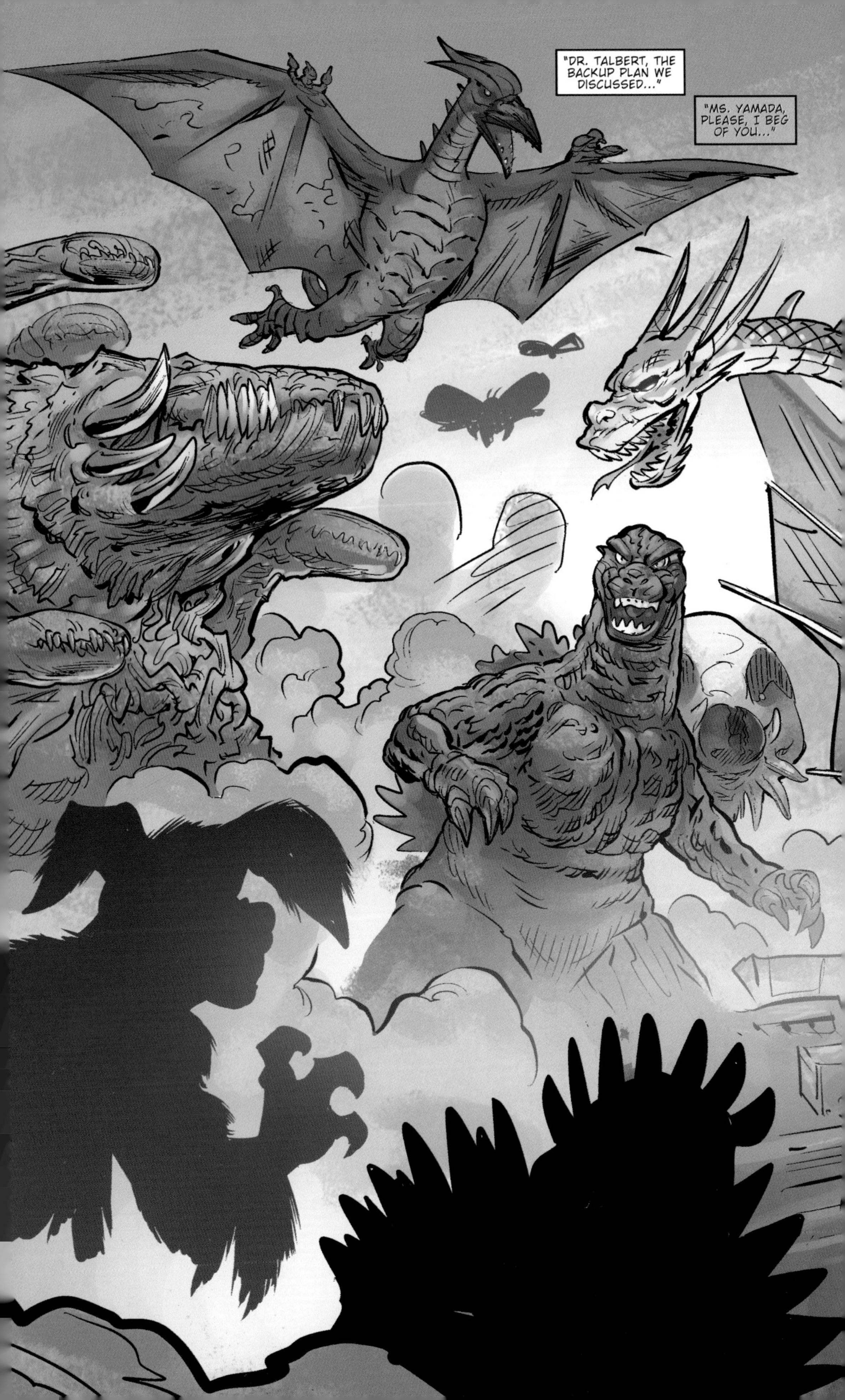
"DR. TALBERT, THE BACKUP PLAN WE DISCUSSED..."
"MS. YAMADA, PLEASE, I BEG OF YOU..."

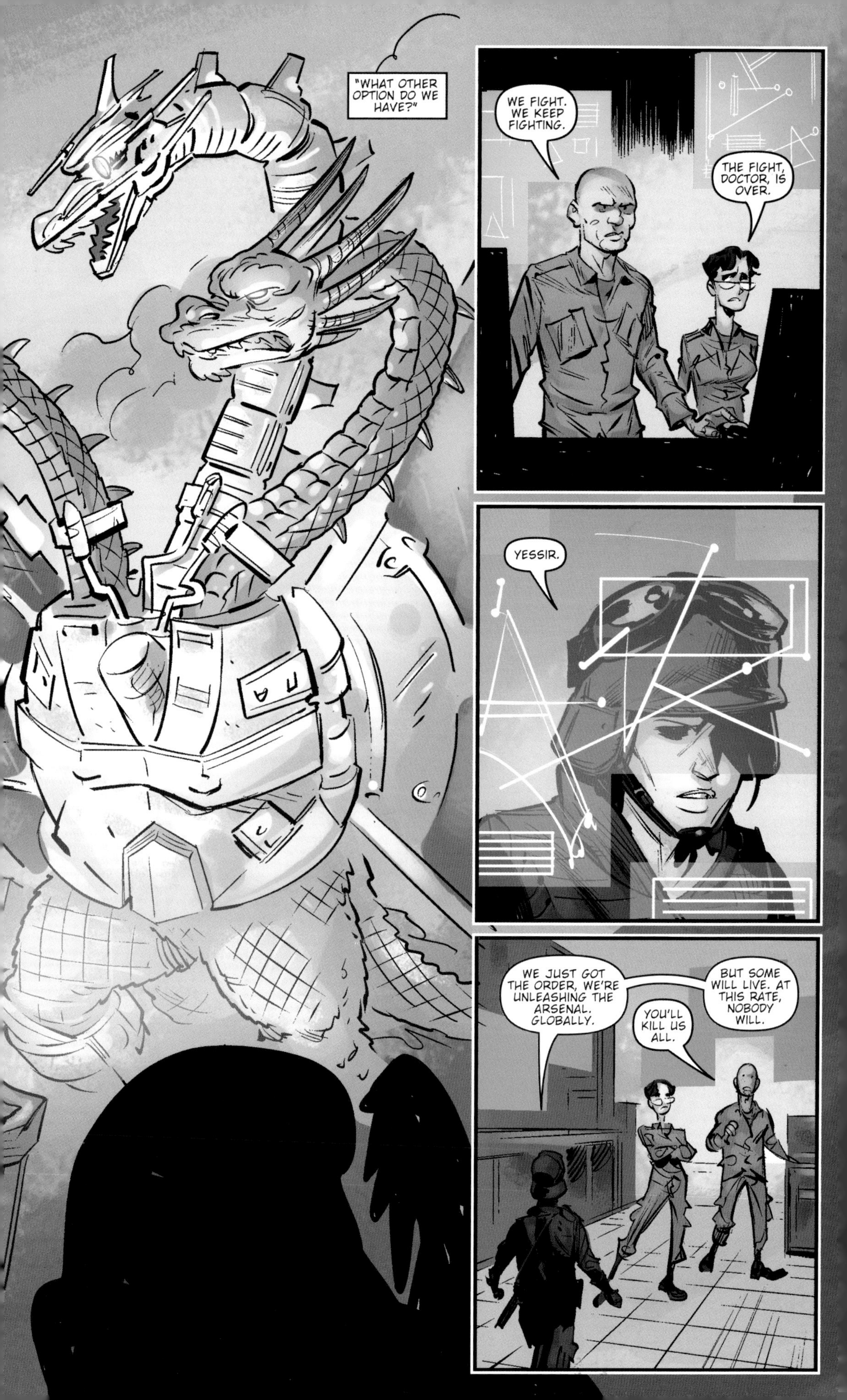
"WHAT OTHER OPTION DO WE HAVE?"
WE FIGHT. WE KEEP FIGHTING.
THE FIGHT, DOCTOR, IS OVER.
YESSIR.
WE JUST GOT THE ORDER, WE'RE UNLEASHING THE ARSENAL. GLOBALLY.
YOU'LL KILL US ALL.
BUT SOME WILL LIVE. AT THIS RATE, NOBODY WILL.

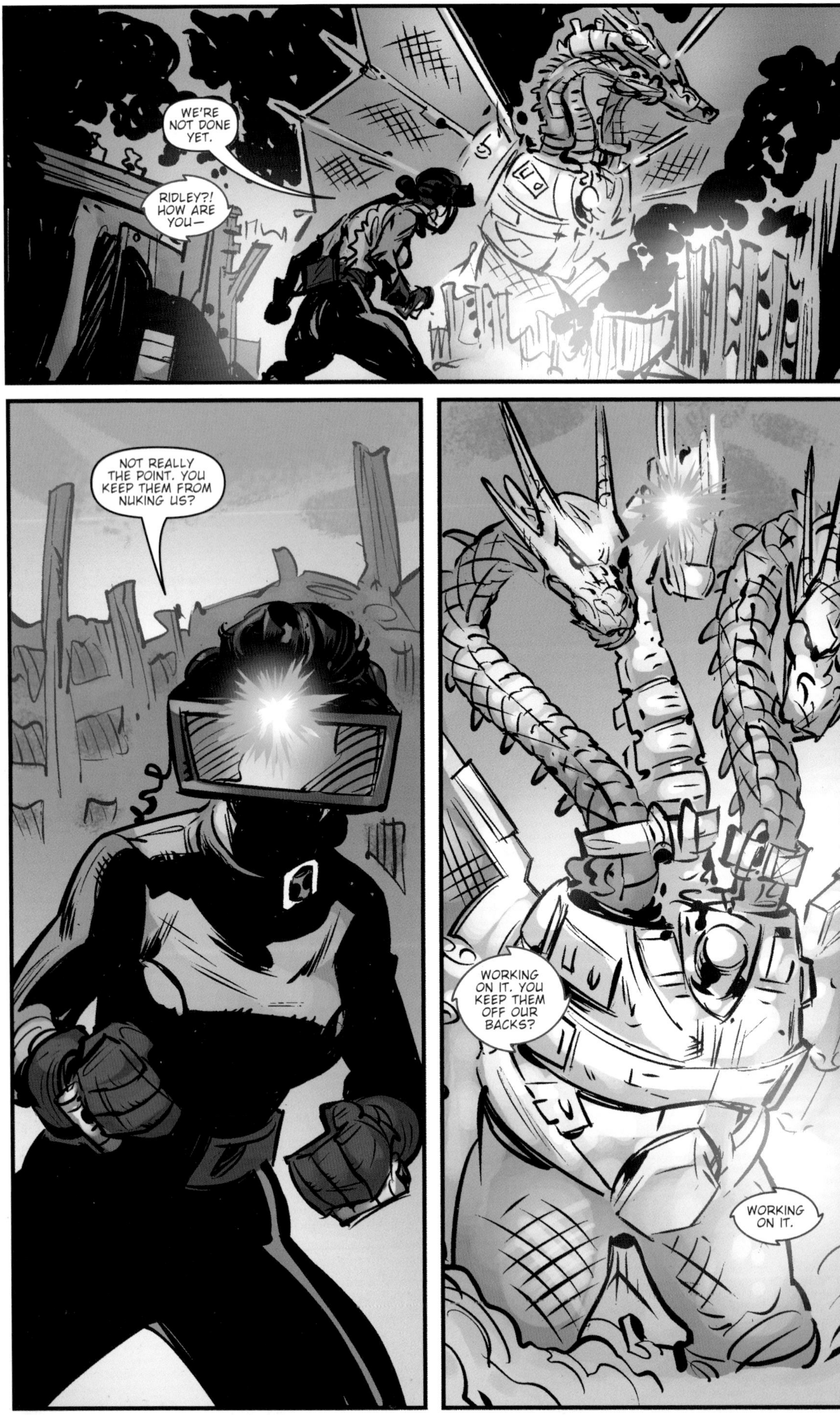
WE'RE NOT DONE YET.
RIDLEY?! HOW ARE YOU—
NOT REALLY THE POINT. YOU KEEP THEM FROM NUKING US?
WORKING ON IT. YOU KEEP THEM OFF OUR BACKS?
WORKING ON IT.

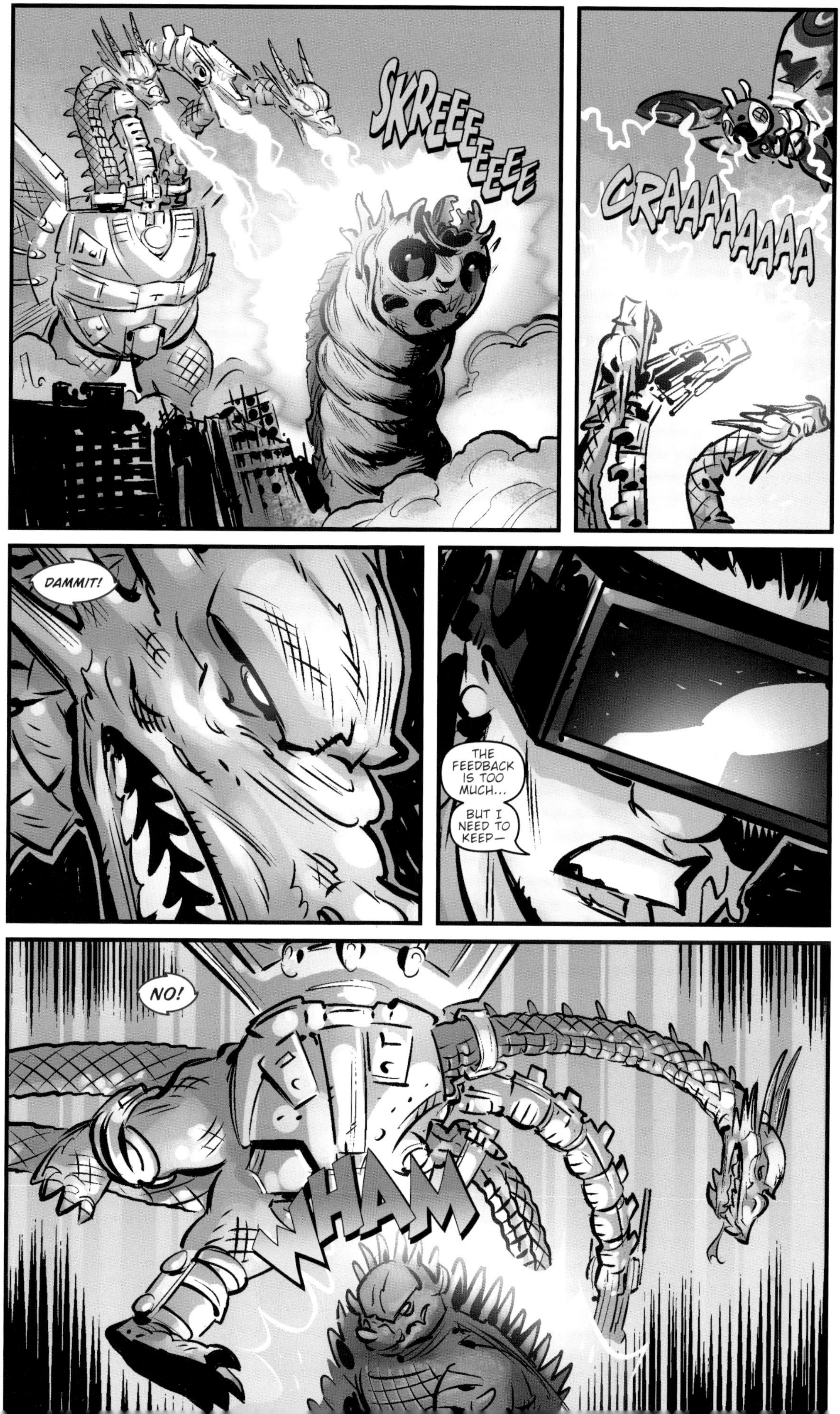
SKREEEEEEEE
CRAAAAAAAAA
DAMMIT!
THE FEEDBACK IS TOO MUCH...
BUT I NEED TO KEEP—
NO!
WHAM

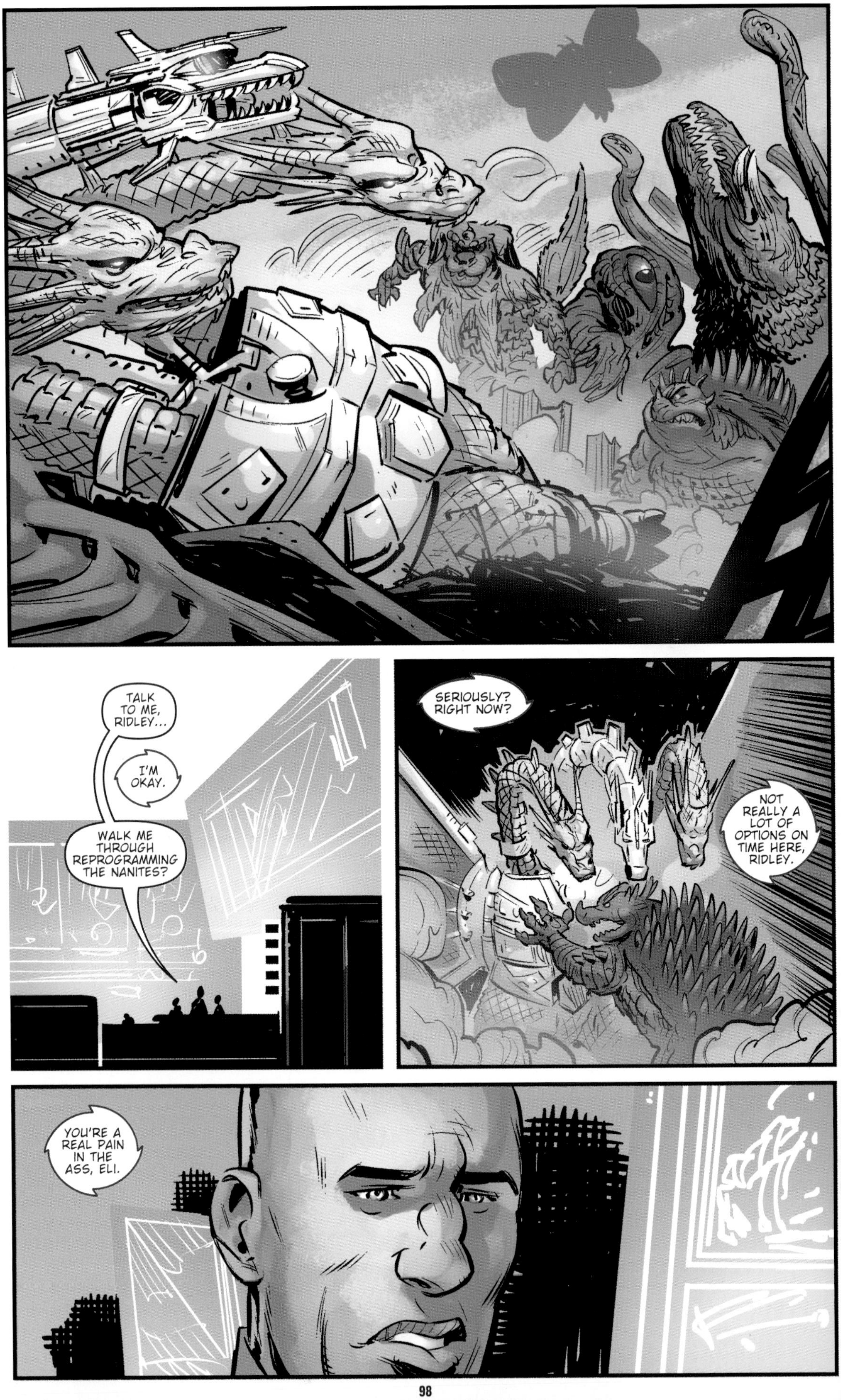
TALK TO ME, RIDLEY...
I'M OKAY.
WALK ME THROUGH REPROGRAMMING THE NANITES?
SERIOUSLY? RIGHT NOW?
NOT REALLY A LOT OF OPTIONS ON TIME HERE, RIDLEY.
YOU'RE A REAL PAIN IN THE ASS, ELI.

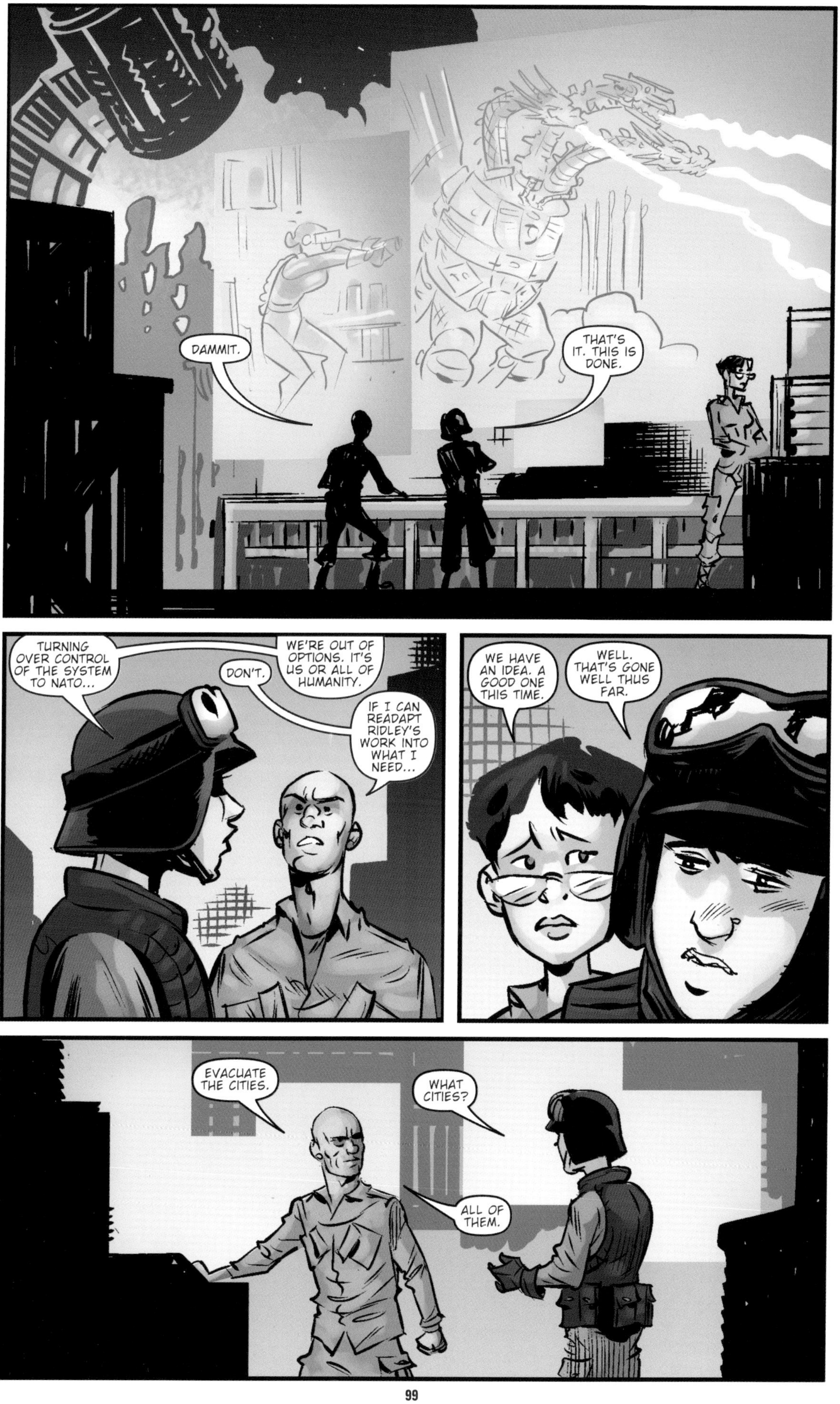
DAMMIT.
THAT'S IT. THIS IS DONE.
TURNING OVER CONTROL OF THE SYSTEM TO NATO...
DON'T.
WE'RE OUT OF OPTIONS. IT'S US OR ALL OF HUMANITY.
IF I CAN READAPT RIDLEY'S WORK INTO WHAT I NEED...
WE HAVE AN IDEA. A GOOD ONE THIS TIME.
WELL. THAT'S GONE WELL THUS FAR.
EVACUATE THE CITIES.
WHAT CITIES?
ALL OF THEM.

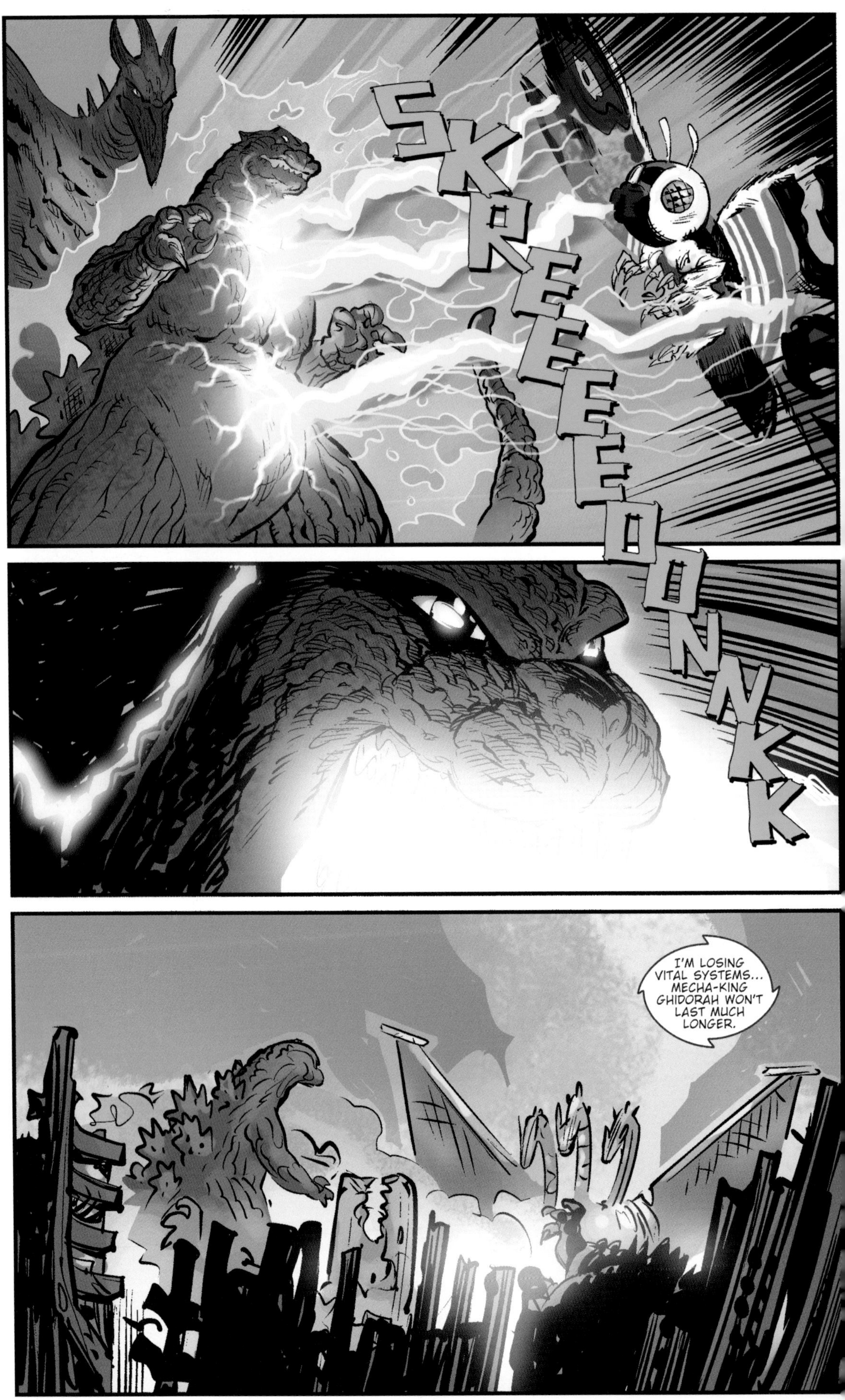
SKREEEEEOONNKK
I'M LOSING VITAL SYSTEMS... MECHA-KING GHIDORAH WON'T LAST MUCH LONGER.

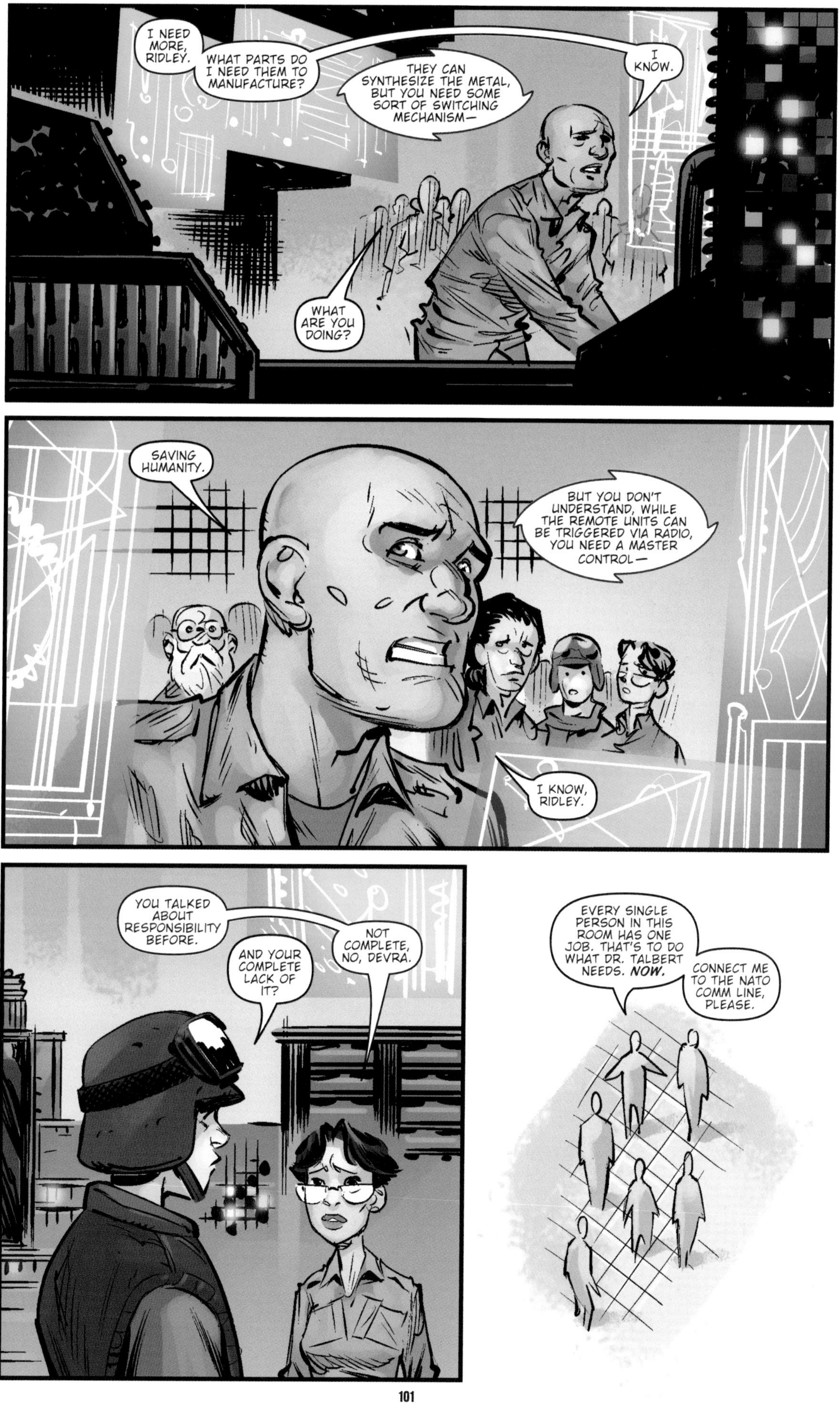
I NEED MORE, RIDLEY.
WHAT PARTS DO I NEED THEM TO MANUFACTURE?
THEY CAN SYNTHESIZE THE METAL, BUT YOU NEED SOME SORT OF SWITCHING MECHANISM—
I KNOW.
WHAT ARE YOU DOING?
SAVING HUMANITY.
BUT YOU DON'T UNDERSTAND, WHILE THE REMOTE UNITS CAN BE TRIGGERED VIA RADIO, YOU NEED A MASTER CONTROL—
I KNOW, RIDLEY.
YOU TALKED ABOUT RESPONSIBILITY BEFORE.
NOT COMPLETE, NO, DEVRA.
AND YOUR COMPLETE LACK OF IT?
EVERY SINGLE PERSON IN THIS ROOM HAS ONE JOB. THAT'S TO DO WHAT DR. TALBERT NEEDS. NOW.
CONNECT ME TO THE NATO COMM LINE, PLEASE.

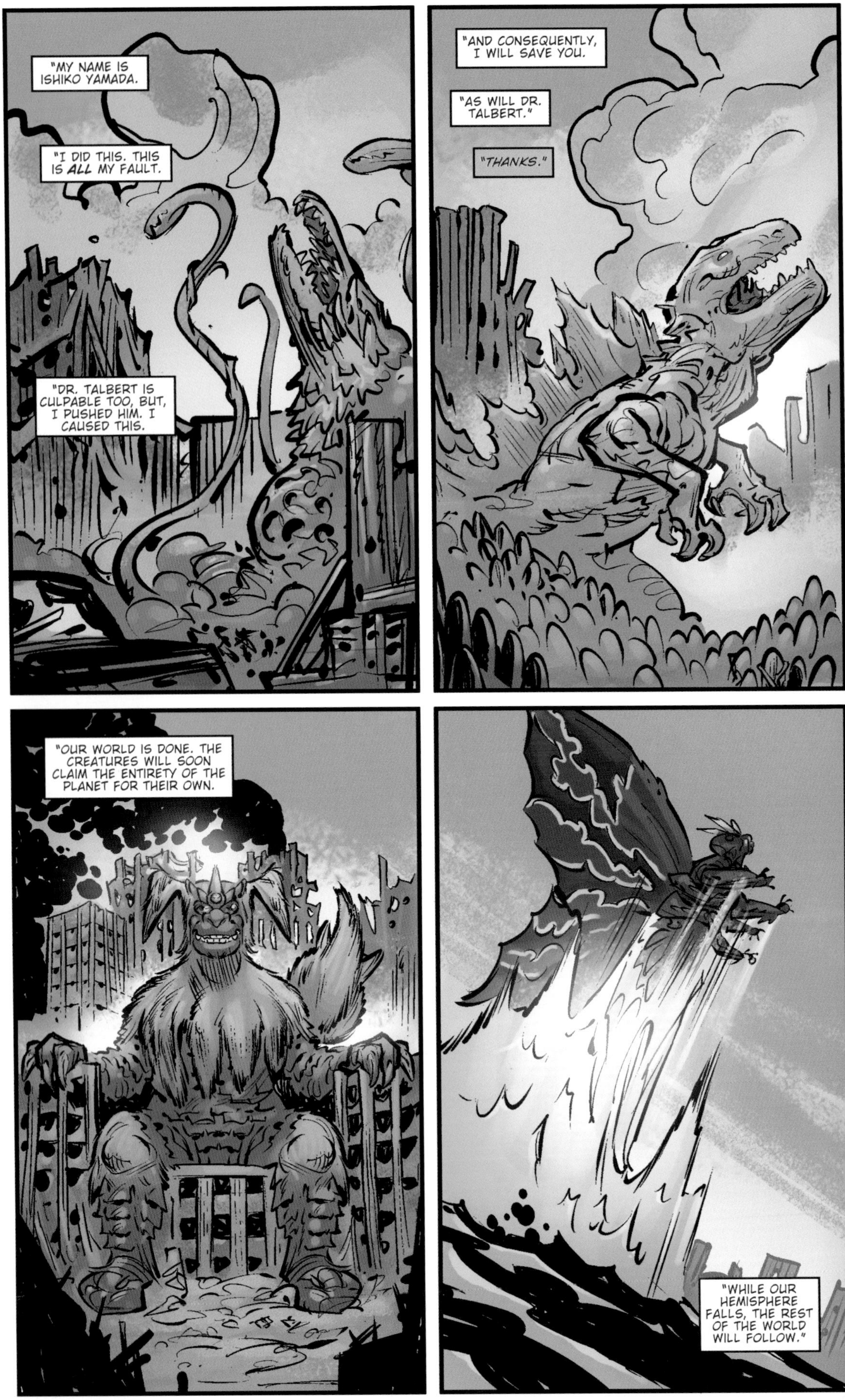
"MY NAME IS ISHIKO YAMADA.
"I DID THIS. THIS IS ALL MY FAULT.
"DR. TALBERT IS CULPABLE TOO, BUT, I PUSHED HIM. I CAUSED THIS.
"AND CONSEQUENTLY, I WILL SAVE YOU.
"AS WILL DR. TALBERT."
"THANKS."
"OUR WORLD IS DONE. THE CREATURES WILL SOON CLAIM THE ENTIRETY OF THE PLANET FOR THEIR OWN.
"WHILE OUR HEMISPHERE FALLS, THE REST OF THE WORLD WILL FOLLOW."

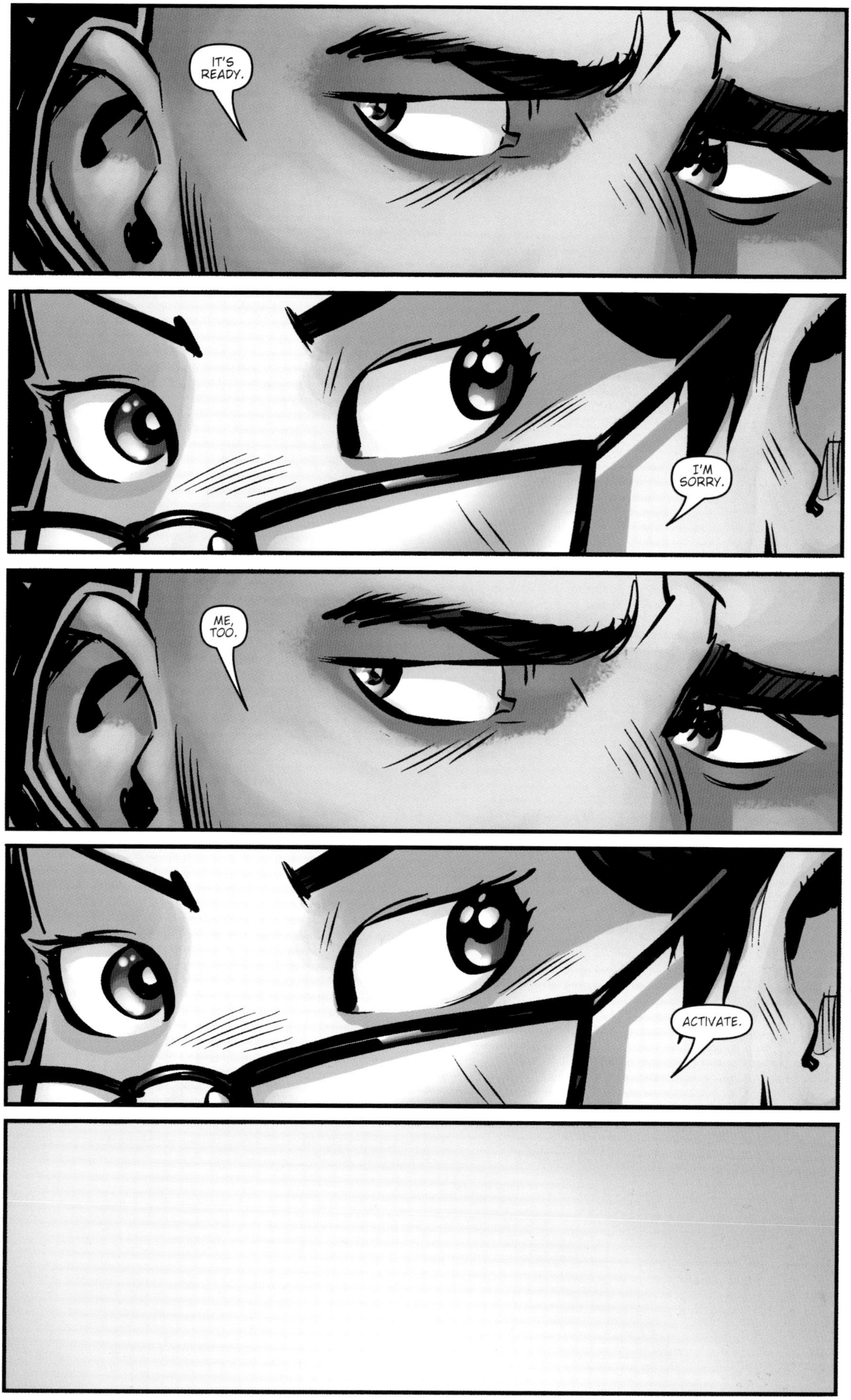
IT'S READY.
I'M SORRY.
ME, TOO.
ACTIVATE.

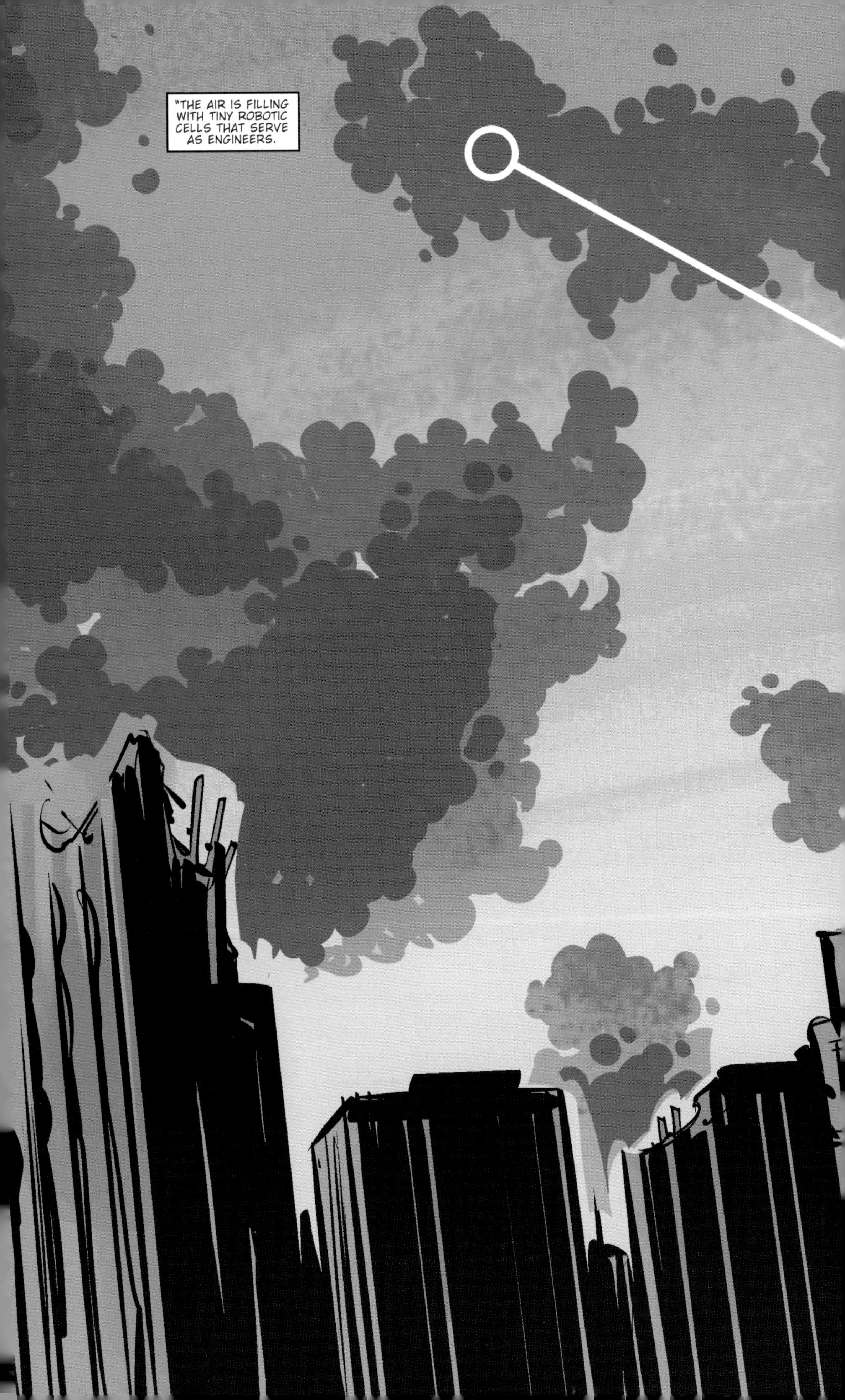
"THE AIR IS FILLING WITH TINY ROBOTIC CELLS THAT SERVE AS ENGINEERS.

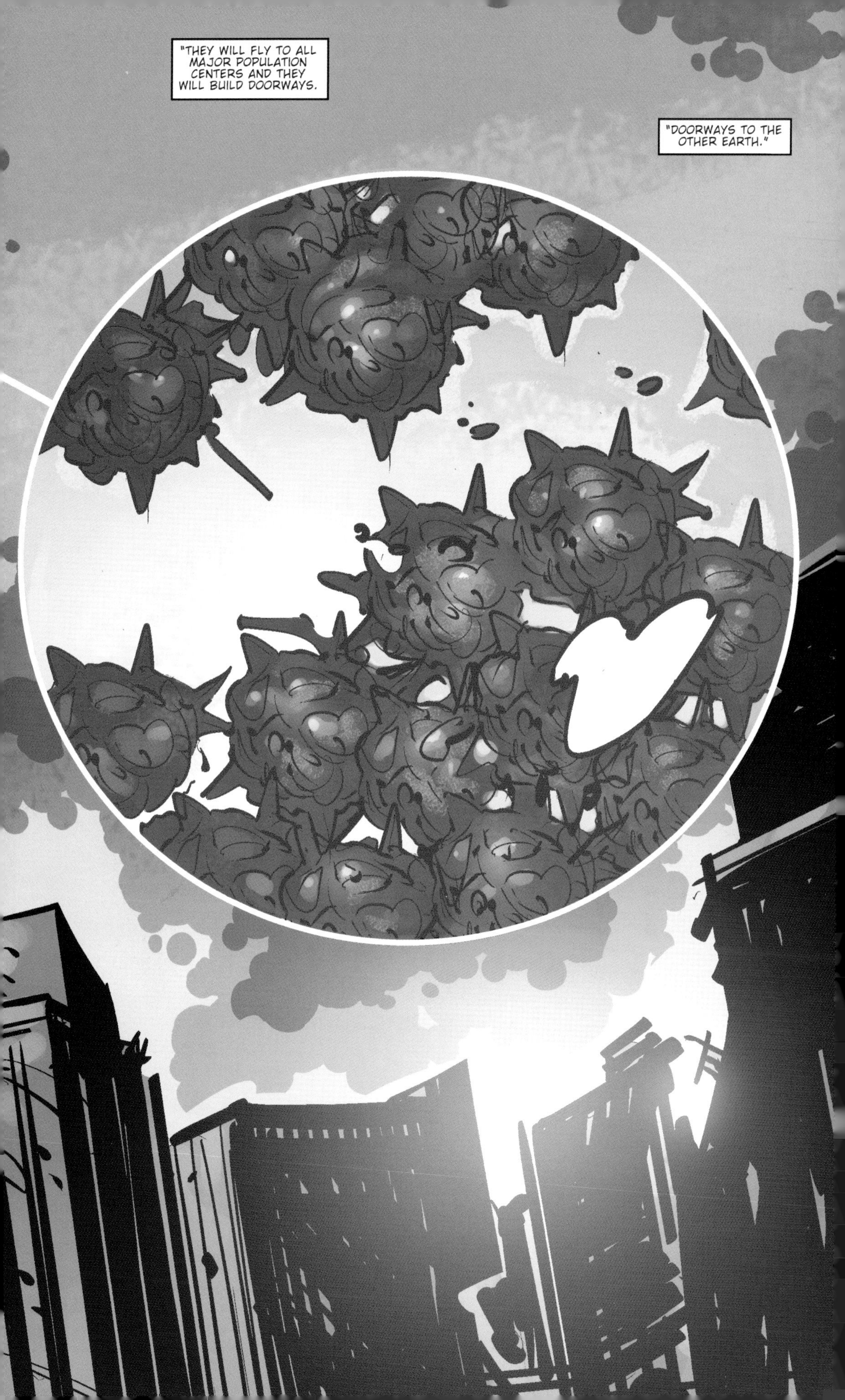
"THEY WILL FLY TO ALL MAJOR POPULATION CENTERS AND THEY WILL BUILD DOORWAYS.
"DOORWAYS TO THE OTHER EARTH."

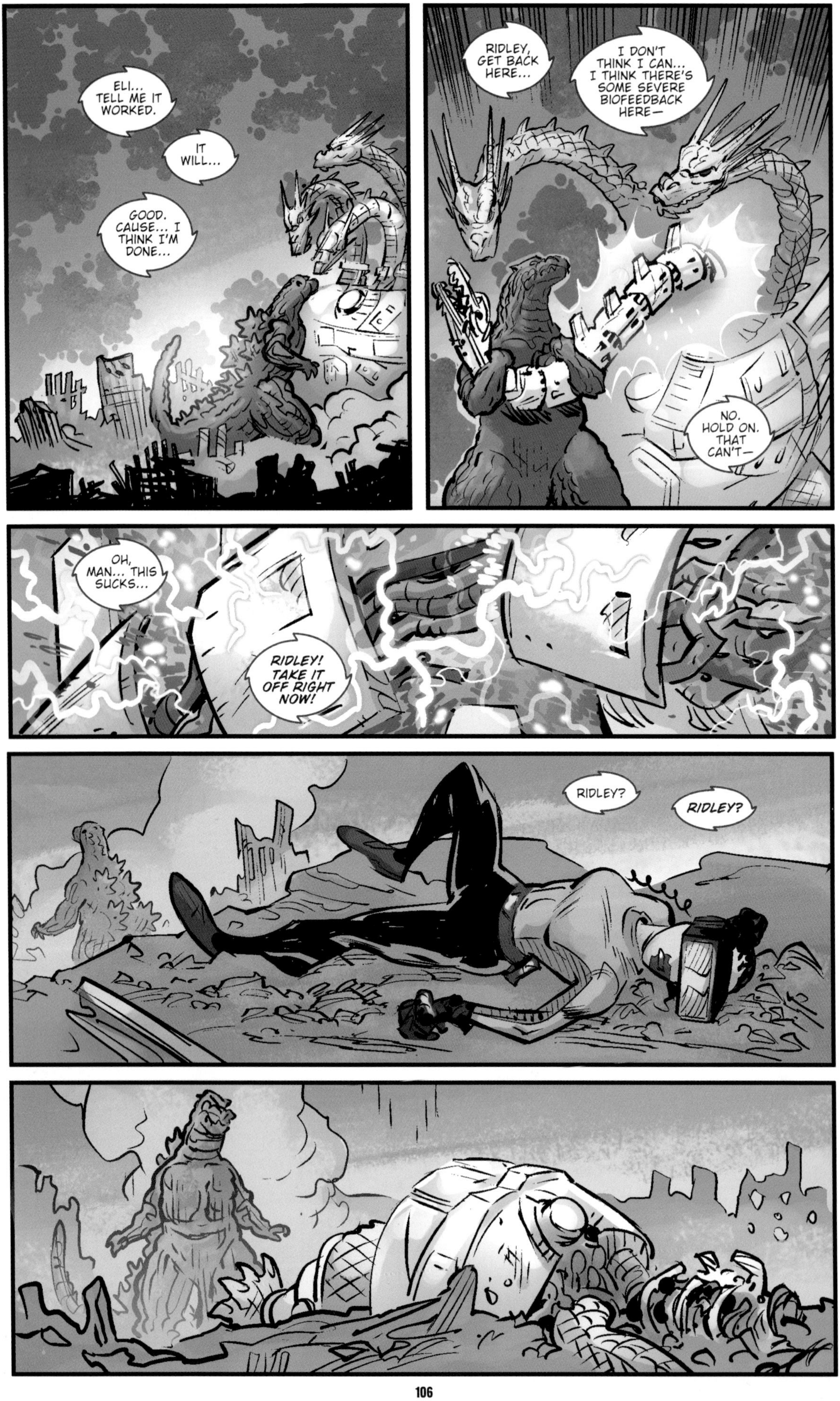
ELI... TELL ME IT WORKED.
IT WILL...
GOOD. CAUSE... I THINK I'M DONE...
RIDLEY, GET BACK HERE...
I DON'T THINK I CAN... I THINK THERE'S SOME SEVERE BIOFEEDBACK HERE—
NO. HOLD ON. THAT CAN'T—
OH, MAN... THIS SUCKS...
RIDLEY! TAKE IT OFF RIGHT NOW!
RIDLEY?
RIDLEY?

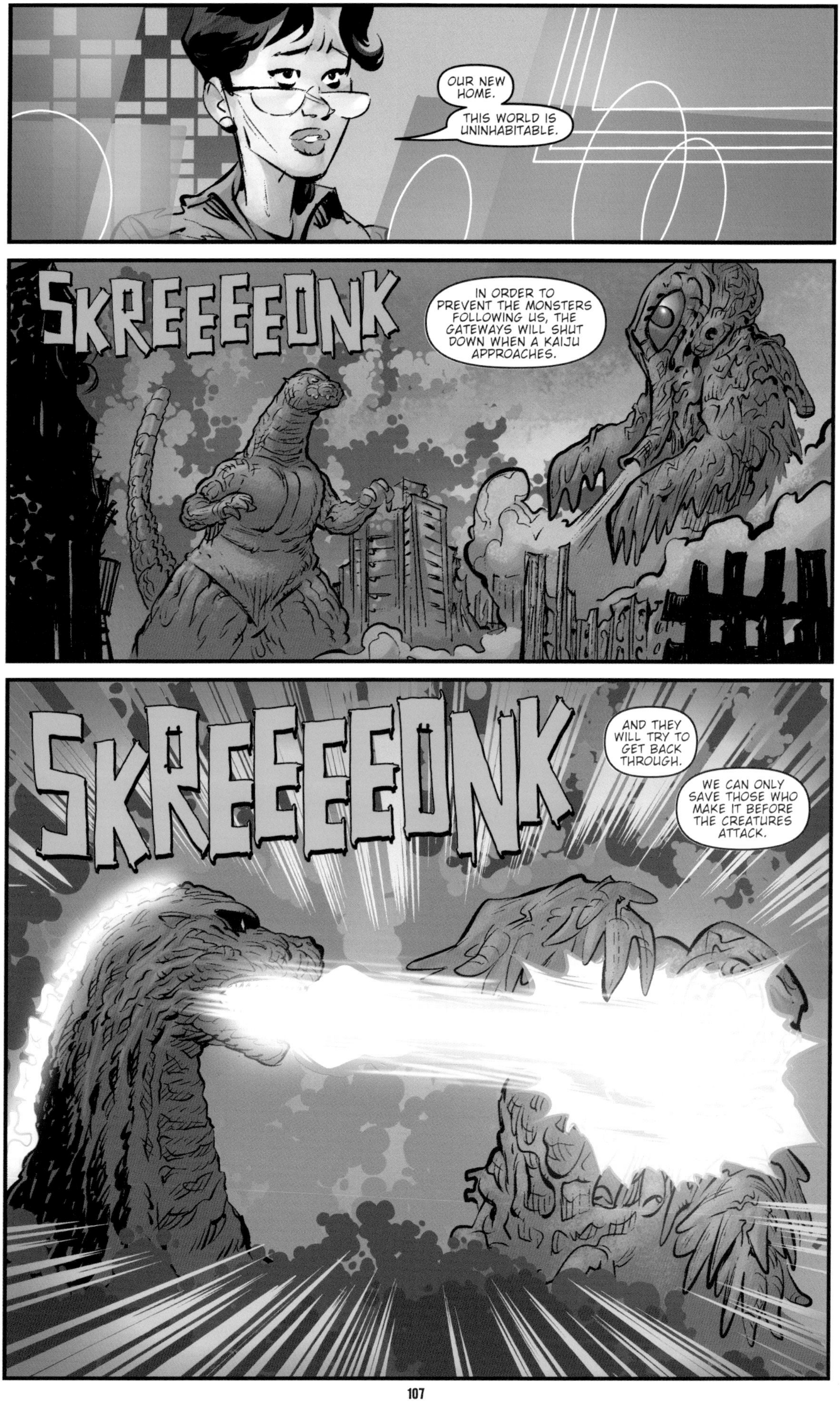
OUR NEW HOME.
THIS WORLD IS UNINHABITABLE.
SKREEEEONK
IN ORDER TO PREVENT THE MONSTERS FOLLOWING US, THE GATEWAYS WILL SHUT DOWN WHEN A KAIJU APPROACHES.
SKREEEEONK
AND THEY WILL TRY TO GET BACK THROUGH.
WE CAN ONLY SAVE THOSE WHO MAKE IT BEFORE THE CREATURES ATTACK.

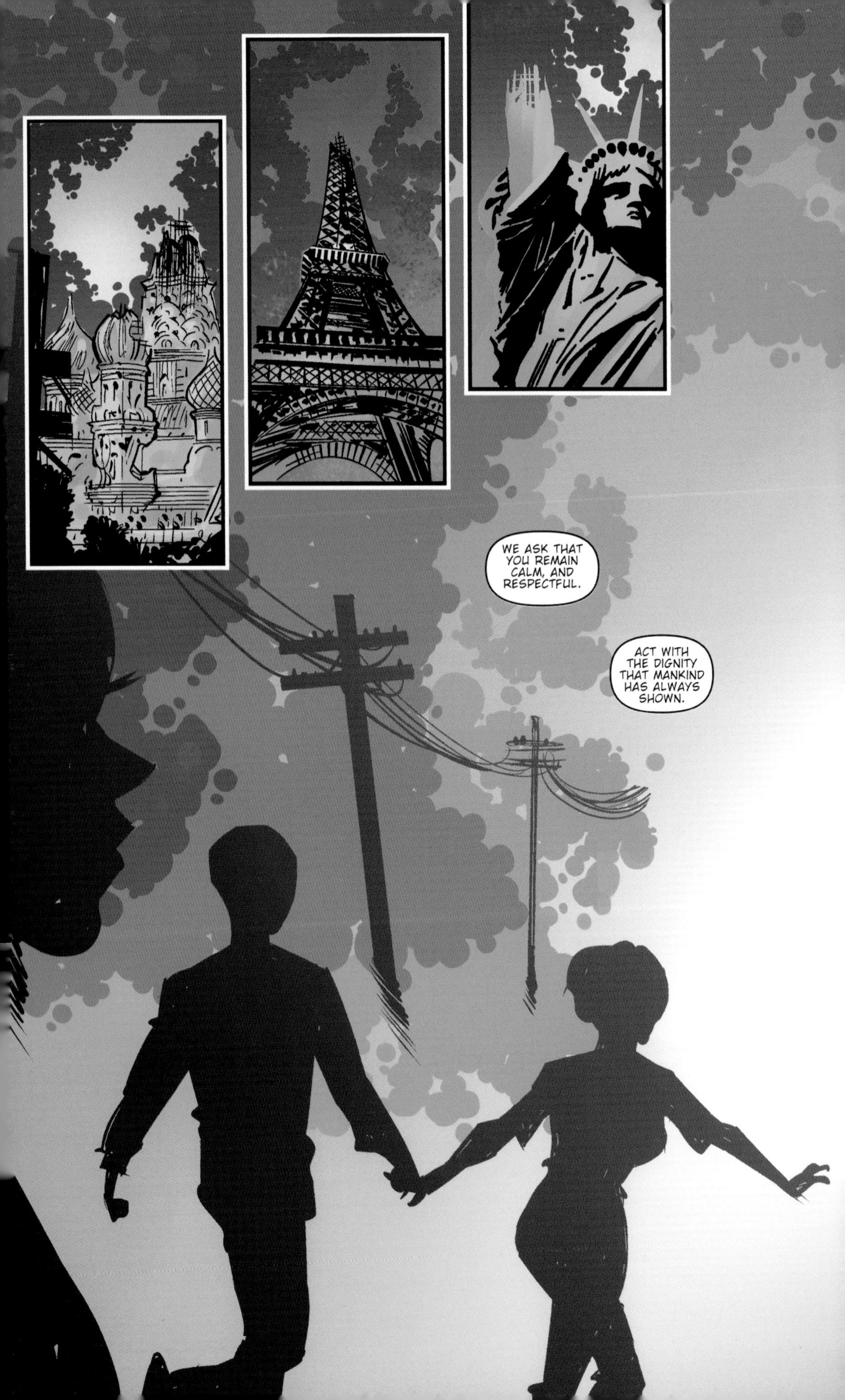
WE ASK THAT YOU REMAIN CALM, AND RESPECTFUL.
ACT WITH THE DIGNITY THAT MANKIND HAS ALWAYS SHOWN.

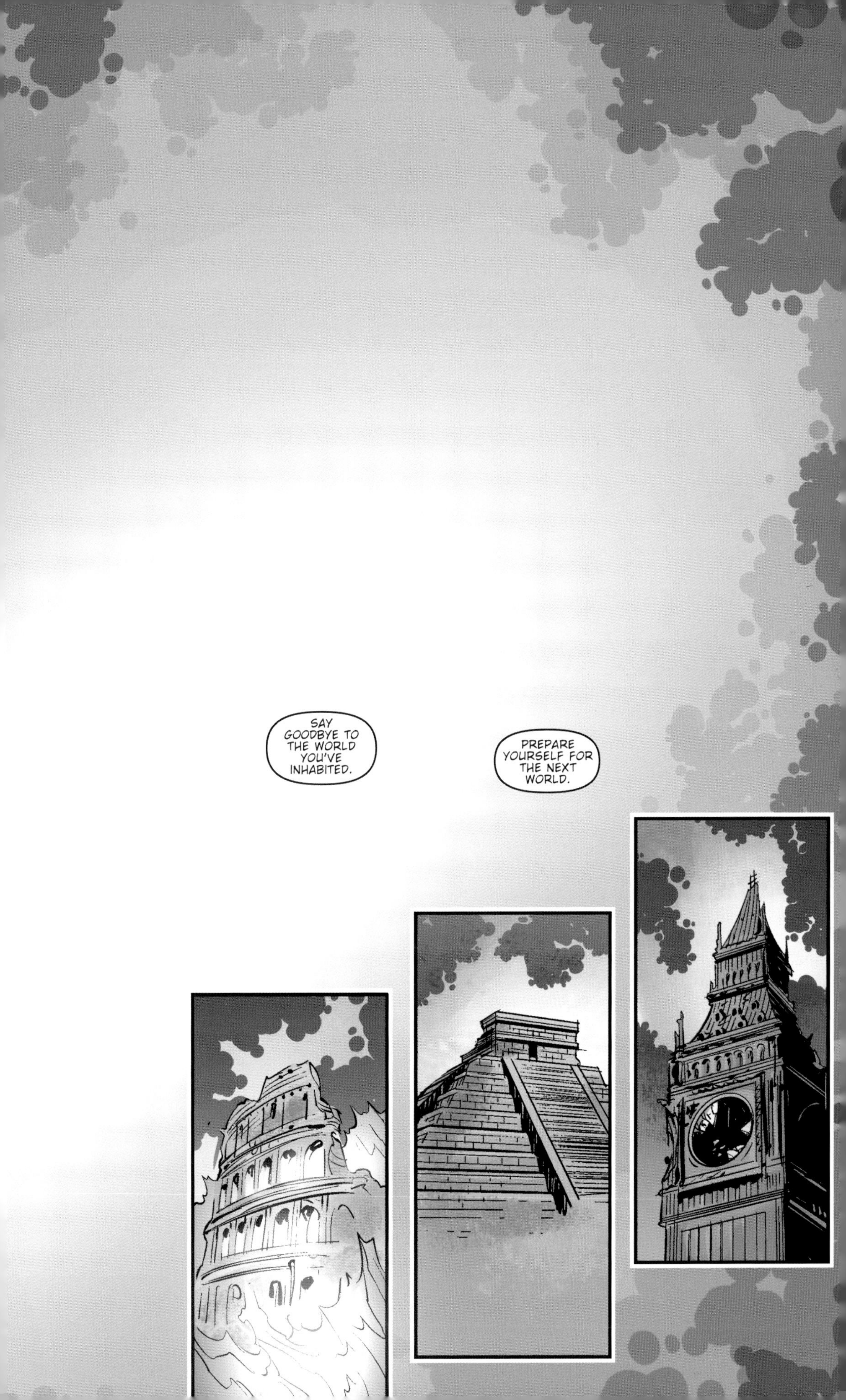
SAY GOODBYE TO THE WORLD YOU'VE INHABITED.
PREPARE YOURSELF FOR THE NEXT WORLD.

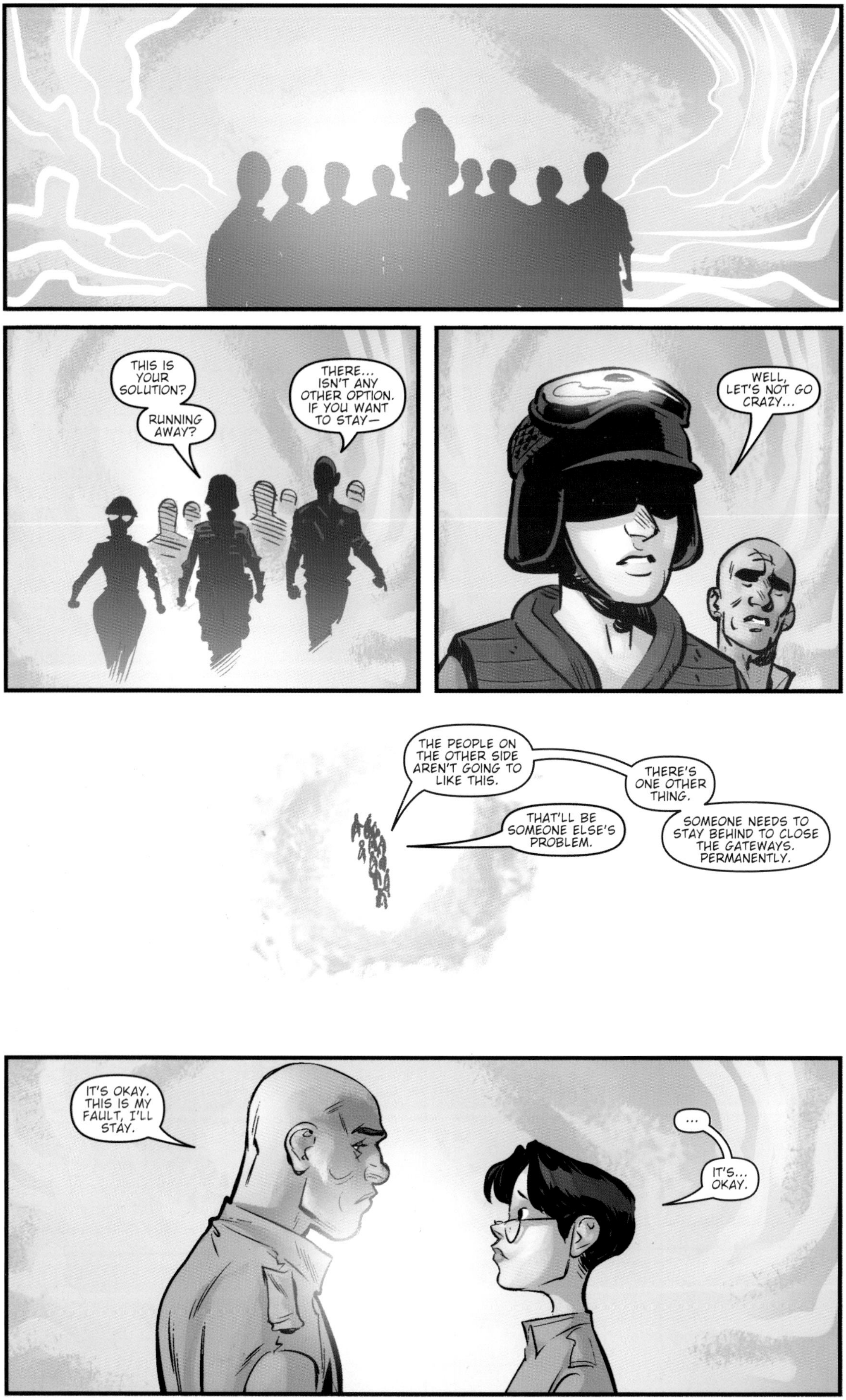
THIS IS YOUR SOLUTION?
RUNNING AWAY?
THERE... ISN'T ANY OTHER OPTION. IF YOU WANT TO STAY—
WELL, LET'S NOT GO CRAZY...
THE PEOPLE ON THE OTHER SIDE AREN'T GOING TO LIKE THIS.
THERE'S ONE OTHER THING.
THAT'LL BE SOMEONE ELSE'S PROBLEM.
SOMEONE NEEDS TO STAY BEHIND TO CLOSE THE GATEWAYS. PERMANENTLY.
IT'S OKAY. THIS IS MY FAULT, I'LL STAY.
...
IT'S... OKAY.

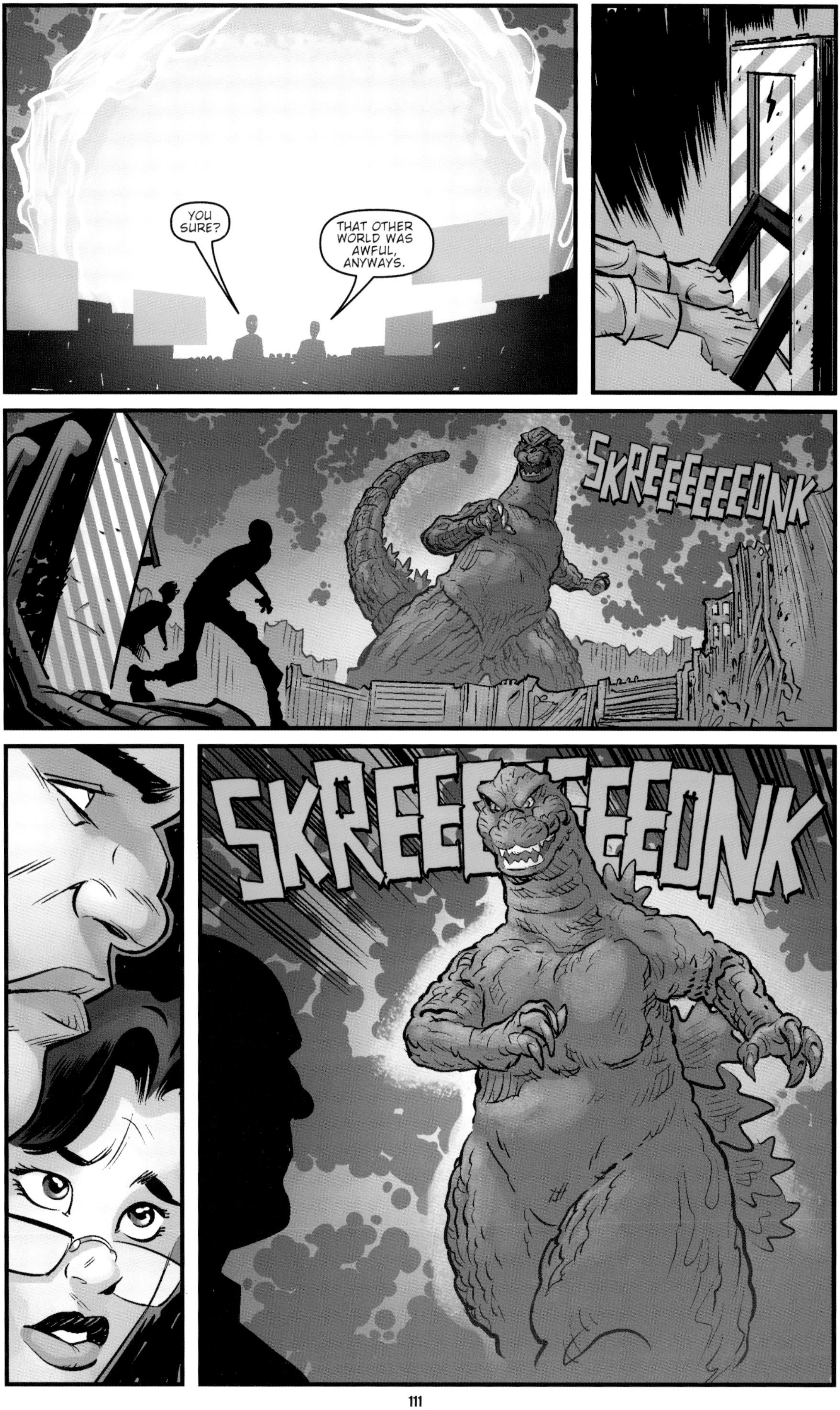
YOU SURE?
THAT OTHER WORLD WAS AWFUL, ANYWAYS.
SKREEEEEEONK

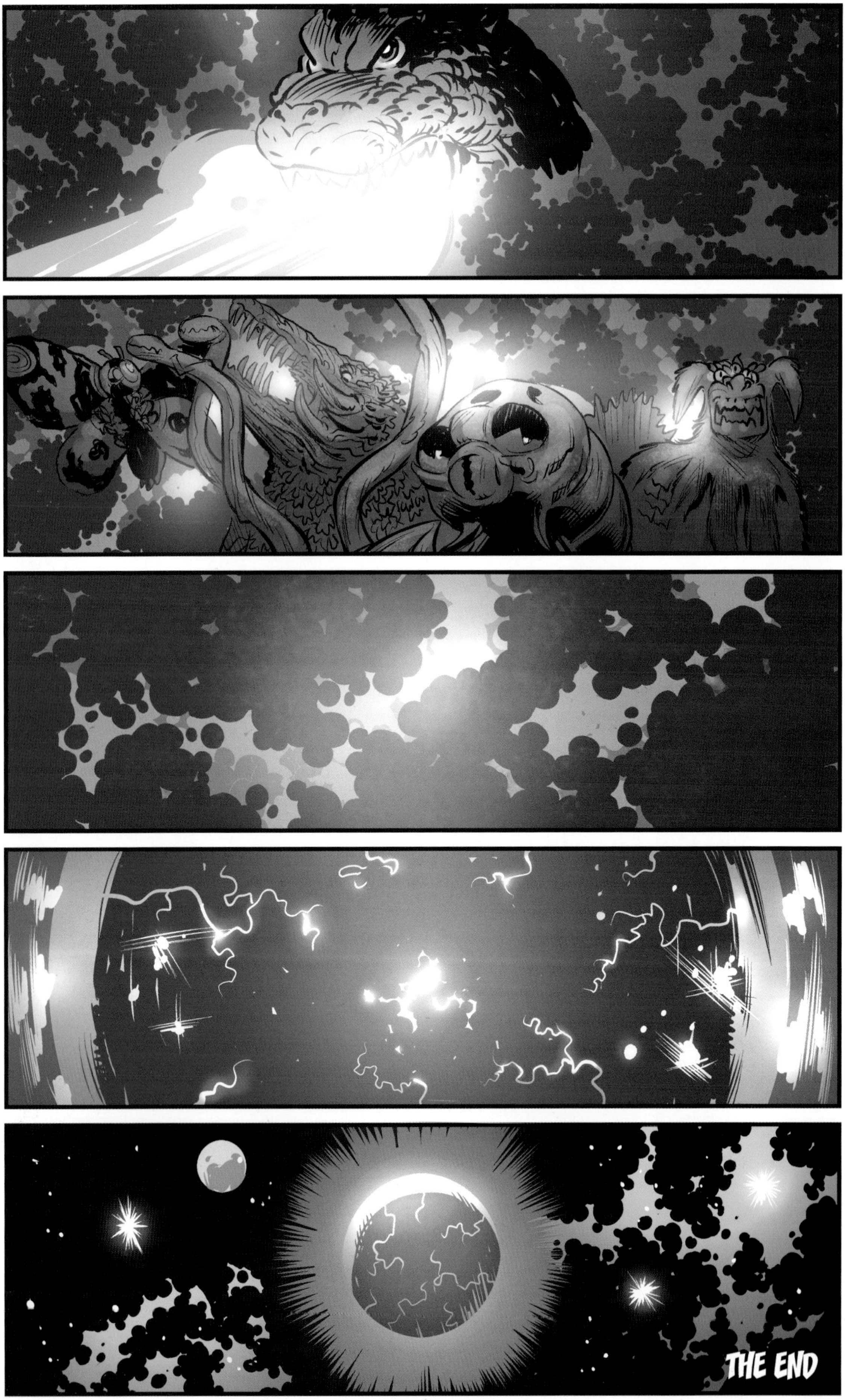
THE END

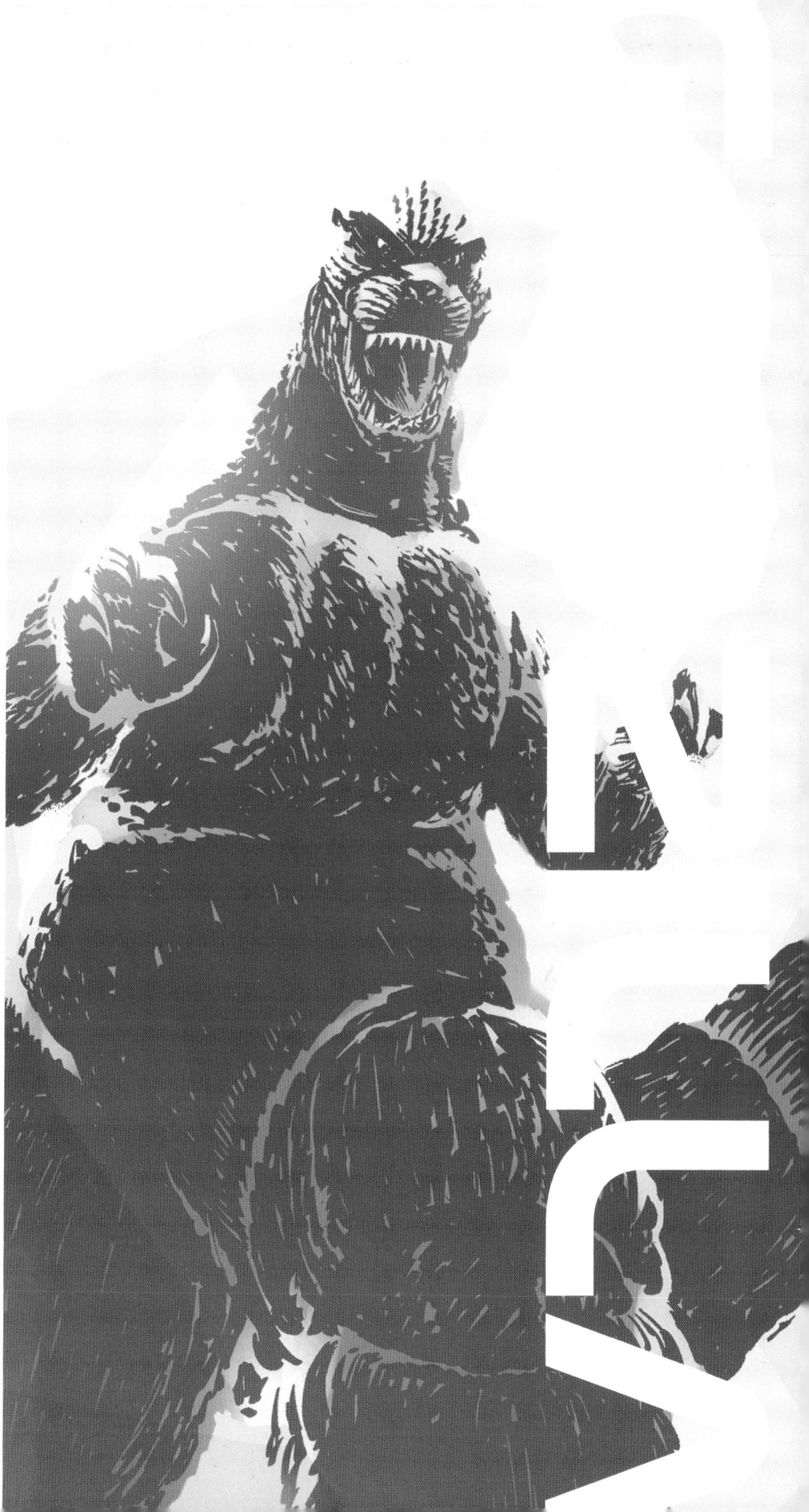

Art by **JAMES STOKOE**

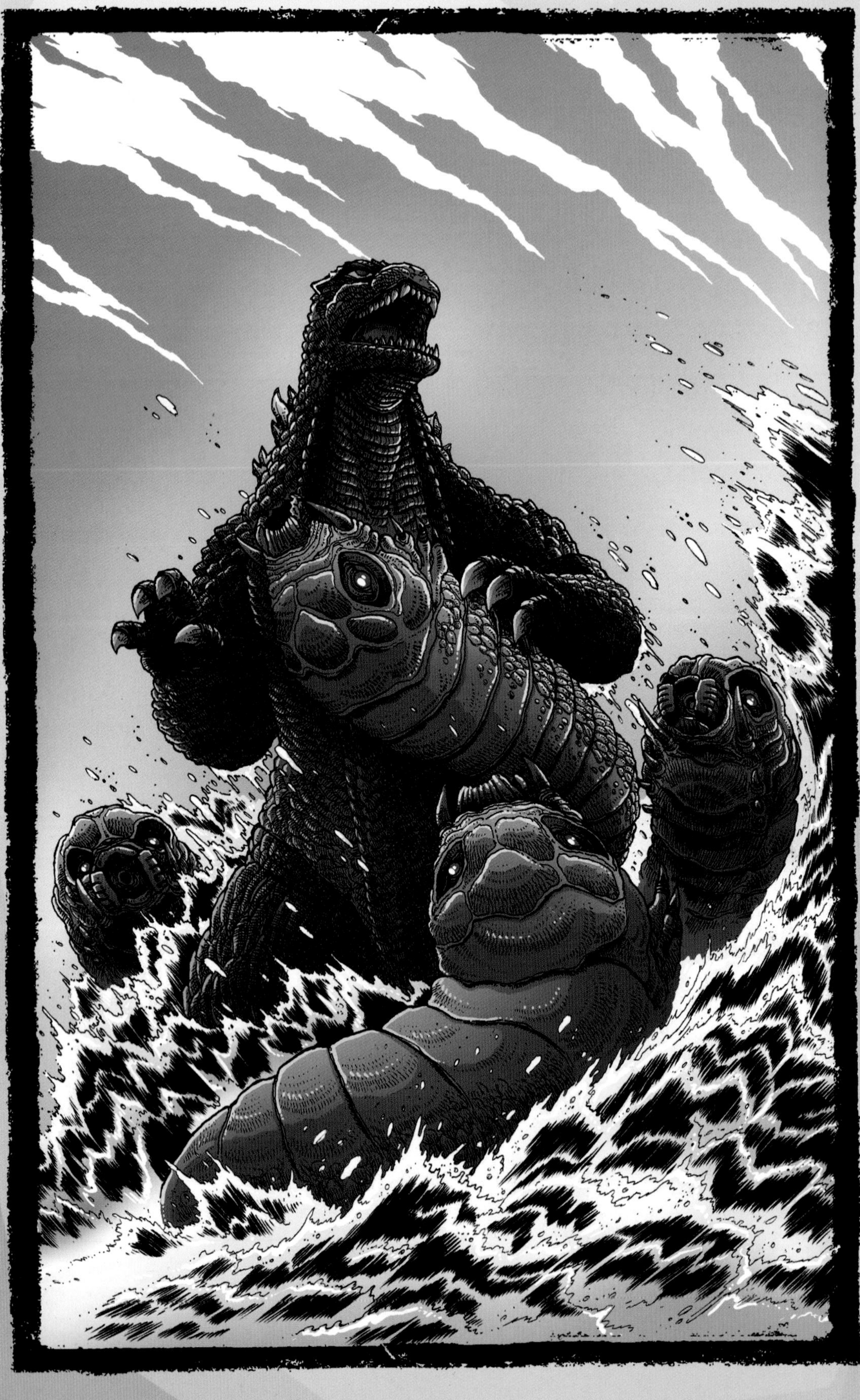

Art by JAMES STOKOE

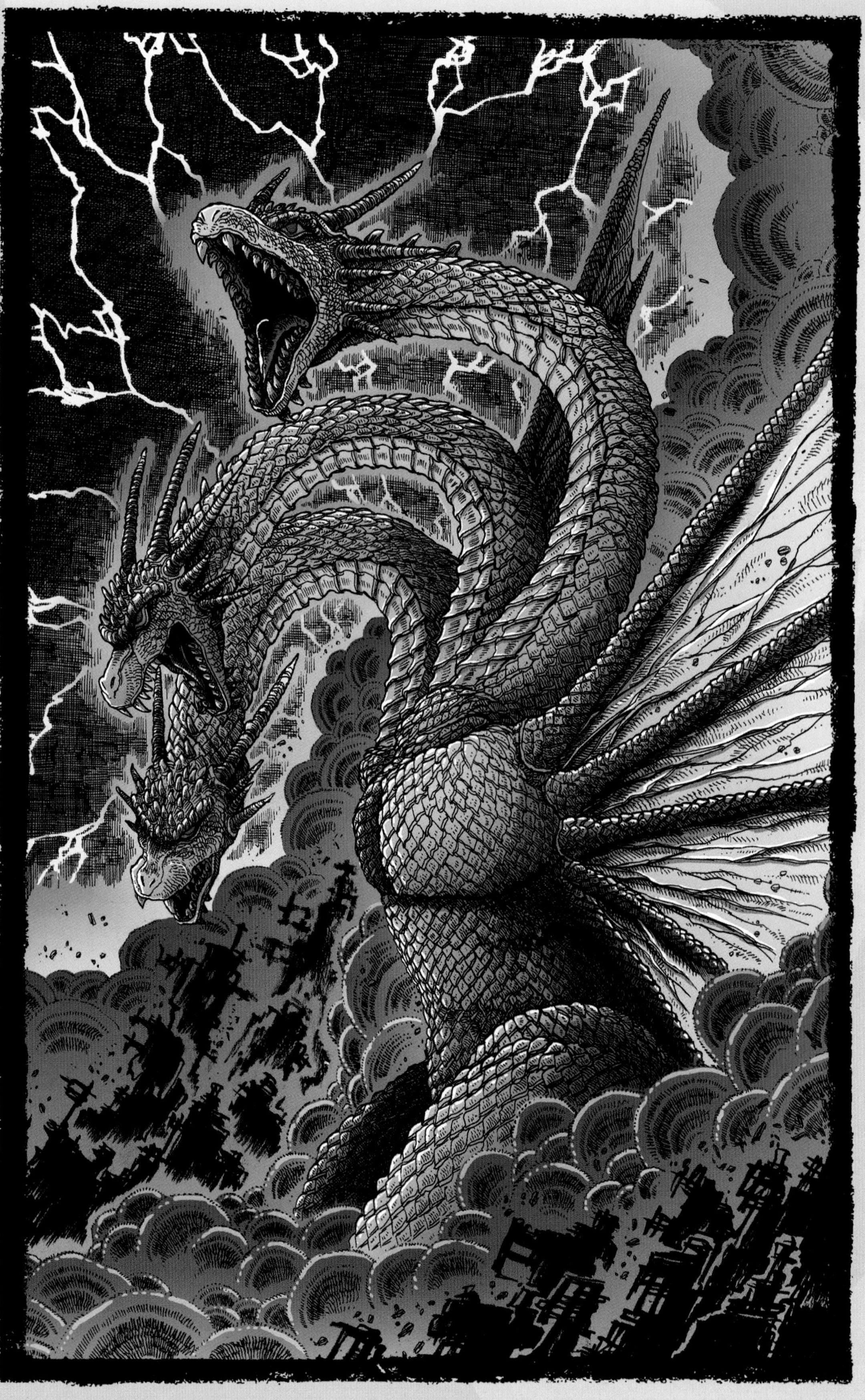

Art by JAMES STOKOE

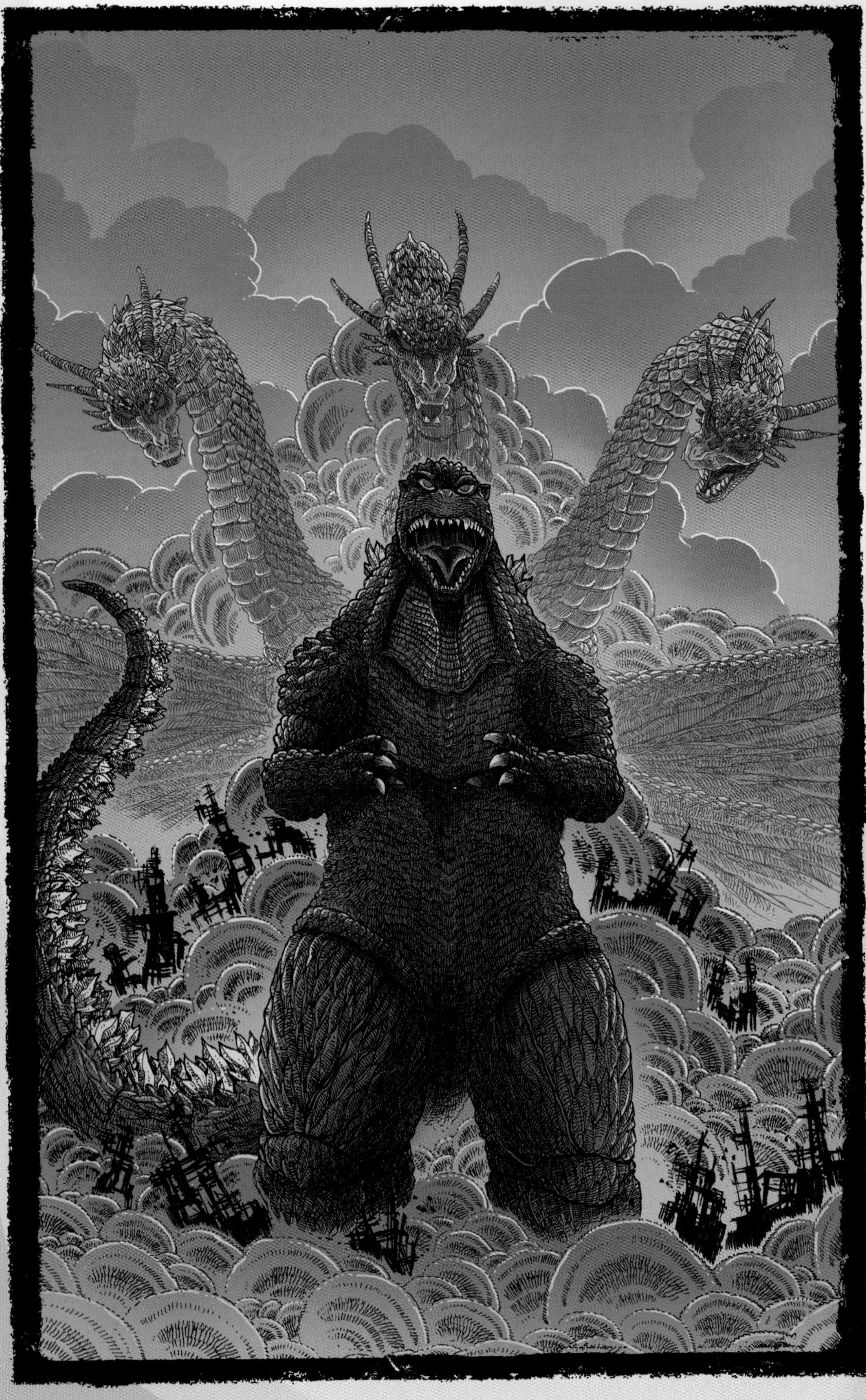

Art by **JAMES STOKOE**

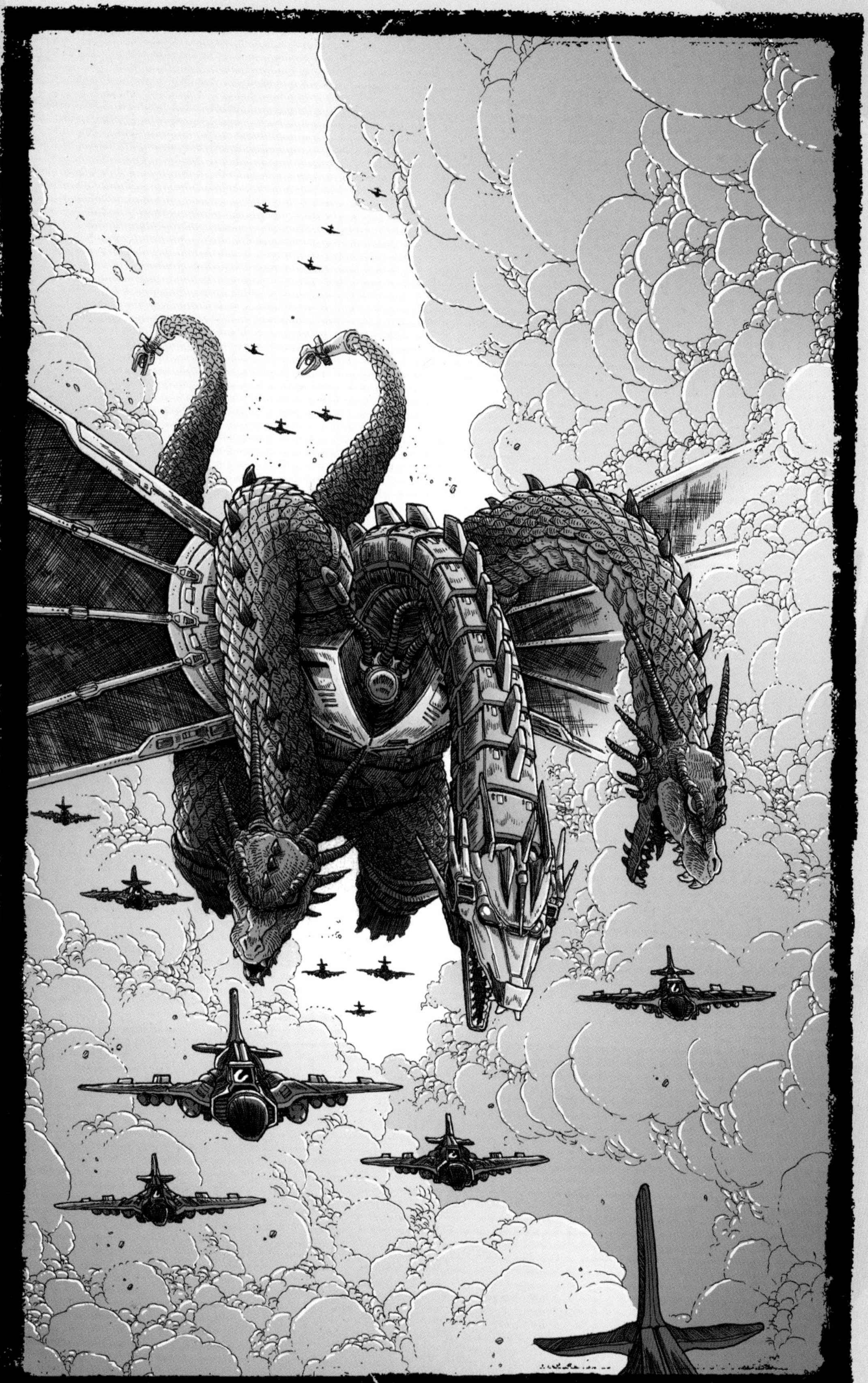

Art by **JAMES STOKOE**

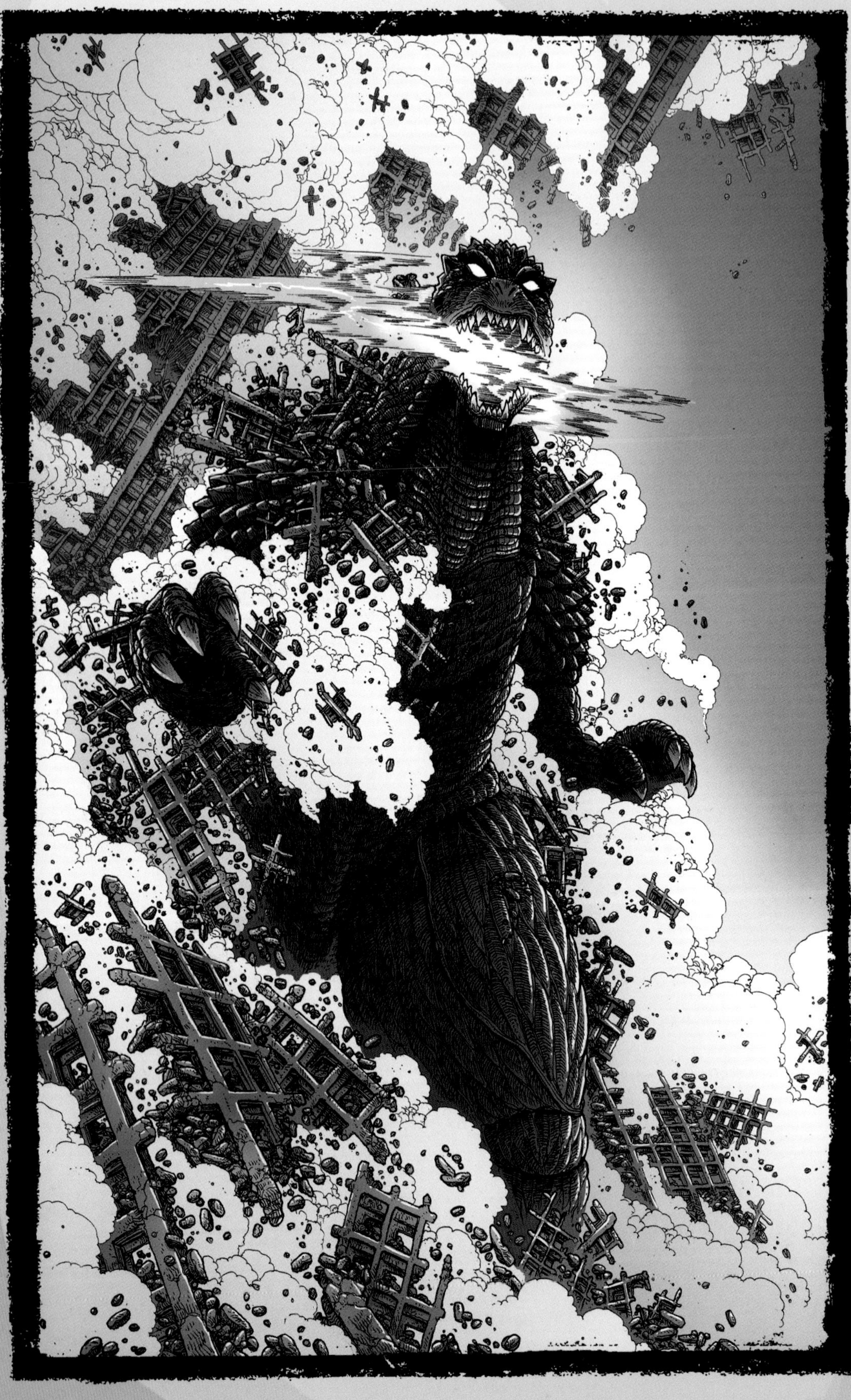

Art by AGUSTIN GRAHAM NAKAMURA

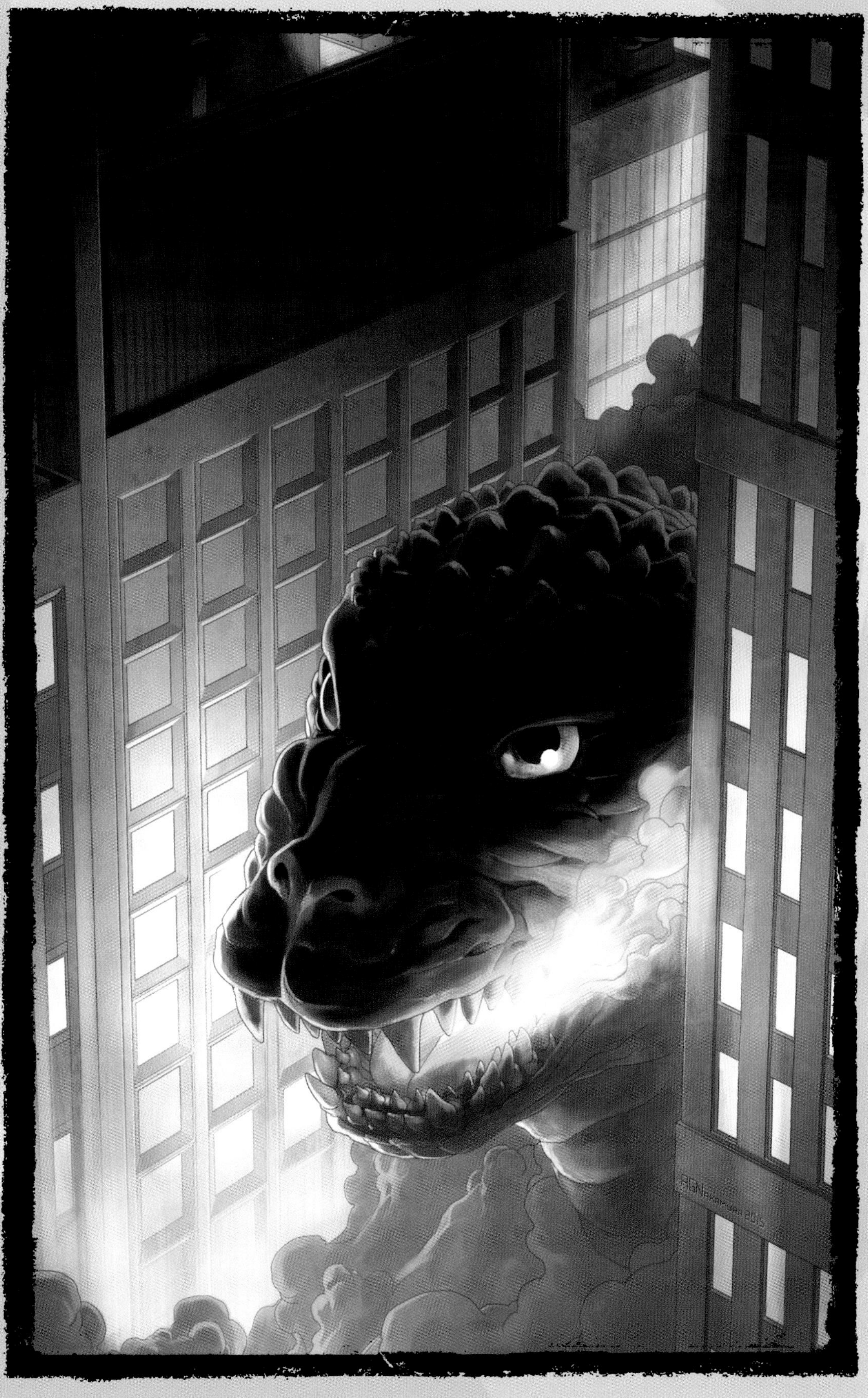
AGNAKAMURA 2015

Art by BRIAN CHURILLA

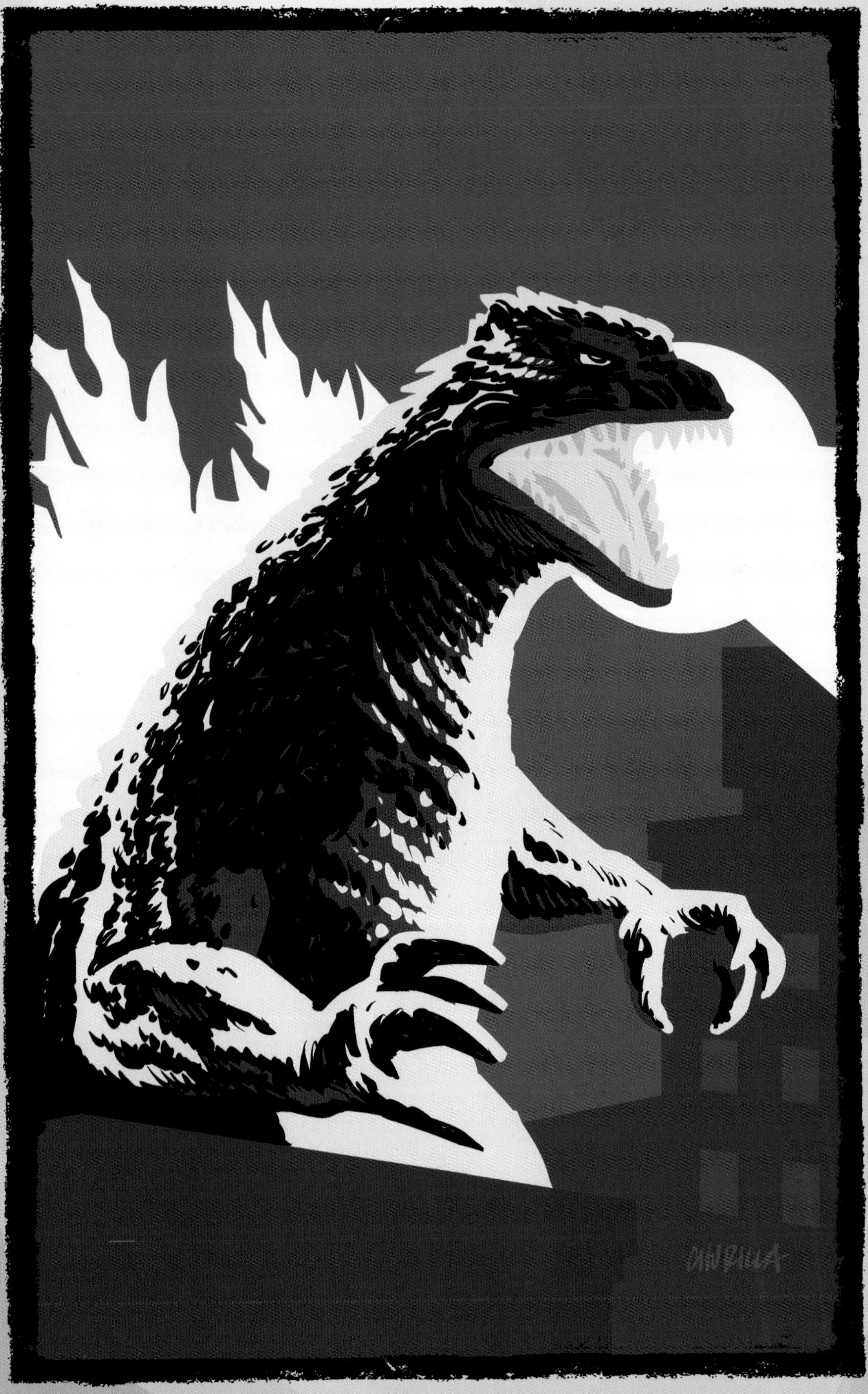
CHURILLA

Art by **JIMBO SALGADO** Colors by **JAY FOTOS**

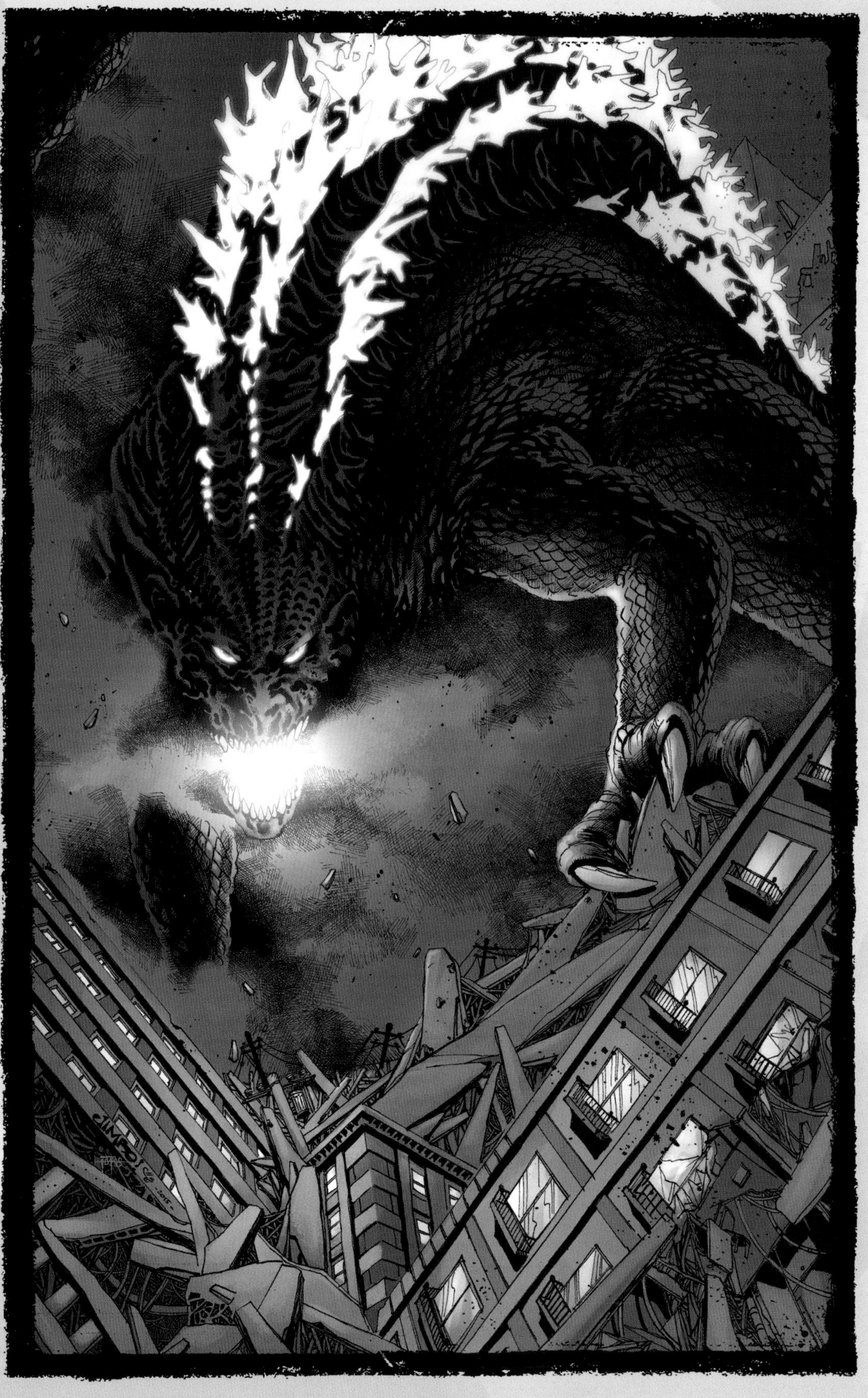

Art by **JOE JUSKO**

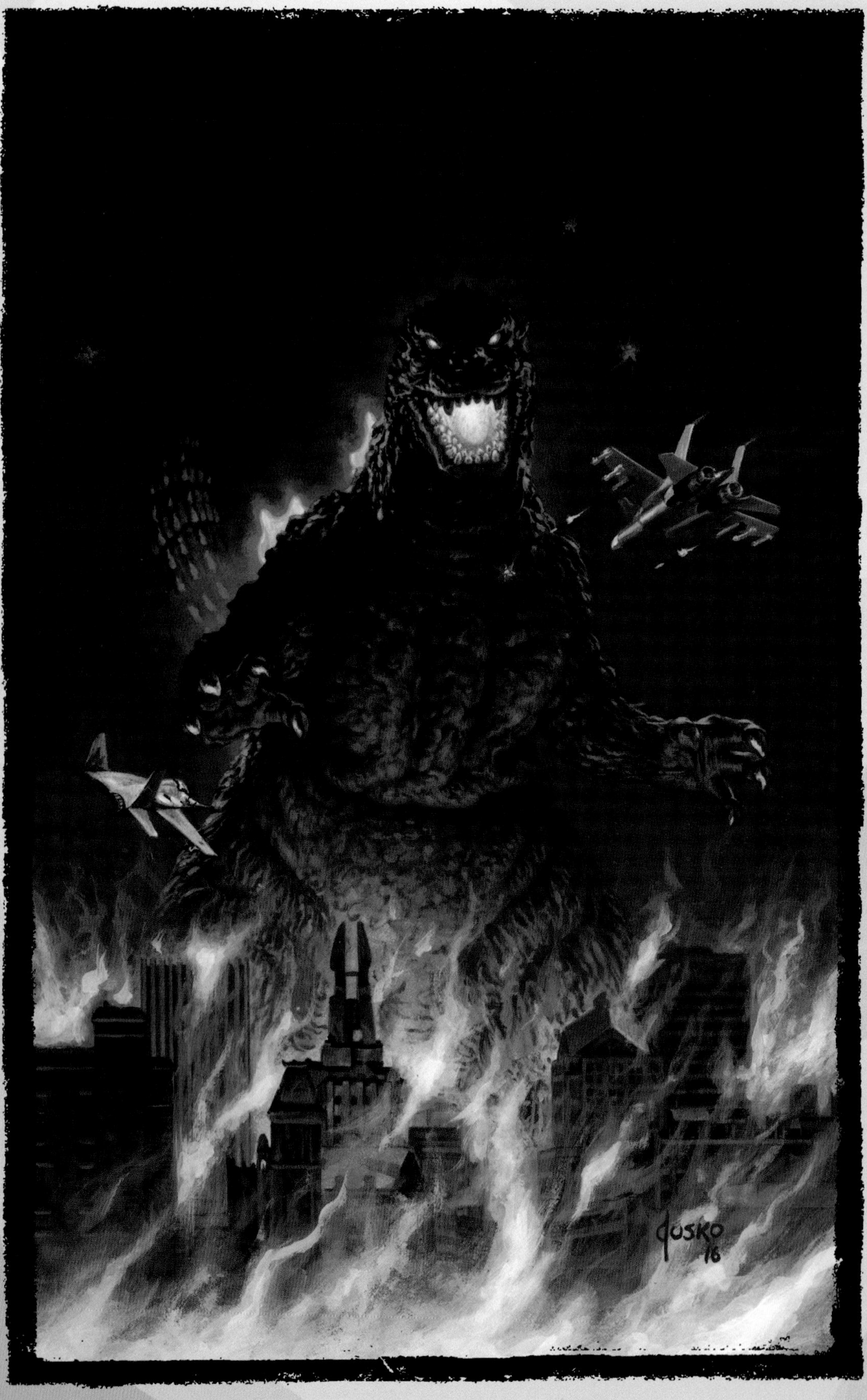
JUSKO
16

Art by **TADD GALUSHA**

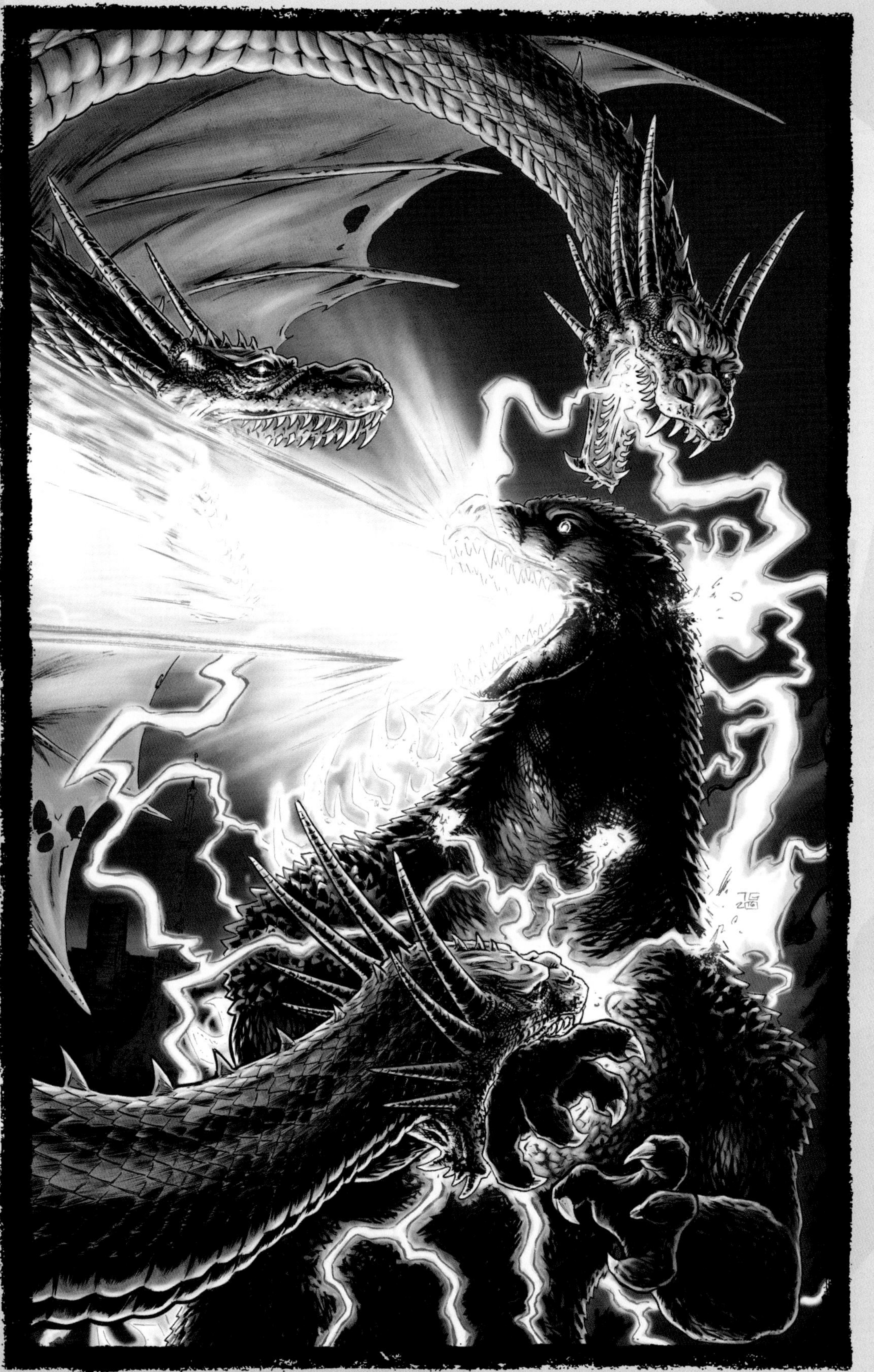

Art by **MICHAEL WALSH**

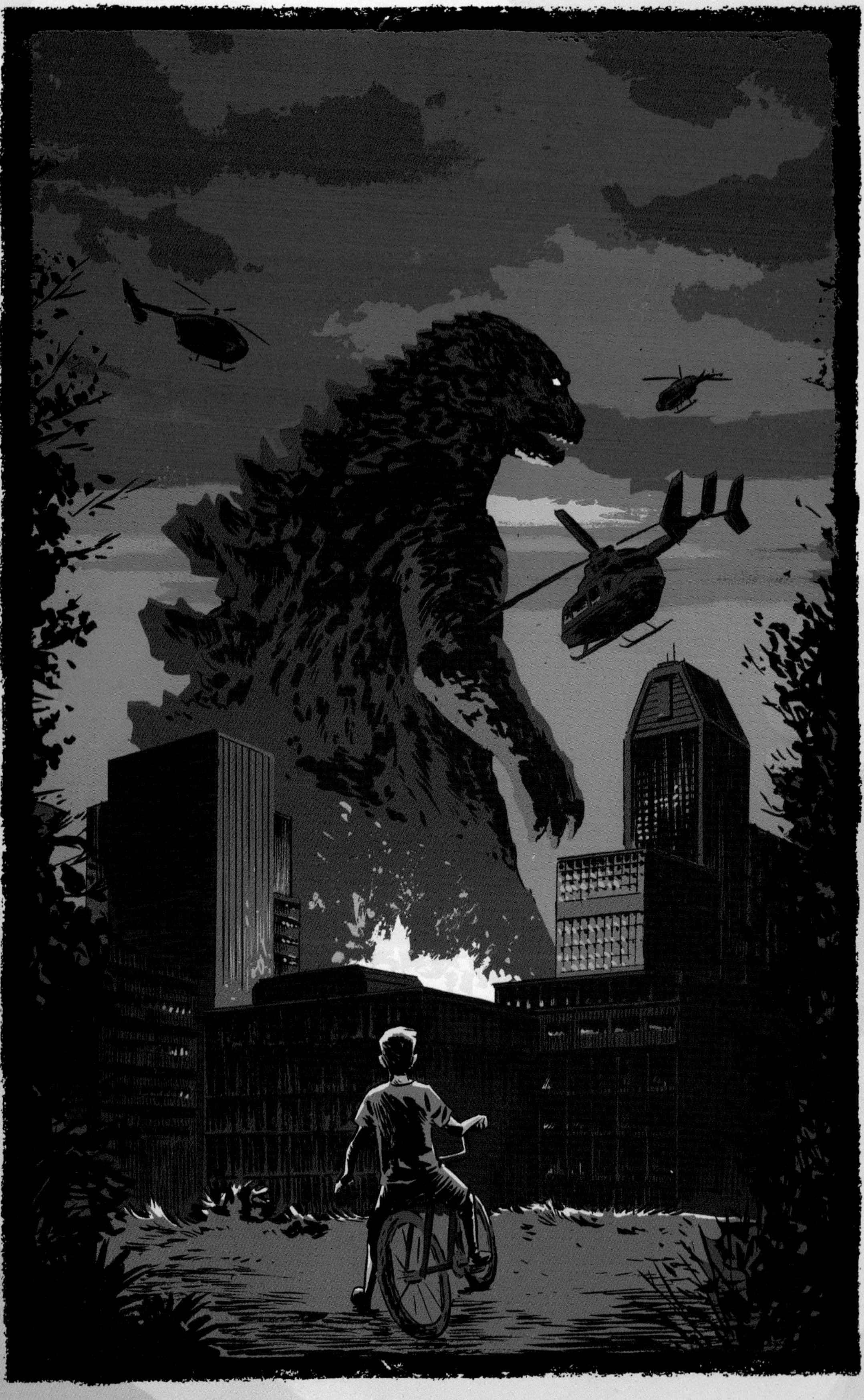

Art by **JEFF ZORNOW**

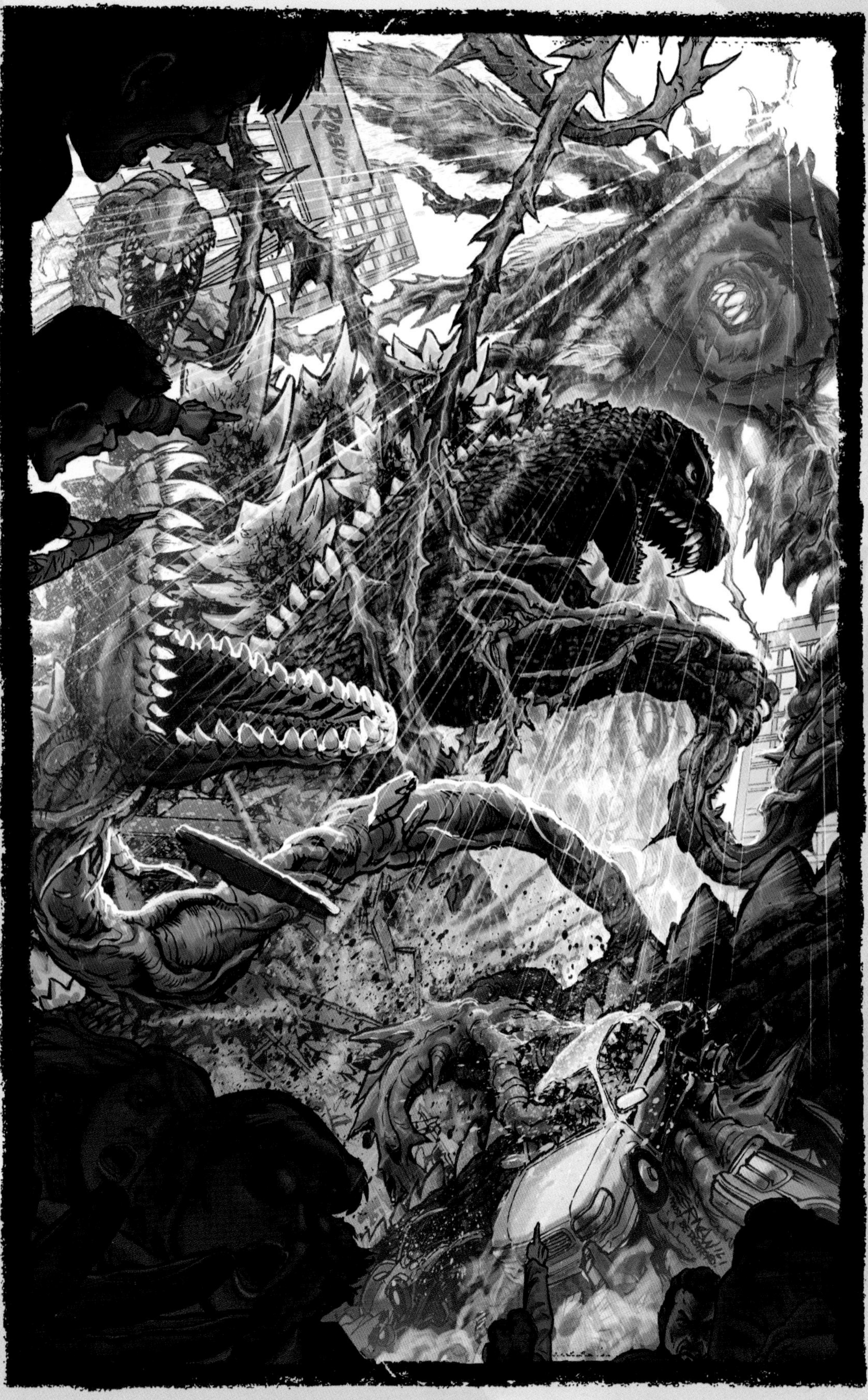

Art by **DAVE WACHTER**

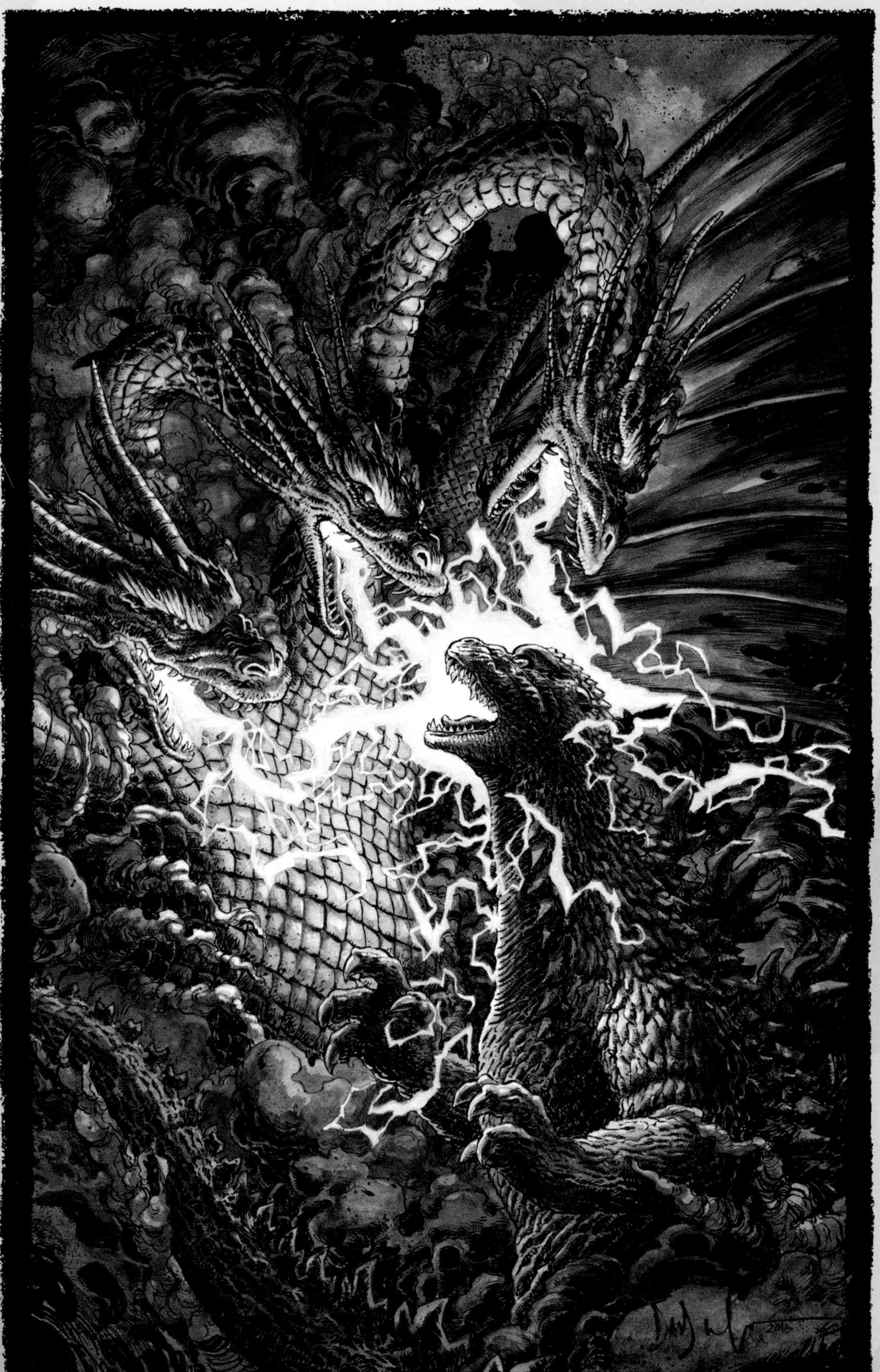

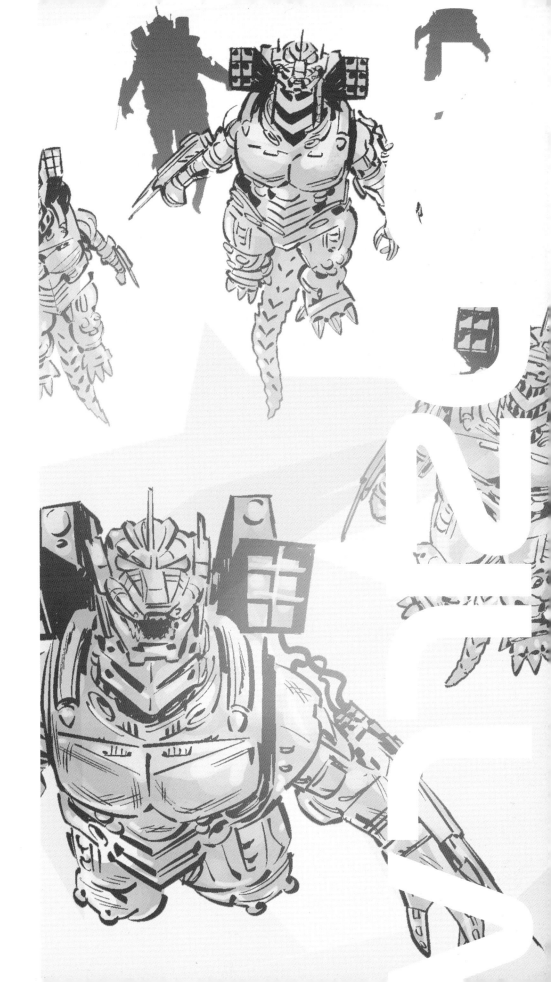

GODZILLA®

MORE TITLES FROM IDW PUBLISHING

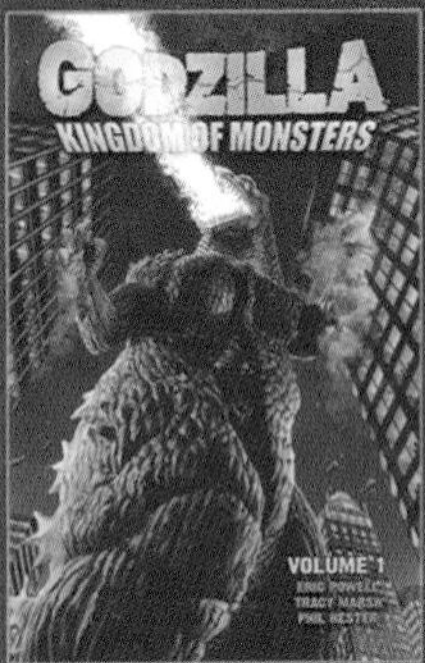
GODZILLA
KINGDOM OF MONSTERS
VOLUME 1

KINGDOM OF MONSTERS, VOL. 1
ISBN: 978-1-61377-016-0

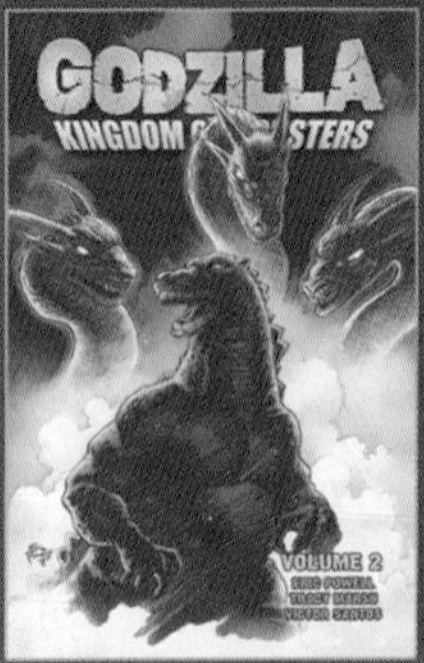
GODZILLA
VOLUME 2

KINGDOM OF MONSTERS, VOL. 2
ISBN: 978-1-61377-122-8

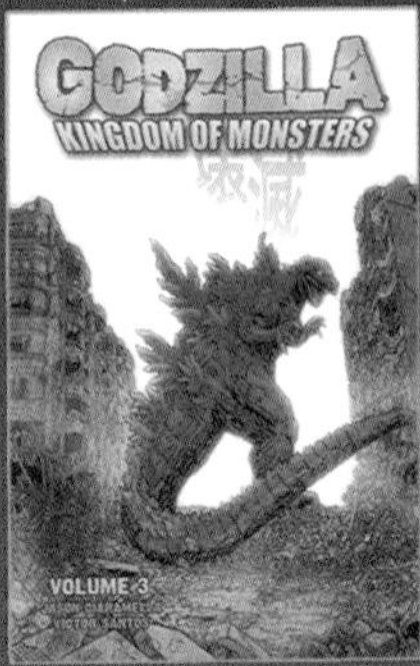
GODZILLA
KINGDOM OF MONSTERS
VOLUME 3

KINGDOM OF MONSTERS, VOL. 3
ISBN: 978-1-61377-205-8

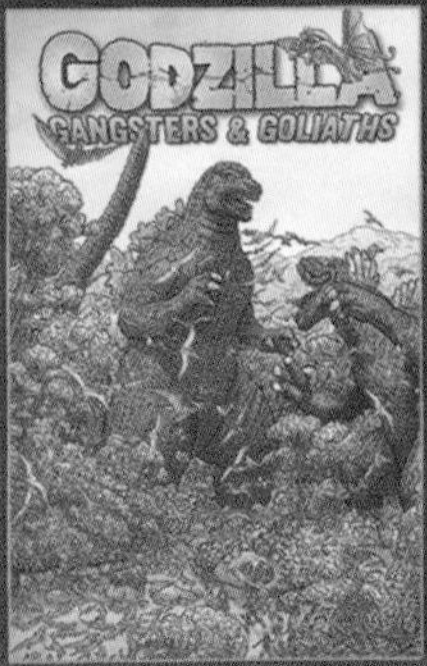
GODZILLA
GANGSTERS & GOLIATHS

GANGSTERS & GOLIATHS
ISBN: 978-1-61377-033-7

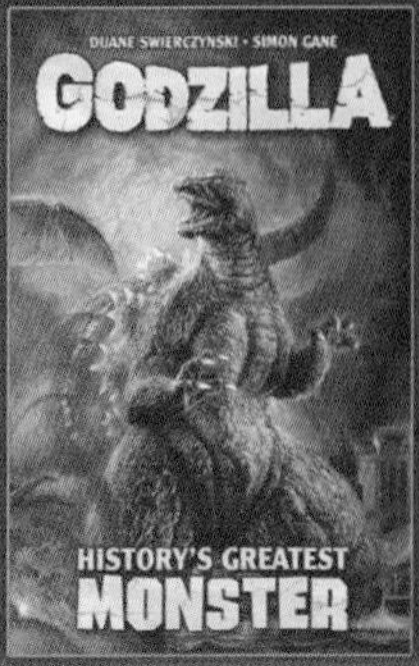
DUANE SWIERCZYNSKI • SIMON GANE
GODZILLA
HISTORY'S GREATEST
MONSTER

HISTORY'S GREATEST MONSTER
ISBN: 978-1-61377-948-4

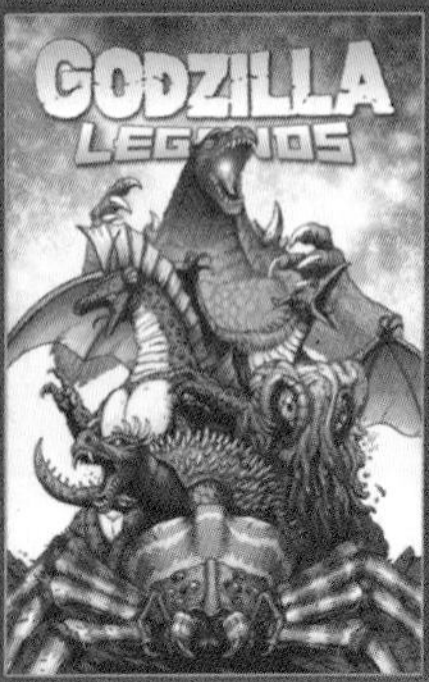
GODZILLA

GODZILLA: LEGENDS
ISBN: 978-1-61377-223-2

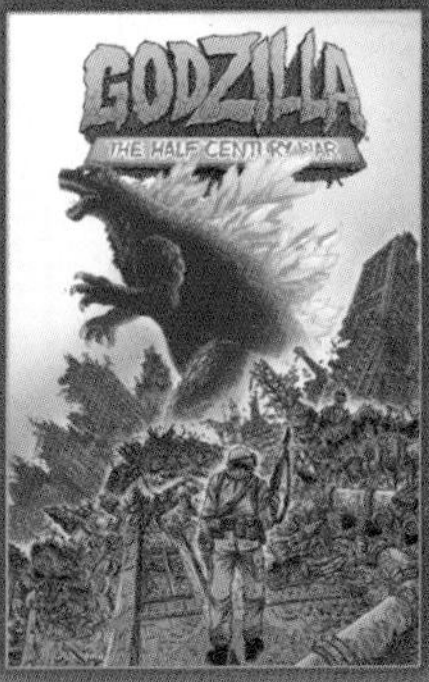
GODZILLA

THE HALF-CENTURY WAR
ISBN: 978-1-61377-595-0

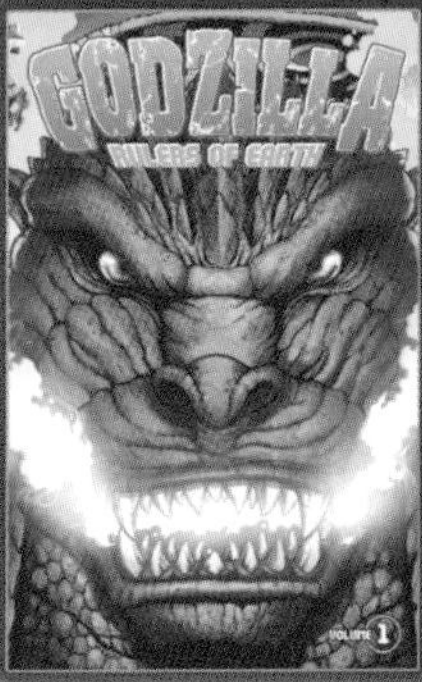
GODZILLA
RULERS OF EARTH

RULERS OF EARTH, VOL. 1
ISBN: 978-1-61377-749-7

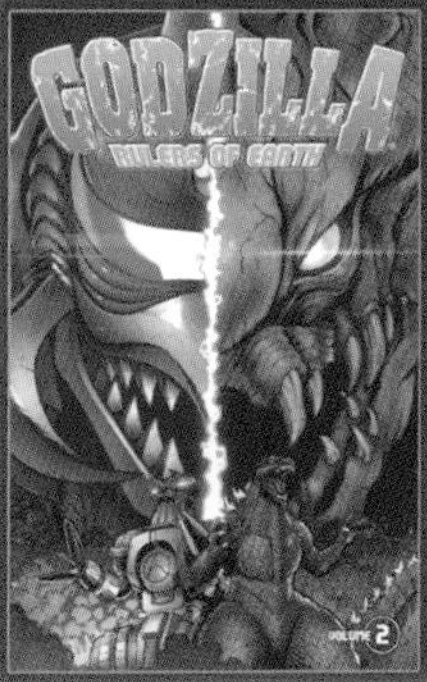
GODZILLA
RULERS OF EARTH

RULERS OF EARTH, VOL. 2
ISBN: 978-1-61377-933-0

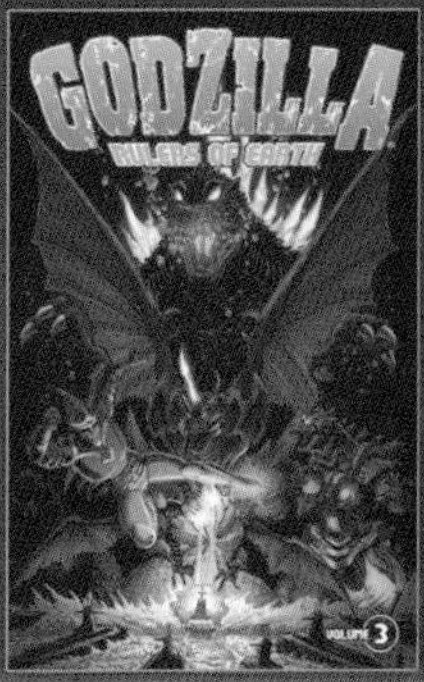
GODZILLA
RULERS OF EARTH

RULERS OF EARTH, VOL. 3
ISBN: 978-1-63140-009-4

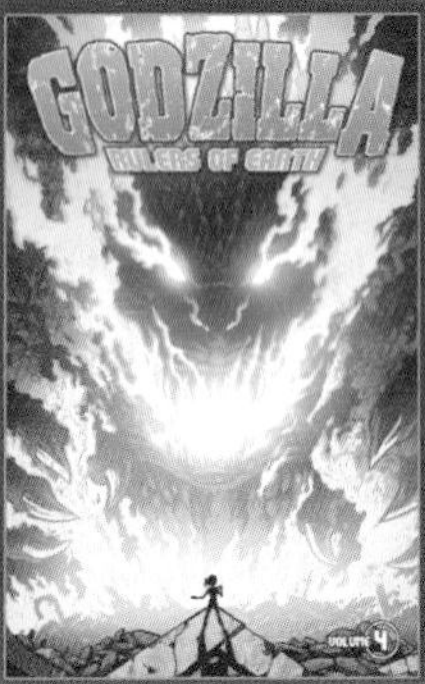
GODZILLA
RULERS OF EARTH

RULERS OF EARTH, VOL. 4
ISBN: 978-1-63140-172-5

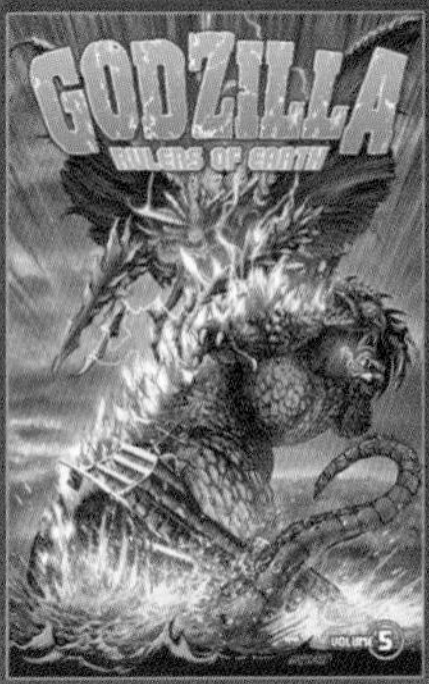
GODZILLA
RULERS OF EARTH

RULERS OF EARTH, VOL. 5
ISBN: 978-1-63140-281-4

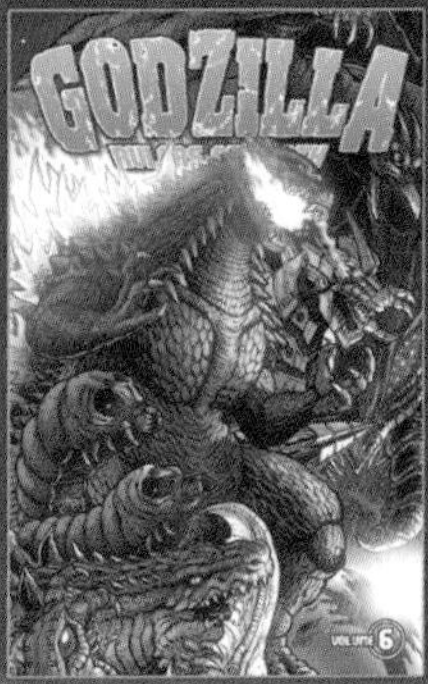
GODZILLA

RULERS OF EARTH, VOL. 6
ISBN: 978-1-63140-407-8

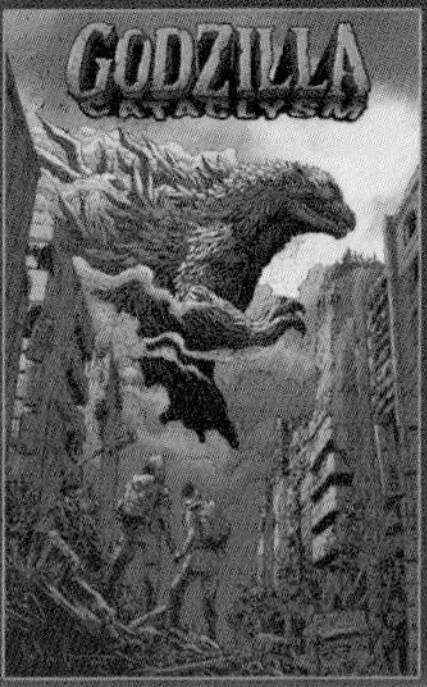
GODZILLA

GODZILLA: CATACLYSM
ISBN: 978-1-63140-242-5

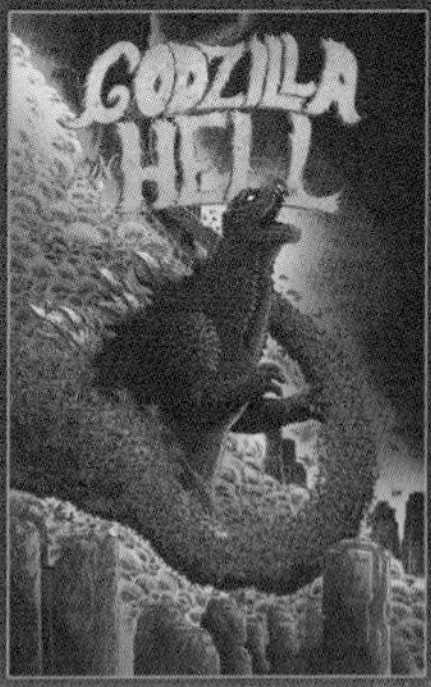
GODZILLA
HELL

GODZILLA IN HELL
ISBN: 978-1-63140-534-1

IDW WWW.IDWPUBLISHING.COM

ON SALE NOW!